RAPTURE:
CASE CLOSED?

RAPTURE:
CASE CLOSED?

STUNNING *NEW* BIBLICAL EVIDENCE

by

Nelson Walters

EXCLUSIVE LEADERSHIP EDITION

Ready for Jesus Publications (Wilmington, NC, 2017)

ISBN-13:978-0692816943

ACKNOWLEDGMENTS

Jesus: I never have a more intimate time of fellowship with you than when I'm immersed with you in your Word. I have enjoyed each moment of writing this book with you. I am so grateful for the privilege of knowing you deeper. Lord, let me know you deeper still!

Laura: Thank you for your patience and unending support throughout this ministry. You are the love of my life and God's greatest gift.

Joseph Lenard: Thank you for your tireless devotion to this project, your insights, your love of Jesus and his followers, and most of all your friendship. This book would not have been the sweet aroma it is before our Lord without you.

Rich Augi, *Bob Brown*, *Sheila Sternberg*, and *Don Zoller*: Thank you for believing in this project enough to invest your hearts and souls into it.

Joel Richardson: Thank you for sparking the interest in me to pursue the Word of God wherever it goes, and for your patient support of my ministry.

All those who read the book and provided insights: Thank you for listening to the Spirit and for providing me with "course corrections" that have made this book what it is.

The Gospel in the End Times Ministries: Thanks to all of you for your voluntary and sacrificial efforts to prepare the world for the return of our King and Savior.

CONTENTS

Appendices:

CONTACT

The Gospel in the End Times Ministries

www.TheGospelInTheEndTimes.com

nelson@thegospelintheendtimes.com

COVER ART

The arresting cover art is a "tongue-in-cheek" rendition of Matt. 24:27-28. The explanation of the relation of this short parable to the rapture can be found in chapter seven: "The Center of the Universe."

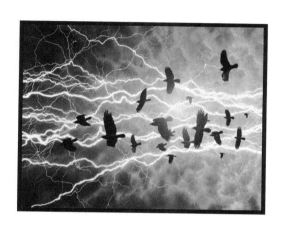

PART ONE:

Pursuing Truth

Chapter One

SOLVING THE "COLD CASE"

(Why Reconsider the Rapture?)

". . . they received the word with great eagerness, examining the Scriptures daily to see whether these things were so." (Acts 17:11)

Will the church face the Antichrist or be safely raptured first? You would think that a question of such fundamental importance would already be resolved. But despite centuries of investigation, the church still isn't sure of the answer; it's evenly split: approximately one-third of Christians believe we will face the Antichrist, one-third believe we won't, and one-third aren't certain.[1] No matter which way the church has looked at this question, the evidence has never been completely consistent. Certain Bible verses seem to support one view, while other verses seem to support another. One thing we are sure of, however, is that *the risks of guessing are significant*:

> 1) If today's churchgoers *won't* face Antichrist, those teaching them that they will may be needlessly scaring seekers out of our pews.
>
> 2) If they *will* face him, hundreds of millions will be woefully unprepared for the greatest challenge in church history; and many may fall away in the type of apostasy both Jesus and Paul described.

1

Not knowing the answer to this question places every Christian in substantial jeopardy—whichever solution proves correct. And right now *every* ministry, *every* church, and *every* believer plans for the future based on what they **think** the return of Jesus will be like.

However, it will not always be this way! Shockingly one day in the future, the church will be completely united on this question.

> *That they may all be one; **even as** you, Father, are in me and I in you*, that they also may be in us, *so that the world may believe* that You sent Me. (John 17:21 NASB emphasis mine)

Jesus asked the Father for the unity of Christians to equal the unity of the Father and the Son! This hasn't happened yet, however, Jesus's prayer *will* be answered. At that time Christians will have perfect unity and a flawless understanding of this book's central question. **I pray this simple work inspires discussion and debate as a step towards that future unity**.

CONSIDERING OLD EVIDENCE WITH NEW EYES

Some readers may be thinking, "Wait a minute! I already know the answer to the central question; in fact, I teach about this topic on a regular basis." These readers *may* hold the correct, biblical understanding, but I'd like everyone to consider two critical facts:

> **1) By *definition*, if churches hold widely divergent views, a vast portion of "the" church doesn't believe the correct biblical view (whatever that proves to be).**
> **2) Perhaps you and everyone else have come to their conclusions without viewing *all* the evidence.**

2

"How can there be fresh, new, *biblical* evidence?" you are probably asking. "The New Testament was written two thousand years ago. Haven't we looked at all the evidence already?"

Christians have poured over the Scriptures for generations, however, in the same way a cold case detective looks at old homicide evidence from a different angle, we can view the ancient Scriptures from a different angle. Just like a cold case, there has never been enough evidence to come to a verdict, but now a new perspective of the old evidence has just turned up that might solve it!

This book, *Rapture: Case Closed?*, is the result of years of research into the testimony of expert witnesses, including Dr. Thomas Ice, Dr. Mark Hitchcock, Dr. John Walvoord, Robert Van Kampen, Marvin Rosenthal, Alan Kurschner, Dr. Renald Showers, Dr. Michael Brown, and dozens of others. Although these experts hold differing opinions, careful examination and exegesis of their biblical testimonies *from a new angle* leads to one, single, inescapable conclusion.

This book contains **147 separate proofs derived solely from Scripture. Dozens and dozens of these proofs are new and never-before published. If you think you have seen all the evidence, let me assure you that you haven't.**

But evidence alone won't solve the case. We need the mind of Christ who is truth (John 14:6). He alone can teach us what the prophecies mean and help us uncover what has been previously hidden. In order to let the mind of Christ teach us, we must humble ourselves and become obedient unto death (Phil. 2:5-8); in this case, it must be the death of our own ideas to be replaced by Jesus's concepts. Thinking we know the answer without viewing all the evidence that Jesus wants us to see is a trap.

ISN'T THIS TOPIC TOO CONTROVERSIAL?

While some readers may think they already know the answer, others may think this topic is too controversial or dangerous to teach in their ministry. But sometimes controversy is necessary. During Jesus's earthly ministry, his greatest disappointment was with the Jewish leaders, primarily because they knew the Scriptures but could not interpret them correctly when it involved his first coming (John 5:45–47).

Now, as Jesus's second coming is fast approaching, we are the leaders. I certainly do not want him to be as disappointed in me as he was with the first-century leaders. So whether or not the material is controversial, I want to be a "good Berean" (Acts 17:11) and examine the Bible to know what it truly says about his second coming. *Jesus expects this of all of us*.

Up to this point in time, the sheep within Jesus's church have been blown in every direction by the winds of the doctrines of men regarding this subject (Eph. 4:14). But we can help them by solving this case together.

WE DON'T KNOW WHEN JESUS RETURNS

Another reason some give for avoiding this issue is the uncertainty of when Jesus will return. They ask, "Why should we even examine this issue if Jesus might not return for a thousand years?"

I agree wholeheartedly that we don't know the day or hour Jesus will return. Nearly every generation has believed that they were to be "the" generation of the end times, yet all previous generations were proved wrong about that assumption. Does the uncertainty of the timing of Jesus's return mean that we should not reopen this cold case?

If we knew with confidence that Jesus would not return for a hundred or even a thousand years, perhaps seeking this answer wouldn't be quite as critical. However, our Lord has not given us the luxury of this information. Quite the opposite, he has told us:

> For this reason *you also must be ready*; for the Son of Man is coming at an hour when you do not think he will. (Matt. 24:44 NASB, emphasis mine)

Jesus specifically commanded us to be ready at all times because he will come when we "do not think he will." Given events on the earth, he could easily return within our lifetimes. But we are not yet ready as a church; we have not solved the case, so we must *urgently* seek the Lord on this issue.

THE ROLE OF LEADERS

You may have noticed this book is an "Exclusive Leadership Edition." This special edition has been *personally* forwarded to you as one of the 1000 top leaders of the Christian faith because those touched by your ministry rely on you and the other leaders for guidance. As we have just seen, we have a Scriptural mandate to examine this issue. Hopefully after testing the proofs and Scriptures in this book, you can resolve this case for yourself. Then *in unity*, we can work together to protect the eternal fate of millions.

APOSTASY PREVENTION OR FEAR MONGERING

So in the spirit of this future unity, let's begin our investigation of the cold case by doing a closer examination of the significant risks we mentioned previously. If the church truly does face Antichrist, the issue is not only that it will be persecuted. The church has a long and glorious history of enduring persecution and testifying to the lordship of Jesus. No, the contention of many is that the *deception associated with this particular persecution will lead churchgoers to apostasy*—a falling away to worship the Antichrist, leading to eternal damnation. The reason these believers suggest this is that Jesus warns us about deception and mentions a great falling away.

> And Jesus answered and said to them, "See to it that no one misleads you . . . At that time [during the reign of Antichrist] *many will fall away* and will betray one another and hate one another. Many *false prophets will arise and will mislead many*. Because lawlessness is increased, *most people's love will grow cold*. (Matt. 24:4, 10–12 NASB, clarification and emphasis mine)

> For false Christs and false prophets will arise and will show great signs and wonders, *so as to mislead, if possible, even the elect*. Behold, I have told you in advance. (Matt. 24:24–25 NASB, emphasis mine)

Jesus is clear that many (or even most) will be deceived and have their love grow cold. If "the elect" that Jesus mentioned includes those currently attending our churches, it will be hard for even them to overcome it. That is why some recommend preparing the church.

On the other hand, although there is no debate as to whether *some* believers will one day face Antichrist, what if current-day Christians will be raptured first and not have to endure these things? If they won't face Antichrist, it is a mistake to teach them that they will! Every week our pews are filled with seekers and new believers trying to figure out what faith in Jesus means. We shouldn't scare these seekers by discussing martyrdom and persecution unless those things might really happen to them.

6

If the church *will* face Antichrist, it is horribly wrong to not prepare our flock. If the church *will not* face him, it is wrong to tell them that they will. ***Jesus has left us no choice but to come to unity.*** So as shepherds of God's flock, we need to pursue this investigation wherever it leads. The eternal fate of millions is at stake—either way.

THE ANTICHRIST AND THE RAPTURE

Although the church is divided on whether it will face Antichrist, a majority are in agreement that a deceiver known as Antichrist will arise. The disagreement stems from an understanding of when the rapture (Gk. *harpazo*) of the church takes place. You may be intimately familiar with this theory or it may have been some years since you thought about it. If you desire to refresh your knowledge, turn to appendix A: "Summary of Rapture Timing Theories" (see page 241 in the appendices section).

Displayed in the form of graphics in appendix A, the differences between the main rapture timing theories seem "stuffy" and "academic." However, they are not academic in their impact. The *pretribulation rapture* theory suggests that Christians will be "caught up" into heaven prior to the rise of Antichrist and avoid his persecutions and deception. The *prewrath rapture* and *post-tribulation rapture* theories suggest that Christians will be subject to the persecution of Antichrist.

NOT AN "ACADEMIC" DEBATE

The Bible says that God will grant Antichrist authority to kill 25% of the earth's population (Rev. 6:7–8). The martyrdom of hundreds of millions is not an academic discussion. The emotions it generates are the reason that the two opposing sides act like this is a street fight. It is the reason a Twitter war has erupted. I'm sure you've seen the posts. They're everywhere, and 99%

of them do nothing but divide the church. This is not the way brothers and sisters in Christ should approach an issue in which the eternal fate of millions is at stake! We may disagree, but "court" is the place to present our case. We as leaders need to examine the evidence rationally and then come to a verdict.

However, despite its emotional component, the timing of the rapture *is* a great proxy for whether or not the church will face Antichrist. For that reason, this book will take on this highly controversial case and examine the biblical evidence for the timing of the rapture. Although that is our approach, the real questions behind the investigation are whether the church faces the Antichrist and whether or not it is our duty to prepare the church for that time. These underlying questions are not academic; they are life or death and worthy of our best efforts. If we are to "feed his sheep," we must know the answers. We must pursue truth with a shepherd's heart.

TRYING TO FIND A MIDDLE GROUND

The following graphic summarizes the current positions in the church on these questions:

Teaching about Facing Antichrist	Rapture Position	Prepare Their Flock for Persecution?
Won't face him	*Pretribulation*	No
Silent, don't discuss	Unsure	No
Will face him	*Prewrath* or *Post-tribulation*	Yes

Figure 1: Teachings about Facing Antichrist

The great divide in Christian culture over these questions has made taking a noncommittal position quite appealing. Frankly, if one is unsure about the timing of the rapture, he/she should remain silent! However, as figure 1 clearly indicates, *remaining silent is still choosing to not prepare your flock.*

This is equivalent to not voting in an election. In the most recent US presidential race (2016), voting wasn't pleasant, but for many it was a sacred duty. Not getting involved in a biblical examination of this issue is similar. Choosing to avoid the issue and not teaching about end times is, by default, choosing to not prepare. You are still making a choice; on this issue *there is no middle ground.*

I have heard that the phrase "in essentials unity, in nonessentials liberty, in all things charity" should be applied to the rapture question. Certainly, I agree that in doctrinal issues that are not essential, this wonderful phrase should apply. Our churches have experienced far too much division. However, this is not a doctrinal discussion where we should sit idly on the sidelines; rather we must all become engaged in seeking God for an answer. After all, the eternal fate of millions is at stake. What could be more important?

FEAR AND TREMBLING

Many leaders take a noncommittal position because they fear that finding the rapture answer might impact their ministry and their relationships. Will it affect attendance or giving? Will it affect your denominational ties or your relationships to other leaders? You may have taken a public position on this issue. What if the new evidence in this book indicates that you may have been mistaken?

Fear is *not* a biblical motivation, but it is a very human reaction to any change. I address how to tackle these specific fears in the final section of the book, "Epilogue for Leaders." Knowing that practical answers wait at the end of the book may be helpful to you.

However, regardless of personal cost, God's shepherds need to examine this issue thoroughly and then take a stand. The perfect love of our Savior casts out all fear. We can trust him.

I don't want to sugarcoat what lies ahead. Some individual churches and even some denominations (Calvary Chapel)[2] make belief in a *pretribulation rapture* an essential doctrine. Rapture expert Marvin Rosenthal has detailed a harrowing experience where he was forced to resign from his position as director of the Friends of Israel Gospel Ministry because of his rapture position.[3] Another rapture expert, Charles Cooper, was a renowned teacher at Moody Bible Institute, which forced him to resign because of his belief in the *prewrath rapture*.[4] Yet another rapture commentator, Dr. Joseph Lenard, resigned from the church *he helped found* because he was unwilling to continue in the denomination with its *pretribulation rapture*–related doctrinal statement.[5]

Conversely, other churches claim the *pretribulation rapture* theory is the greatest threat to Christians today. Others assert those proclaiming the church will not face Antichrist are false teachers. Brothers and sisters on both sides of the rapture discussion have faced persecution.

RIGHT OR WRONG OR SLEEPING?

If this book is going to attempt to prove one of the three main rapture timing theories is "right," that would mean the other theories are "wrong." But that type of thinking is a trap we must not fall into. Our Western mindsets like to express every decision as black or white and every person holding an opinion as right or wrong. But that is not how Jesus viewed those with differing views. He viewed them as "blind" or "asleep."

How we view those we disagree with determines our strategy. If someone is wrong, we correct them. If someone is blind, we guide them. If someone is sleeping, we wake them up. This book will take the position that all of us who hold a rapture timing position are brothers and sisters in Christ and *all of us* need helpful guidance—not harsh correction on this issue.

Jesus's seminal teaching on the state of the church prior to his return is the parable of the ten virgins (Matt. 25:1–13). This parable is about ten virgins (churchgoers) who are keeping themselves pure as they await the return of their bridegroom (Jesus). The fact Jesus is symbolized by a bridegroom (not as a husband) indicates this parable takes place *prior* to the marriage of the Lamb and the rapture. We are told five of the virgins are wise and five are foolish. We then learn something *absolutely incredible*:

> Now while the bridegroom was delaying, they *all* got drowsy and *began to sleep*. (Matt. 25:5 NASB, emphasis mine)

Jesus's parables are usually about contrasts between the righteous and the wicked, but in this parable *both* groups fall asleep waiting for the return of the bridegroom! Both the foolish and the wise are probably sleeping right now, meaning that most of us are slumbering in regard to the return of our Lord. That is a humbling statement. Jesus did not say those who ascribe to our preferred rapture timing theory are awake and the others are asleep, he said *all of us* are asleep. *We need to hold onto this humbling truth as we proceed throughout this book.*

Jesus then tells us the fate of the foolish and the wise:

> But at midnight there was a shout, "Behold, the bridegroom! Come out to meet him." Then all those virgins rose and trimmed

11

their lamps. The foolish said to the prudent, "Give us some of your oil, for our lamps are going out." But the prudent answered, "No, there will not be enough for us and you too; go instead to the dealers and buy some for yourselves." And while they were going away to make the purchase, the bridegroom came, and *those who were ready went in with him to the wedding feast*; and the door was shut. (Matt. 25:6–10 NASB, emphasis mine)

At some point right before the return of Jesus, both the foolish *and* wise virgins wake up. The difference between them is that the wise have enough oil (Holy Spirit) for their lamps, and the foolish do not. Because the foolish run out of oil, their lamps burn out. It is for this very reason that the foolish miss the rapture (where only *those who were ready went in with him to the wedding feast*).

In this parable, Jesus has conclusively answered any question of "what difference does rapture timing make?" The foolish virgins (the seekers and the unsaved within our churches) are at risk of being shut out of the wedding feast. Unfortunately, the wise virgins are asleep and cannot help them!

Jesus was speaking metaphorically, but if our churches truly contain up to 50% "foolish virgins," they are the greatest mission field imaginable. My goal in writing this book and the passion of my life is to awaken churchgoers for what is to come—to be a *fountain of life* (Prov. 10:11). If you and I are awakened to this reality, perhaps we can work this mission field together and impact the eternal destiny of millions.

SO WHAT IS THE RAPTURE ANSWER?

In my home church, we frequently use this expression: "Some questions require an answer; others necessitate a conversation." This question demands an in-depth conversation. We are going to spend the rest of this book discussing it.

SUMMARY

We have explained that the timing of the rapture is a good proxy for whether or not Christians will face Antichrist. If the rapture occurs before he begins his persecutions (*pretribulation rapture*), the church will not face him. If the church is raptured after the Antichrist begins his persecutions (*prewrath* and *post-tribulation rapture*), the church will face him.

We must remember that this disagreement within the body of Christ is *not* an academic one.

> **The *eternal destiny* of millions of churchgoers is at stake in the answer.**

We cannot ignore the debate (even if we would like to), and we cannot rely solely on our previous understanding and assume we're correct. But rather, we must press on to uncover all the biblical evidence to solve the case with absolute biblical certainty. Too much is at stake to do otherwise. Knowing the timing of the rapture with relative *certainty* allows the church to plan accordingly. This is important stuff. God *wants* us to know the answer. We *need* to know the answer.

The emotions engendered by this debate have led many of us to fall into the trap of viewing those who disagree with us as "wrong." Jesus views them as sleeping (parable of the ten virgins). In humility, I ask every reader to lay aside the "dreams" of the rapture timing we all have developed while we were sleeping and to awaken to the truth of Jesus's Word.

In the next section, we will begin our specific examination of rapture proofs. It is only logical that given the importance of the timing of the rapture that Jesus will not allow his church to enter the time of the end without giving us conclusive evidence of that timing in his Word. He will give us his mind, the "mind of Christ," on this issue. So it isn't surprising that the Bible is amazingly specific about this event. In the next chapter, we are going to uncover the "smoking gun": new, never-before-published evidence that proves which of the rapture timing theories is correct, and by extension, whether the church will face Antichrist. Then throughout the rest of the book, we will support our findings with additional Scripture witnesses.

The cold case of whether the sheep in our pews will someday face the wolf (Antichrist) may sometimes feel like a street fight; however, as shepherds of God's flock, we have a responsibility to discover the biblically correct answer. God has promised us unity and that we will find the answer (John 17:21)! Please join this endeavor in faith that God will provide what he has promised.

PART TWO:

THE RAPTURE TIMING ANSWER

Chapter Two

HIDDEN TREASURE

(Ultimate Proof of Rapture Timing)

> *As he was sitting on the Mount of Olives, the disciples came to*
> *Him privately, saying, 'Tell us, when will these things happen,*
> *and what will be the sign of your coming, and of the end of the*
> *age?' (Matt. 24:3 NASB)*

Sometimes the most effective place to hide an object is right out in plain sight. In 2009, Hungarian art historian Gergely Barki was watching a DVD of a children's movie at home with his young daughter. As the movie, *Stuart Little*, unfolded, his daughter sat enraptured. Barki was almost nodding off, but then he saw *it*. In the movie scene hanging on the wall behind the actors appeared to be a famous painting—a missing masterpiece. Barki, an expert on Hungarian art, was sure this was *Sleeping Lady with Black Vase* by avant-garde painter Róbert Berény. The painting was last seen in 1928. Barki rewound the video. It certainly appeared to be the missing masterpiece.

It took Barki a year to hunt down the painting, but he did. The set designer for *Stuart Little* had purchased the painting for $500 to use in the movie. She liked the painting so much, she had bought it from Columbia at cost to hang in her own apartment; and that's where it was when Barki called her.[6] The painting was sold at auction for €229,500 (about $330,000).

Something of much greater value has lain hidden in the middle of one of the most famous end-time passages in the Bible. For millennia, Christians searching for rapture evidence have passed over this simple proof

17

and missed it. The definitive proof of rapture timing was right where you'd expect it to be, except the setting was so familiar it was passed right over— literally, hidden in plain sight. As we stated in chapter one: "Solving the Cold Case," it's logical that Jesus himself would provide his church with irrefutable proof of proper rapture timing. So, it only makes sense that this proof would be found in Jesus's great teaching on end times: the Olivet Discourse (Matt. 24).

At this moment, I am sure that every proponent of the *pretribulation rapture* is taking exception to my claim that the definitive rapture proof is in the Olivet Discourse. If you are not aware, *pretribulation rapture* advocates claim that the Olivet Discourse in Matt. 24 was given only for the Jews. Pretribulationalists have constructed an elaborate set of evidence to confirm this. We will discuss this evidence later in the book, in chapter six: "The Backfire Effect (*Pretribulation Rapture* Arguments)." At this point, however, we do not need to evaluate the validity of these claims. The proof presented in this chapter is totally independent of the intended audience of the Olivet Discourse. It is even valid if the audience *was* exclusively meant to be the Jews!

The fact that this proof is found in the Olivet Discourse, however, is pertinent. Because *pretribulation rapture* theorists have discounted the Discourse as relevant for the church, it has lain under examined for decades. Additionally, because this proof involves looking at the Discourse in a way that *post-tribulation rapture* exponents do not usually view it, they also have been blind to the evidence hidden right before their eyes. When I discovered this proof, I was dumbfounded. *Why hadn't anyone seen this proof before? It could have solved so many arguments.* The answer might be that all of us have been looking to prove ourselves correct rather than seeking truth. For this reason, I implore you to empty yourself of your preconceived notions of rapture timing, at least for the next half hour as you explore this chapter. Imagine that you are listening to Jesus's words for the first time without the layers of baggage that endless rapture arguments have created. Look beyond what you already know to see the "scenery of the room." Only then will you notice the masterpiece waiting to be discovered.

After you have heard the argument with fresh ears, only then do I ask you to reengage your mind to explore it and contest it. Remember, we are ten virgins and we are all asleep.

THE OLIVET DISCOURSE—A SPRING AFTERNOON

Let us first set the context for Jesus's sermon on end times: the Olivet Discourse (Matt. 24; Mark 13; Luke 21). Jesus gave this sermon on one of the last afternoons before he was betrayed. He had just had a heated exchange with the established Jewish leaders in Jerusalem. As our Lord and his disciples left the temple area, the disciples were stunned by the interchange they had just witnessed. They tried to break the tension by commenting on the majestic temple architecture, but Jesus rebuffed them by saying that soon not one of those magnificent stones would stand upon another.

On their way back to their "camp" on the Mount of Olives, Jesus's disciples tried to put the day's events in perspective. After his triumphant entry on Palm Sunday, they had expected Jesus to be recognized as Messiah and king. Now everything was falling apart. Jesus and the leaders of the nation had just had a knock-down war-of-words from which there was no going back. Not only that, Jesus had just prophesied that the temple where the Messiah would someday sit as king would soon be destroyed. How could Jesus be crowned king after that day's events? Their vision of the

19

future had just been smashed into a million pieces like Jesus's prophecy about the temple stones.

I can imagine Jesus's closest disciples whispering under their breath, "If Jesus isn't going to become king, what will happen to us?" They finally got up the nerve to ask their master about the future. Jesus responded with the Olivet Discourse, an amazing prophetic sermon about his return (second coming). It began with the simple question that was quoted at the beginning of this chapter:

> As he was sitting on the Mount of Olives, the disciples came to Him privately, saying, "Tell us, *when will these things happen, and what will be the sign* of your coming, and of *the end of the age?*" (Matt. 24:3 NASB, emphasis mine)

The disciples' question was the same as ours is today: "When will these things happen?" Jesus did not rebuff his disciples and say, "Prophecy is none of your business." Rather, Jesus wants his listeners to understand the timing of events. He went into great detail about the signs that would precede his return. That return is pictured dramatically at the climax of the Discourse:

> The sign of the Son of Man will appear in the sky, and then all the tribes of the earth will mourn, and *they will see the Son of Man coming on the clouds of the sky with power and great glory.* And He will send forth His angels with a great trumpet and they will gather together His elect from the four winds, from one end of the sky to the other. (Matt. 24:30–31 NASB, emphasis mine)

This event is believed to be the physical second coming of Jesus by 96% of the church. Both the *pretribulation rapture* and the *post-tribulation rapture* camps believe that. They believe the same events are also depicted in Revelation in the following passage:

> I saw heaven opened, and behold, a white horse, and He who sat on it is called Faithful and True, and in righteousness He judges and wages war. His eyes are a flame of fire, and on His head are many diadems; and He has a name written on Him which no one knows except Himself. He is clothed with a robe dipped in blood, and His name is called The Word of God. And *the armies which are in heaven, clothed in fine linen, white and clean were following Him on white horses.* From His mouth comes a sharp sword, so that with it He may strike down the nations, and He will rule them with a rod of iron; and He treads the wine press of the fierce wrath of God, the Almighty. And on His robe and on His thigh He has a name written, "KING OF KINGS, AND LORD OF LORDS" . . . And I saw the beast and the kings of the earth and their armies assembled to make war against Him who sat on the horse and against His army. (Rev. 19:11–16, 19 NASB, emphasis mine)

Both the *pretribulation rapture* camp and the *post-tribulation rapture* camp consider this second passage where Jesus rides a white horse and comes to do battle with the Antichrist at Armageddon to be the physical second coming. I agree with them. Both camps also claim the event depicted in Matt. 24:30–31 is *this same event.* But what if they are both mistaken? What if the event in Matt. 24:30–31 is something else? In fact, ***the two events as*** *they are portrayed in Scripture couldn't be more dissimilar!* These differences are seen in following graphic.

Events in Matt. 24:30–31	Events in Rev. 19:11–16, 19
Jesus comes on the clouds	Jesus rides a white horse
Jesus blows a trumpet	Jesus has a sword coming from his mouth
Jesus comes with his angels	Jesus is followed by the saints on white horses
Jesus comes to gather the elect	Jesus comes *with* the elect to destroy Antichrist

Figure 2: Contrasts in Matthew 24:30–31 and Revelation 19:11–16, 19

This obvious disparity with traditional interpretation is why I am recommending you set aside all your preconceived notions about timing and events and hear Jesus's words as if for the first time. If you haven't done that yet, now is the time.

SIGNS OF HIS RETURN

Hopefully, I have gotten your attention. But before I can prove to you that the event in Matthew 24:30–31 *is not* the physical second coming of Jesus, we need to set the stage. As I stated earlier, the Olivet Discourse (in Matt. 24) is organized as a series of signs that precede the return of Jesus. These signs are followed by this event in Matthew 24:30–31. Together they form the first clue in solving the case for rapture timing. Pictorially, this might look like the following graphic on the next page:

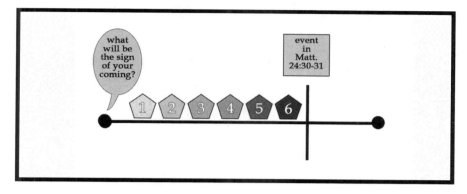

Figure 3: The Olivet Discourse

As detectives, let's examine the scene which Scripture has meticulously preserved for us behind the yellow tape of its inspired words. The Discourse begins with the disciples' question, "When will these things happen and what will be the sign of your coming?" It ends with the event depicted in Matthew 24:30–31 which the *pretribulation rapture* and *post-tribulation rapture* camps claim is the physical second coming of Jesus, but that I contend is something else. In between are six signs that Jesus gave to his disciples that precede his coming. These signs were given in direct response to the question they asked about what would be the sign of his coming. They asked for one sign; Jesus gave them six. These six prophetic events are listed on the following page.

Sign	Pattern of Seven Events[7]	Matt. 24	Additional References in Matt. 24
1	Deception by False Messiahs	vv. 4–5	vv. 23–26
2	War, Bloodshed, and Chaos	vv. 6–7	
3	Famine and Economic Collapse	v. 7	
4	Abomination and Death	v. 9	vv. 15–21
5	Martyrdom and Apostasy	vv. 9–14	
6	Celestial Earthly Disturbance	v. 29	

Figure 4: Six Signs in the Olivet Discourse

These six signs are represented by the six numbered pentagonal boxes in figure 3: "The Olivet Discourse." When viewed in this manner, the organization of the Olivet Discourse jumps to life. Jesus gave his disciples the first five signs in exact order in Matthew 24:4–14. He then expounded on two of these signs in Matthew 24:15–26, and then he gave the final sign in Matthew 24:29. After this series of six signs, Jesus described his return to the disciples in Matthew 24:30–31.

These six signs are not unique to Matthew 24. This assessment may be new to you, but Bible commentators have long been aware of the amazing parallel between Matthew 24 and the first six seals of Revelation 6. Both *pretribulation rapture* and *post-tribulation rapture* proponents seem to agree on the comparison.

In his commentary on Revelation, *pretribulation rapture* supporter John Walvoord, along with his editors Mark Hitchcock and Phillip Rawley, state, "There is a remarkable parallel between the progress of chapter 6 (Revelation) as a whole and the description given by our Lord of the end of the age in Matthew 24:4–31."[8] Other *pretribulation rapture* supporters Andreas J. Köstenberger, L. Scott Kellum, and Charles L. Quarles present an impressive table showing the exact mirror image between prophecies of the seals of Revelation 6 and the Olivet Discourse on page 834 of their classic book *The Cradle, the Cross, and the Crown*.[9] Ron Bigalke of the Pre-Trib. Research Center also supports this view,[10] and in a recent debate, Thomas Ice, director of the Pre-Trib. Research Center, confirms that the signs in Matthew 24 are equivalent to the six seals in Revelation 6.[11]

Post-tribulation rapture supporter William Daniel Kelly also points out the amazing parallels of the six signs in Matthew 24 to the six seals in Revelation 6 in his book *Shadow of Things to Come*.[12] The academic and theological community is mostly unified in its acceptance of this association. The graphic on the next page summarizes these comparisons.

Sign	Pattern of Seven Events	Matt. 24	Rev. 6
1	Deception by False Messiahs	vv. 4–5, 23–26	vv. 1–2
2	War, Bloodshed, and Chaos	vv. 6–7	vv. 3–4
3	Famine and Economic Collapse	v. 7	vv. 5–6
4	Abomination and Death	v. 9, 15–21	vv. 7–8
5	Martyrdom and Apostasy	vv. 9–14	vv. 9–11
6	Celestial Earthly Disturbance	v. 29	vv. 12–17

Figure 5: Six Signs in Matthew 24 and Revelation 6

Of greater interest to me, however, is what Jesus *didn't say* were signs. On that spring afternoon, this was all new information to the disciples; they didn't have the Book of Revelation so they had no basis on which to question the signs. But fifty to sixty years later, Jesus's vision to John provided much more detail about end-time events. We now have this additional information at our fingertips. We have *references*. (In appendix A: "Summary of Rapture Timing Theories," we discuss the scriptural interpretation method known as **sense and reference**. If you are not familiar with this method, check out the discussion beginning on page 249).

In John's vision in Revelation, Jesus provided John with twenty-one major end-time prophetic events or signs: seven seals (found in Rev. 6–8:1 that we already have seen include the six signs of the Olivet Discourse), seven trumpet judgments (Rev. 8–11), and seven bowl judgments (Rev. 16). The trumpet and bowl judgments contain extremely severe punishments. The first trumpet judgment, for instance, includes fire, blood, and hail, which burn one-third of the land and grass on the planet (Rev. 8:7). The fifth trumpet judgment lasts five months and includes what appear to be demonic stinging locusts that cause many of the inhabitants of the earth to wish for death that doesn't come (Rev. 9:1–6). The sixth trumpet judgment results in the death of one-third of mankind (Rev. 9:18). The bowl judgments which directly follow are even more severe than the trumpet judgments.

These judgments would be undeniable signs of the soon return of Jesus; yet, he chose to ignore them and *did not list a single one* in the Olivet Discourse as a sign of his coming. What are we to make of this? Why is the Olivet Discourse silent on the trumpet and bowl judgments and only lists the first six seals as signs? Obviously, Jesus and the Holy Spirit were omniscient and fully aware of these coming plagues. So we must conclude Jesus *intentionally* did not include the trumpet and bowl judgments in the Olivet Discourse as "signs." Also even more obviously, Jesus would not purposely mislead the church (or even the Jews) by giving an incomplete list of signs. No, Jesus has left us with *only one possible conclusion*:

> **The trumpet and bowl judgments are not given as signs of the coming of our Lord because these judgments occur *after* his coming. His coming *precedes* them.**

The disciples asked Jesus what would be the sign of his coming. Jesus responded with all six signs (the first six seals of Rev. 6:1–17) that would *precede* it; and he didn't give a single sign that would *follow* it (the trumpet and bowl judgments).

Let's take a moment to consider the implications of what we have just uncovered. We know from Revelation that the battle of Armageddon and the physical second coming take place sometime *after* the sixth bowl:

> The sixth angel *poured out his bowl* on the great river, the Euphrates; and its water was dried up, so that the way would be prepared for the kings from the east . . . ("Behold, *I am coming* like a thief. Blessed is the one who stays awake and keeps his clothes so that he will not walk about naked and men will not see his shame.") And they gathered them together to the place which in Hebrew is called Har-Magedon. (Rev. 16:12, 15–16 NASB, emphasis mine)

From this passage, we learn that Jesus is still coming ("I am coming") *after* the sixth bowl is poured out and *prior* to Armageddon. From this we can deduce without a doubt that the physical second coming occurs *after* the trumpet and bowl judgments. Yet, we have just learned that the event in Matt. 24:30–31 occurs *before* the trumpet and bowl judgments. What event is it? It obviously cannot be the physical second coming. Jesus, again, has left us only one option: it's the rapture! ***This is a radical new understanding for the church!***

The rapture is a *harpazo* (the Greek word found in 1 Thessalonians 4:16–17 from which we get the word rapture). Harpazo means a forceful, visible, and sudden rescue, and that's exactly what is depicted in Matthew 24:30–31.

This new information is hard to assimilate all at once. Let's return to our previous graphic of the *Olivet Discourse* and add what we have learned, shown in the following graphic, so we can visualize it.

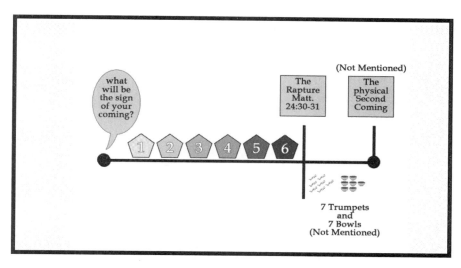

Figure 6: Olivet Discourse with Trumpets and Bowls Added

This graphic helps our understanding. Let's look at the structure of the Olivet Discourse:

- The disciples initiate the Discourse by asking, "When will these things happen and what will be the sign of your coming?"

- Jesus then responds with the six signs that precede his coming that are the same as the first six seals of Revelation 6:1–17.
- Jesus then depicts his coming in graphic terms that are forceful, visible, and sudden—just like the word harpazo.
- Jesus does *not* depict the trumpet judgments or bowl judgments or the physical second coming in the Olivet Discourse because these events come *after* his arrival (his *parousia*) at the rapture.

THE OLIVET DISCOURSE = THE *PREWRATH RAPTURE*

I don't know if you have noticed it yet, but the Olivet Discourse is an exact depiction of the *prewrath rapture*. Let us overlay the graphic of the *prewrath rapture* (see appendix A, pp. 269–271) on the one we have now developed for the Olivet Discourse so you can see the perfect fit of this rapture theory with the model of the Discourse.

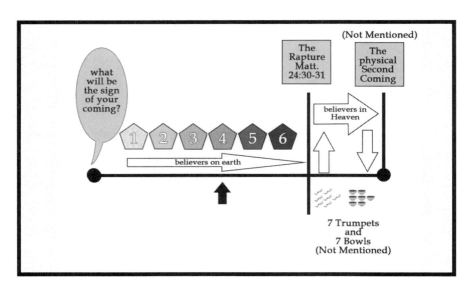

Figure 7: Perfect Match of the Olivet Discourse and the Prewrath Rapture

The first six signs occur while the believers are still on the earth (so they can see the signs of his coming!). The last three of the six signs perfectly match the timing of the great tribulation, which follows the midpoint (black arrow) of the Seventieth Week (or Tribulation), as depicted in the graphic. Note that *the rapture occurs after the sixth sign,* as it does in Matthew 24:29–31. The believers are insulated from the wrath of God (the trumpet and bowl judgments) by the rapture, as prophesied in 1 Thess. 1:10 and 1 Thess. 5:9.

> The Olivet Discourse is the *ultimate and definitive proof of rapture timing.* It makes mute all other rapture theories and proofs.

In summary, the Olivet Discourse is an elegant proof for the *prewrath rapture* and disproves both the *pretribulation rapture* theory and *post-tribulation rapture* theory. **This alone should close the "rapture timing case."** However, we provide much more evidence in this book.

Admittedly, entrenched doctrine positions are difficult to change, and additional biblical evidence is helpful for some to change their position. Let's demonstrate in the section below some sample arguments from the other rapture theory camps to show how this is true.

CONTRARY RAPTURE TIMING POSITIONS:

1) *PRETRIBULATION RAPTURE* ARGUMENTS

Pretribulation rapture proponents will be quick to point out that they also believe the rapture occurs before the trumpet and bowl judgments—long before. This is correct; however, they must then identify the event taking place in Matthew 24:30–31. We have conclusively shown it cannot be the physical second coming of Jesus, as Revelation 16:12, 15–16 quotes, "I am coming" after the sixth bowl is poured out. If it isn't the physical second coming, and if pretrib rapture proponents say it isn't the rapture, what event is it? They have no answer for this argument.

A great weakness of the *pretribulation rapture* position is that it is an inferred position, and supporters of this theory cannot point to a single passage of Scripture that clearly depicts the rapture happening before the so-called "tribulation." In our legal system in the USA, we honor habeas corpus, which gives a suspect the right to be presented before a judge. The *pretribulation rapture* supporters cannot present their suspect before us as judges. The proof in this chapter has shown that the depiction of the rapture was always there in Matthew 24:30–31; unfortunately, most have missed it—**hidden in plain sight**.

Additional *pretribulation rapture* arguments are discussed in chapter six: "The Backfire Effect (*Pre-Tribulation Rapture* Arguments)."

2) *POST-TRIBULATION RAPTURE* ARGUMENTS

Many *post-tribulation rapture* proponents (and *some pretribulation rapture* supporters) believe the seals, trumpets, and bowls happen concurrently. They do not believe that the trumpet and bowl judgments occur only at the end of the Seventieth Week of Daniel as pictured in the preceding graphics. At the conclusion of this chapter, we will present numerous proofs that their theory on concurrent seals, trumpets, and bowls is incorrect. However, right now, those proofs are unnecessary. All we need to understand at this point is that Jesus did not mention the trumpet and bowl judgments as a sign of his return in the Olivet Discourse. Thus, he must return *before* a single trumpet is sounded and before a single bowl is poured out or the Discourse has seriously misled the church. Although whether the seals, trumpets, and bowls are concurrent or consecutive is important, it is *immaterial* to **this proof** of rapture timing. That is the elegance of this rapture proof.

Post-tribulation rapture supporters also argue that the celestial earthly disturbance and, by extension, the rapture must take place after the great tribulation. "After the tribulation of those days, the sun will be darkened . . ." (Matt. 24:29). I agree. But, they mistakenly claim that the entire last three and a half years of the Seventieth Week is the great tribulation. It is not. As we state in appendix A: "Summary of Rapture Timing Theories," Jesus only said that after the midpoint of the Seventieth Week that there would *be* great tribulation, not that the entire three and a half years would be "the" great tribulation. We will discuss this further in chapter seven: "Center of the Universe (*Post-Tribulation Rapture Arguments*)." But like the discussion above, all that is critical at this point is that Jesus did not mention the trumpet and bowl judgments as signs of his coming. He either misled the church, or his return is *prior* to those judgments as well as prior to the physical second coming. The takeaway message here is: ***his return (rapture) is before the trumpet and bowl judgments***.

Seals, Trumpets, and Bowls

However, because organization of the seven seals, seven trumpets, and seven bowls is certainly a lingering question in the minds of many, we will discuss it now rather than later in the book. There is great debate within the church as to whether the seals, trumpets, and bowls are all *concurrent* (they occur interspersed throughout the seven-year period) or whether they are *consecutive* (the seals occur first, the trumpets second, and finally the bowls). I must thank Alan Kurschner[13] for his outstanding investigation into this issue, which conclusively shows they are consecutive. Below you will find graphics of each of the two models of the order of seals, trumpets, and bowls:

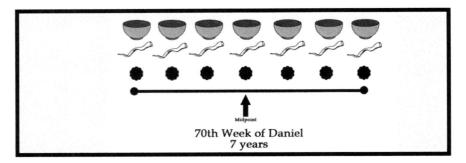

Figure 8: Concurrent Seals, Trumpets, and Bowls Model

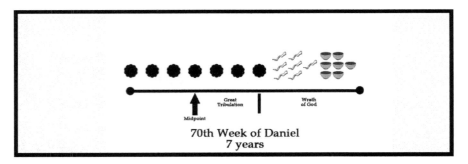

Figure 9: Consecutive Seals, Trumpets, and Bowls Model

(not to scale)

The concurrent theory is consistent with what is known as a *post-tribulation rapture*. This theory states that Jesus will return at the end of the Seventieth Week of Daniel, rapture his church, save all of Israel on that last day, and then fight the battle of Armageddon. This *post-tribulation rapture* theory requires that the seventh seal, the seventh trumpet, and the seventh bowl all occur at about the same time (essentially on the last day of the Seventieth Week). This is necessary to mitigate inconsistencies in their position and the

34

obvious sense of Scripture that the resurrection and rapture occur *after* the sixth seal, and that the day of the Lord (God's wrath) unfolds before the battle of Armageddon. Most believers in a concurrent theory of the seals, trumpets, and bowls believe that the *seventh trumpet* is the *last trumpet* referred to by Paul in 1 Corinthians 15 that accompanies the rapture. We discuss the last trumpet and its true identity in chapter seven: "Center of the Universe (*Post-Tribulation Rapture* Arguments)."

The consecutive theory of seals, trumpets, and bowls is consistent with a *prewrath rapture*. When the seventh seal is opened, it reveals the seven trumpet judgments. When the seventh trumpet is blown, it reveals the seven bowl judgments. The seventh seal and seventh trumpet are like nesting dolls that contain the next series of events within them. This concept is further developed in my book, *Revelation Deciphered*[14]

The Evidence

This chapter is the **ultimate proof** that the trumpet and bowl judgments follow the seals, but there are other proofs of a consecutive timing of seals, trumpets, and bowls as well. The following graphic provides the majority of Alan Kurschner's published reasons why the seals, trumpets, and bowls must be consecutive and not current:

Reason	Implication
Rev. 15:1 claims the seven bowls are the *last* aspect of God's wrath	If the seven bowls are the last aspect of God's wrath, another aspect (the trumpet judgments) must precede them

Reason	Implication
Rev. 8:1 clearly shows that the seven trumpets are given to the angels *after* the seventh seal is broken	If the seven trumpets are blown after the seventh seal, the seals precede the trumpets
Silence occurs after the seventh seal is broken. In Zeph. 1:7, silence precedes the day of the Lord (God's wrath)	If silence follows the seventh seal, yet precedes God's wrath, all the seals precede God's wrath
Each of the septets (seals, trumpets, bowls) are progressively worse than the preceding	This implies a progressively worsening order of events
At the fifth seal, the martyrs under the altar are told to wait for God's avenging of their murders	By extension, God's wrath (trumpets and bowls) cannot have occurred prior to the fifth seal
The celestial earthly disturbance occurs at the sixth seal. In Joel 2:30–31 we are told that this precedes the day of the Lord (God's wrath)	By extension, God's wrath (trumpets and bowls) cannot have occurred before the sixth seal
In Rev. 7:3, God instructs his angels to not damage the earth or the seas or the trees prior to sealing the 144,000	The first three trumpets damage the earth, seas, and trees; by extension the trumpet judgments must follow this sealing event

Figure 10: Evidence for Consecutive Seals, Trumpets, and Bowls (Based on analysis by Alan Kurschner)

SUMMARY

The question arises as to why centuries have gone by without anyone noticing the Olivet Discourse doesn't include the trumpet and bowl judgments? The answer is similar to why only Gergely Barki was able to identify the Hungarian masterpiece in the movie *Stuart Little*. It was "hidden in plain sight" and required someone whose knowledge and interests were centered on Hungarian art. Noticing the significance that the Olivet Discourse does include the first six seals but *does not* include the trumpet and bowl judgments required someone with a knowledge and interest in the *prewrath rapture* theory to see it.

The first testimony of this fact was by Charles Cooper, director of the Prewrath Resource Institute, in a footnote found in his book *God's Elect and the Great Tribulation*,[15] although he did not expand this observation to its implications on the timing of the rapture.

The beauty of this simple and elegant rapture-timing proof is that it **categorically disproves both the *post-tribulation rapture* and the *pretribulation rapture* in one proof**. If you are not yet 100% convinced, I recommend you reread this chapter. It contains a lot of new information and is a radically new way of looking at the Olivet Discourse.

The major takeaway from this chapter, however, is not which theory is correct and which ones are "mistaken." The takeaway is that this chapter presents seemingly irrefutable proof that the church of Jesus Christ *will* face the Antichrist and his great tribulation. The implications of this proof are enormous.

If the conclusions of this chapter are correct, then the entire strategy of most churches must change.

Millions or even hundreds of millions of churchgoers are at risk of entering the greatest period of persecution the world has ever known without any preparation at all! The results of this persecution are mind-blowing. When faced with their own or their family's starvation, torture, or death or with denying Jesus, which will our churchgoers choose? Will their love of our Savior exceed their love of their earthly lives? Obviously many will choose Jesus. But the vast majority of the unprepared may choose to worship Antichrist rather than suffer. Jesus tells us *most* people will fall away, and their love for him and others will grow cold:

> At that time many will fall away and will betray one another and hate one another. Many false prophets will arise and will mislead many. Because lawlessness is increased, *most people's love* will grow cold. (Matt. 24:10–12 NASB, emphasis mine)

Consider your church and congregation. Can we let them enter this period without being ready? In the final section of this book, we have included a chapter on preparation: chapter eight: "Brethren, What Shall We Do?" that gives detailed suggestions on what we need to teach in order to prepare the flock God has entrusted to each of us.

We cannot end our discussion with this one proof, however. With so much at stake, we must dig in and examine the full testimony of Scripture and every proof of every theory. We must know what God's Word says and not assume. I highly encourage you to read this entire book because that is its goal: to illuminate the entire case for whether the church faces Antichrist.

We will begin by exploring **whether Scripture provides a "second witness"** for the proof we have just witnessed. The Bible never gives us just one witness to a prophecy. "On the evidence of two or three witnesses a matter shall be confirmed" (Deut. 19:15 NASB). In the next chapter, we'll discover a second-witness Scripture that utilizes "sense and reference" to enable us to decipher Scripture in its most accurate and majestic form.

Chapter Three

MOVING PICTURES

(Explicit Rapture Depiction in Revelation)

"These are the ones who come out of the great tribulation, and they have washed their robes and made them white in the blood of the Lamb." (Rev. 7:14 NASB)

The word "movie" came from a much older term: "moving pictures." I remember my grandmother always referring to a movie as a "moving picture." In a way, this is exactly how old celluloid movie film worked. Individual pictures or frames were illuminated by light. As the pictures were set in motion in front of this light, the image on the screen appeared to move. Thus the term "moving pictures" was born.

The individual images made of celluloid are called "cels." Cels from animated movies are among the most sought-after movie memorabilia. A single cel from Walt Disney's 1935 classic animated movie *The Band Concert* sold for a reported $420,000 in 1999. The top ten most valuable movie cels of all time were also from Disney movies.[16]

Well, not quite. There is a much more valuable moving picture found in the pages of Scripture that will provide us with our second witness of rapture timing. We will bring this witness to the stand shortly.

EVERY EYE SHALL SEE HIM

In chapter two: "Hidden Treasure (Ultimate Proof of Rapture Timing)," we discussed how Jesus gave John 21 prophetic end-time events or signs in the form of seven seals, seven trumpets, and seven bowls. In that previous chapter, we also discussed how the first six seals are the exact same events as the six signs of Jesus's return presented in the Olivet Discourse.

The following graphic displays that this amazing parallelism *continues* after the sixth seal is opened, showing that the events in Matt. 24:29-30 and Rev. 6:12-17 are depicting the same things.

Events in Matt. 24:29-30		Events in Rev. 6:12-17	
The sun is darkened	Matt. 24:29	The sun is black	Rev. 6:12
The moon doesn't give its light.	Matt. 24:29	The moon becomes like blood	Rev. 6:12
Stars fall from the sky	Matt. 24:29	Stars fall from the sky	Rev. 6:13
The powers of the heavens are shaken	Matt. 24:29	Sky is split and rolled up like a scroll	Rev. 6:14
The tribes of the earth mourn	Matt. 24:30	The inhabitants of the earth ask the rocks of the mountains to fall on them	Rev. 6:16
They will see the Son of Man coming on the clouds	Matt. 24:30	The inhabitants of the earth ask to be hidden from the *face* of God	Rev. 6:17

Figure 11: Parallelism after Opening the Sixth Seal

The final similarity in these six parallel events is stunning. Jesus is present in the sight of all people after the opening of the sixth seal!

> They said to the mountains and to the rocks, "Fall on us and hide us from the presence [Gk: *prosopou*, meaning "face"] of Him who sits on the throne, and from the wrath of the Lamb." (Rev. 6:16 NASB)

The Greek word translated "presence" is prosopou, which means "face." The inhabitants of the world will see Jesus's face. How can this be explained other than that this is the point at which Jesus comes on the clouds of heaven and is seen by all as his angels rapture his elect?

Jesus is seen by all the inhabitants of the earth after the opening of the sixth seal.

This incredible passage (Rev. 6:16) discounts both *pretribulation rapture* and *post-tribulation rapture* theories; neither theory expects Jesus to be seen prior to the physical second coming. Yet, he obviously will be.

In 2015, a debate on the rapture was held between Alan Kurschner, a leading prewrath expert, and Dr. Thomas Ice, pretribulationalism's leading voice and the Director of the Pre-Trib. Rapture Institute. In that debate, Dr. Ice claimed this appearance of Jesus in Rev. 6:16 will only be a "theophany" (appearance of God to a human) prior to the physical second coming.[17] This is a desperate attempt to deny the obvious conclusions of this verse; that this is the moment "every eye shall see him" (Rev. 1:7). Many other Scriptures imply Jesus will not leave heaven to be revealed until his parousia ("return") making the "theophany" theory impossible:

41

For I say to you, from now on you will not see Me until you say, "Blessed is He who comes in the name of the Lord!" (Matt. 23:39 NASB)

That He may send Jesus, the Christ appointed for you, whom heaven must receive until the period of restoration of all things. (Acts 3:20–21 NASB)

Christ also, having been offered once to bear the sins of many, will appear a second time for salvation without reference to sin, to those who eagerly await Him. (Heb. 9:28 NASB)

Behold, He is coming with the clouds, and every eye will see Him, even those who pierced Him; and all the tribes of the earth will mourn over Him. So it is to be. Amen. (Rev. 1:7 NASB)

Additionally, passages like Luke 17:29-30 and 2 Thessalonians 1:6–8 utilize the word "reveal" in regard to the return of Jesus. Calling his return the revealing of Jesus implies it is the first sighting of Jesus and that it occurs when he comes on the clouds. The fact that these scriptures indicate Jesus will not be seen by humans until his coming on the clouds is the very reason that pretribulationalists claim their vision of the rapture will be a "silent" and "invisible" one. Again, Rev. 6:16 cannot simply be a "theophany."

So as unlikely as it is that the appearance of Jesus to every inhabitant of the world (in a section of Scripture that exactly parallels Matthew 24) is only a theophany, the "moving picture" we are about to discuss disproves that theory entirely by demonstrating the rapture immediately follows this sighting of Jesus.

"MOVING PICTURE" OF THE RAPTURE

Based on this exact parallel between the Olivet Discourse and Revelation 6 that we have seen thus far, this section of Scripture is a likely place to look for our "second witness" to *prove* rapture timing. In the Olivet Discourse, the rapture occurs in Matthew 24:31 after the six events in Matthew that follow the sixth seal as listed in figure 11. It is my hypothesis that the rapture will also be recorded in Revelation after the *six parallel events* in Revelation 6:12–17. If this hypothesis is correct, we need to look in Revelation 7 for this second witness Scripture.

As we look for evidence of the rapture, we must remember this portion of Scripture is a vision of events happening *in heaven*. Therefore, we must look for evidence of what occurs in heaven at the time of the rapture. Matthew 24:31 depicts what occurs on earth after Jesus descends *out of heaven*. The events of Matthew 24:31, the sounding of the trumpet of God and the gathering together by the angels, are unlikely to be seen in the Revelation vision.

Before we are able to examine our evidence, however, we must ascertain the broad context of the passage in Revelation 7. Only in the full perspective of this passage can the truth of rapture timing be uncovered. The opening of the seals in Revelation 6 exists in the greater setting of Revelation 4–8. At the beginning of Revelation 4, John the Revelator is called up into heaven "in the spirit" to observe an extended vision. In that vision, John is ushered into the throne room of God, and he witnesses the seven-sealed scroll being handed to Jesus and then opened.

And in the context of the heavenly vision of Revelation 4–8, there *is* evidence that demonstrates the rapture occurs at the *very point we expect it* based on our discussion in the previous section: after the sixth seal of Revelation and after Jesus manifests himself before the inhabitants of the earth. In fact, this evidence presents itself as a "moving picture" that we can evaluate.

When we say the evidence is a moving picture, what we mean is that two scenes, or cels, are found in Scripture. These cels are almost exactly the same. The only difference is that one of the items in the cels will have moved. That will be the moving aspect of this moving picture.

As an example of this principle, let's say we are looking at two consecutive cels of an animated Disney moving picture cartoon. First, let us say all aspects of the cels are held constant except one. Second, let's say that in the first cel Mickey Mouse is on the side of the lake and in the second cel he is in the lake. Mickey Mouse, then, is the moving aspect of the moving picture. He will have moved *from* the side of the lake and *into* the lake.

In the extended biblical passage in question (Rev. 4–8), there are two such similar cels. If we carefully look at verses in Revelation 5, we see the first cel generated:

> And they sang a new song, saying, "Worthy are you to take the book and to break its seals; for you were slain, *and purchased for God with Your blood men from every tribe and tongue and people and nation* . . ." Then I looked, and I heard the voice of *many angels around the throne and the living creatures and the elders*; and the number of them was myriads of myriads, and thousands of thousands, *saying* with a loud voice, "Worthy is the Lamb that was slain to receive *power* and *riches* and *wisdom* and *might* and *honor* and *glory* and *blessing*." (Rev. 5:9, 11–12 NASB, emphasis mine)

Then if we continue to examine this vision in Revelation 4–8, a nearly identical cel is found later; except this time it is *after* the sixth seal:

> I looked, and behold, *a great multitude* which no one could count, *from every nation and all tribes and peoples and tongues*, standing before the throne and before the Lamb, clothed in white robes, and palm branches were in their hands; and they cry out with a loud voice, saying, "Salvation to our God who sits on the throne, and to the Lamb." And *all the angels* were standing *around the throne* and around *the elders and the four living creatures*; and they fell on their faces before the throne and worshiped God, *saying*, "Amen, *blessing* and *glory* and *wisdom* and thanksgiving and *honor* and *power* and *might*, be to our God forever and ever. Amen." (Rev. 7:9–12 NASB, emphasis mine)

Scripture interprets Scripture. These two passages are *nearly identical quotes* of each other. They are given to us like two consecutive scenes from a movie with almost every aspect held constant, the only difference being the location of the saints. All the characters in the scenes are the same:

- The saints are described by the phrase "**every tribe and tongue and people and nation**"
- The angels are listed second in the two cels as "**many angels around the throne**" and "**all the angels . . . around the throne**"
- The **living creatures** and the **elders** are listed next
- The moving picture has a sound track. They sing the *same song* in both cels with six of the seven praise words being identical in the Greek (**blessing, glory, honor, wisdom, power**, and **might**).

45

The only significant difference between these two passages is that in the second cel, a great multitude of saints has been added to the picture. This is the moving picture aspect of this Bible study. The saints move into the second scene just as Mickey Mouse moved into the lake in our earlier example. ***This is the most explicit proof in Revelation for the timing of the rapture***. In the first passage, the great multitude of the church isn't in heaven. They are referred to as the ones Jesus purchased with his blood, but they're not seen. In the second cel, John sees the multitude; they have moved in heaven. This process is depicted in the following figure:

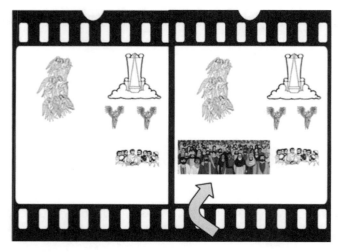

Figure 12: Throne in Heaven Moving Picture in Revelation

In the first movie cel of this graphic, we see the throne, the living creatures, the myriads of angels, and the elders. This cel represents what we find in Revelation 5:9–12. In the second cel, all the original participants are still there but the "vast multitude" of raptured saints has been added to the cel. They have moved into the picture. This second cel represents Revelation 7:9–12.

The timing for this transition is *after* the sixth seal (the celestial earthly disturbance) and after the manifest appearance of Jesus, which coincidentally also happens to be the timing of the rapture in the Olivet Discourse (Matt. 24:29–31), exactly where we predicted it would be found! It not only is exactly where we predicted it would be found, it is also the rapture as seen from heaven's perspective *just as we predicted* it would be.

John then asks one of the elders about this multitude and is given a second clue about the timing of the rapture:

> And he said to me, "These are *the ones who **come out of the great tribulation***, and they have washed their robes and made them white in the blood of the Lamb." (Rev. 7:14 NASB, emphasis mine)

This is the exact timing given in the Olivet Discourse for the rapture as well:

> But immediately ***after the tribulation*** of those days the sun will be darkened, and the moon will not give its light, and the stars will fall from the sky, and the powers of the heavens will be shaken. (Matt. 24:29 NASB, emphasis mine)

The timing of the rapture is the same in both witness accounts: *after* the sixth seal, *after* Jesus's appearance, and *after* great tribulation. Then immediately upon the completion of this scene, Jesus breaks the seventh seal (Rev. 8:1) and the angels begin to blow the trumpet judgments. The order of events in Revelation is exactly the same as it is in Matthew:

- Six signs/seals (the same events) precede the return of Jesus.

- The rapture occurs *after* the sixth sign/sixth seal, *after* the appearance of Jesus, and *after* great tribulation.
- The trumpet judgments take place *after* the rapture (they are not mentioned in Matthew so they must take place after the events that are depicted).

CONTRARY RAPTURE TIMING POSITIONS:

1) *PRETRIBULATION RAPTURE* ARGUMENTS

The only argument that *Pretribulation rapture* theorists have devised to cross-examine our scriptural witness is to contend that the vast multitude in Rev. 7 are simply the souls of martyrs ("tribulation saints") who came out of the great tribulation and not the raptured church. One of these theorists is Dr. Renald Showers, a pastor, author, and a Bible teacher for The Friends of Israel Gospel Ministry. Dr. Showers has served on the faculties of Lancaster Bible College, Moody Bible Institute, and Philadelphia College of the Bible.

Before we look at Dr. Shower's specific arguments, however, we must examine his theory biblically. First, we notice that John visualizes the great multitude as a unit, as if they showed up *en masse*: "I looked, and *behold*, a great multitude" (Rev. 7:9 NASB). John doesn't see them arriving one by one as would be true if they were the souls of those martyred in the great tribulation; rather he is shocked by their sudden appearance which is consistent with the rapture.

Second if *pretribulation rapture* theorists are correct, we must question why John's vision would focus on the celebration a relatively small group of "tribulation saints" and would ignore the earlier celebration of vast "multitudes" of saints from all the ages when *they* first entered into the presence of God. *Pretribulation rapture* theorists cannot claim that a single resurrected saint is included in this later group before the throne because we

48

are specifically told they have come out of the great tribulation. Yet, this vast multitude are the ones that God covers with his tabernacle (Rev. 7:15), and they are the ones in wild celebration.

Third, the vast multitude do not exhibit the traits of "souls." Earlier, at the opening of the fifth seal, we *do* observe the souls of martyrs prior to them receiving resurrection bodies. We are specifically told that these individuals are "souls." This is a term that is used twice in Revelation (Rev. 6:9, Rev. 20:4), and in both instances it is specifically used for the spirits of deceased saints prior to a resurrection.

The following graphic provides the sharp contrast of those souls under the altar at the fifth seal and the saints of Rev. 7:9–17.

Martyrs under the Altar (Rev. 6: 9–11)	Saints before the Throne (Rev. 7:9–17)
Called "souls"	They stand, wave palm branches, and wear garments; they have bodies
They are under the altar	They're before the throne
They cry out for justice	They praise God
They are given white robes but told to wait	They are wearing white robes
Told to rest until the number of martyrs is completed	Serve God day and night
Called martyrs	Praise God for salvation
John recognizes who they are	John has to ask who they are

Figure 13: Beneath the Altar and before the Throne
Based on the teaching of Marvin Rosenthal[18]

Due to these emphasized differences, it is *impossible* to imagine that both of these groups represent the same "souls." The saints in Revelation 7:9–17 are not called souls and they're no longer beneath the altar, but have moved to before the throne. It is obvious they are in their resurrection bodies because they stand, they wave, and they wear garments. They no longer cry out for justice but are in wild celebration and praise. They no longer are told they have to wait to wear their white robes, but they have them on. At the fifth seal, John knew who the souls were, but after the sixth seal John has to ask who the multitude is. A change has taken place, and that change is the one that takes place at the resurrection and rapture (1 Cor. 15:51-52)!

Those who discount that the vast multitude are not the raptured saints must explain *all* these fundamental differences. An important point to note, however, is that the great multitude *includes* the souls beneath the altar of the fifth seal. After the sixth seal, they were resurrected first and then raptured into heaven with all the rest of God's elect.

Now let's return to Dr. Shower's specific arguments, which in contrast to the case we have just presented, appear quite weak. The first exception that Dr. Showers presents is that we are told the vast multitude came "out of" the great tribulation.[19] Dr. Showers reasons that this would exclude all the saints who died prior to this period. What this learned man has overlooked, of course, is that the resurrection of the righteous dead from all the ages takes place immediately prior to the rapture (1 Thess. 4:16–17). In this way, the living *and* the resurrected will meet the Lord in the air, and all the saints of all the ages will "come out of" the great tribulation together *at the same time.*

Second, Dr. Showers also takes exception to the translation of the word "came" in Revelation 7:14. He indicates that the present participle translated "came" in the statement: "These are they who *came* out of the

50

great tribulation" is a *verb* that indicates continuous action and should be translated "are coming." As we mentioned before, he suggests that the vast multitude are souls of martyrs who come out of the great tribulation one by one through death, not all at once as in the rapture of the church.[20]

Let's examine this theory. The fact that the word "came" is utilized as a *participle* and not as a verb is incredibly important. A verb determines action, but a participle does not indicate action at all. In this case the participle phrase functions as a noun (predicate nominative). Only the context of the participle phrase—nothing in the grammar—indicates how and when the "came" occurs in Rev. 7:14[21]. And as we have just seen in the numerous proofs presented earlier in this section, the context of Rev. 7:14 clearly indicates the vast multitude were raptured at one moment in time. They did not come before the throne incrementally.

In conclusion, we are told these raptured saints in Revelation 7 have "come out of the great tribulation" *after* the sixth seal and *prior* to trumpet and bowl judgments. It was a *prewrath* resurrection and rapture. This is proof that neither the *pretribulation* nor *post-tribulation rapture* theories are correct.

THE ELDERS

In contrast to this highly logical and likely scenario that the great multitude are the raptured church, *pretribulation rapture* proponents claim that in the cel we looked at in Revelation 5, the twenty-four elders are the church or at least representatives of the church. One of the proponents of this position is Dr. David Hocking. Dr. Hocking has pastored numerous churches, has taught Greek and theology in Bible institutes, and is a teacher for the "Hope for Today" radio broadcast. In a featured article on Pre-Trib Research Center's website, he had this to say about the twenty-four Elders:

There is no doubt that the issue of the 24 elders is critical to the whole argument of Pre-tribulationalism.[22] —Dr. David Hocking

Dr. Hocking is correct; pretribulationalism rests on this point. After the rapture, saints will "always be with the Lord" (1 Thess. 4:17). If the rapture occurs prior to the opening of the seven-sealed scroll at the beginning of the Seventieth Week of Daniel as the *pretribulation rapture* theory says it should, the saints must always be present with the Lord from that point on. However, a big problem for this position is that there are no saints depicted before the throne in Revelation 4 and 5, prior to the opening of the seals. If the twenty-four elders are not the newly raptured saints or at least newly raptured representatives of the saints, there is no *pretribulation rapture*. It is as plain and simple as that.

And to me, the notion that the twenty-four elders are the newly raptured church is very hard (if not impossible) to accept. First, there are only twenty-four of them (Rev. 4:4). Hocking has suggested that the number twenty-four may have some symbolic significance of the vast multitudes of saints. Despite my respect for him, this suggestion borders on the absurd. In Revelation 5:11, we are told John sees myriads of myriads of angels. In Revelation 7:9, John sees a vast multitude of saints. These massive numbers of individuals are not accounted for by a symbolic number; so by comparison, the twenty-four elders are simply twenty-four in number, as Scripture states.

By logic, they also cannot be newly raptured representatives of the saints because we are told in 1 Thessalonians 4:17 that after the rapture, *all* the saints are "always with the Lord." It is unimaginable that immediately after the rapture, Jesus and a few representatives retire to a back room to open the seven-sealed scroll while the rest of the saints wait outside (for the majority of seven years)!

I do, however, agree with my brothers who hold to a *pretribulation rapture* theory that these twenty-four elders might be human, and raptured humans at that. One theory is that they may have been raised and raptured with Jesus in the first century as part of the first fruits resurrection, as Matthew 27:52–53 so states:

> The tombs were opened, and *many bodies of the saints* who had fallen asleep were raised; and coming out of the tombs after His resurrection they entered the holy city and appeared to many. (Matt. 27:52–53 NASB, emphasis mine)

"The saints" which were raised may include many of the Old Testament prophets, patriarchs, and kings; and perhaps even John the Baptist is among their ranks. They very well might be a part of the fulfillment of the first fruits resurrection of Jesus.

Marvin Rosenthal, in his groundbreaking book *The Pre-Wrath Rapture of the Church*, shows how twenty-four is the number of courses or groups of Levite priests in the Old Testament. Each course would send a spokesperson elder as the people's representative before God.

The twenty-four elders are wearing white garments in Revelation 4–5. John and his contemporaries in the first century would all know that the high priest took off his priestly robes and donned a white garment to enter the Holy of Holies on each Yom Kippur, signifying being in the presence of God. The twenty-four elders are also fulfilling priestly duties of intercession by carrying bowls of incense that are the prayers of the saints. These prayers rise like incense before God at the seventh seal.[23]

Conversely, Dr. Michael Heiser, resident scholar at Faithlife (makers of Logos Bible Software, my personal Bible software choice) takes the position that the twenty-four elders are not humans but are heavenly beings and make up the divine council referenced in Psalm 82:1–6.[24] It is possible that the twenty-four courses of Levitical priests was an earthly copy of this heavenly divine council. He points out that these elders are referred to as God's elders in Isaiah in an apocalyptic context:

> Then the moon will be abashed and the sun ashamed [the sixth seal], for the Lord of hosts will reign on Mount Zion and in Jerusalem, And His glory will be before *His elders*. (Isa. 24:23 NASB, clarification and emphasis mine)

In either instance, whether they are saints resurrected in the first century or heavenly beings, the twenty-four elders are *not* representatives of the newly resurrected and raptured church depicted later in Revelation (Rev. 7:9–17).

2) *POST-TRIBULATION RAPTURE* ARGUMENTS

In addition to the argument above that the saints pictured in Revelation 7:9–17 are souls not yet raptured (discussed in the previous section), *post-tribulation rapture* theorists may also argue that the order of the seals—trumpets—bowls is not sequential. In chapter two: "Hidden Treasure (Ultimate Proof of Rapture Timing)," we have already proven that the seals—trumpets—bowls are sequential and consecutive.

Some *post-tribulation rapture* supporters do favor a proper sequential order of the seals—trumpets—bowls, but they must take extreme measures to overcome the difficulties presented by the sixth seal. In his recent book, *Rapture Verdict*, Michael Snyder—attorney, author, and renowned speaker—takes the position that the sun and moon darkening events in Matthew 24:29 and the sixth seal are not the same event. Mr. Snyder points out that in the Matt. 24 and the Rev. 6 versions of the event, the Greek words for "black" are different. He also observes that in Matthew 24, the moon does not give its light, while in Revelation 6, the moon is turned to blood red.[25]

In my opinion, these extremely *minor* differences in wording are the reflection of two different witnesses recording Jesus's testimony about the same events in slightly different terms. What Mr. Snyder misses are the other identical, "fingerprint" similarities between the two versions of the celestial earthly disturbance (see figure 11). In both versions of the event, the stars fall and the sky is split open (Matthew calls it the powers of the heavens being shaken). Most importantly, however, Jesus is visibly seen by everyone on the planet, and the unrighteous mourn. These similarities prove unmistakably that these are the same events—and that these events are followed by the *prewrath rapture*.

SUMMARY

We have shown in this chapter three: "Moving Pictures (Explicit Rapture Depiction in Revelation)" that Revelation 4–9 is a perfect second-witness Scripture for the Olivet Discourse's *prewrath rapture*. As we have seen in chapter two, the rapture is preceded by six parallel signs, which are recorded in both the Olivet Discourse and in Revelation 6 (see figure 5). The last three of these six signs take place during the great tribulation. After the opening of the final sign, the sixth seal, we demonstrated six additional parallel events occur (see figure 11). The rapture takes place after these parallel events, as seen in Revelation 7:9–17. The trumpet and bowl judgments then take place after the rapture. It is as simple and clear as that.

But just as we discussed in the conclusion to our previous chapter, the takeaway to this "second witness" proof is not only which rapture theory is correct; it is the implications of that theory. The vast majority of churchgoers today are completely unprepared for the persecution and deception that is coming. Rapture expert Sheila Sternberg has detailed three ways that unpreparedness may lead to churchgoers falling away[26]:

- Deny that the Antichrist truly is the Antichrist because "Christians aren't supposed to face him (so this can't be the Antichrist.)"
- Reject Christianity entirely because they were misled them about rapture timing. They may think, "If the Pastor was wrong about something so basic, might he also be wrong about Jesus?"
- Fall away due to a lack of time for preparation when the Great Tribulation takes them by complete surprise.

We must never forget those whom we fellowship with every Sunday. God has given us this foreknowledge of what is to come to help prepare them; and God has made us **accountable** for their preparation!

In light of the seriousness of that charge, the next chapter, chapter four: "Synchronous Fireworks (Same-Day Salvation and Wrath)," will present yet a third, newly presented proof that the event in Matthew 24:31 is the rapture and not the physical second coming—still further evidence for the *prewrath rapture* position. Our goal is to systematically analyze all the major proofs of all the rapture theories. Only then can we come to a biblically based verdict and close the rapture case.

Chapter Four

SYNCHRONIZED FIREWORKS

(Same-Day Salvation and Wrath)

"On the day that Lot went out from Sodom it rained fire and brimstone from heaven and destroyed them all. It will be just the same on the day that the Son of Man is revealed" (Luke 17:29–30 NASB)

W hen I was much younger, my neighbor worked for the Zambelli Fireworks Company, which produces large extravaganza displays as you may have seen in major cities. At the time, Zambelli specialized in fireworks that were synchronized to music. It used to be a Fourth of July tradition for the local symphony orchestra to play Tchaikovsky's "1812 Overture" (complete with cannons) while the fireworks burst overhead. My friend's job was to fire specific firework shells at the precise moment required to synchronize with the music. In today's computerized world, this synchronization is accomplished by a computer program, but in those days, my neighbor had to accomplish it manually.

Today's firework displays still require a designer. The first step in the process is inputting the songs that will be used into the software. Then the designer selects from the hundreds of explosive shell types in the software's database, matching them to specific segments of the song. The software digitally places a code on the music track and then fires electronic signals as each code is played during the song. These electronic signals launch the shells at the appropriate moment, taking into account the time it takes the shell to launch to its full height and explode. Current fireworks

57

software is accurate up to 0.01 of a second. This allows amazing synchronization of music and fireworks. Audiences love it and appreciate the accuracy and timing necessary to achieve the event.

GOD'S FIREWORKS

God's timing is even more perfect and amazing. Most Christians are aware that God plans to someday judge the wicked of this world with *fire* that will fall from heaven on the *day of judgment* at his perfect timing:

> But by His word the present heavens and earth are being reserved for *fire*, *kept for the day of judgment* and destruction of ungodly men. (2 Pet. 3:7 NASB, emphasis mine)

> But a terrifying expectation of *judgment and the fury of fire* which will consume the adversaries. (Heb. 10:27 NASB, emphasis mine)

> Upon the wicked He will rain snares; *fire and brimstone and burning wind* will be the portion of their cup. (Psalm 11:6 NASB, emphasis mine)

God has planned this judgment of "fire-works" to *synchronize* with the rest of his redemptive plan. This fiery judgment will not be random, but will occur at a precise, preplanned moment. God's accuracy is much greater than the computer's accuracy of 0.01 second. The passage at the beginning of this chapter gives us that exact timing:

58

> On the day that Lot went out from Sodom it rained *fire and brimstone* from heaven and destroyed them all. *It will be just the same on the day that the Son of Man is revealed*. (Luke 17:29–30 NASB, emphasis mine)

From this we learn that on the day that Lot was taken out of Sodom by the angels, fire and brimstone fell upon the cities of the plain (Sodom, Gomorrah, and other cities). More incredibly, we learn that it will be *just the same* on the day that Jesus is revealed. The righteous will be saved and then later *on that same day*, fire and brimstone will fall on the wicked. This makes the falling of fire and brimstone from heaven a time marker for the salvation of the righteous!

Although the judgment poured out as the wrath of God in Noah's day was water, it is a depiction of the judgment that will fall in the final wrath of God. There are numerous references to that judgment being a same-day salvation and wrath as well:

> They were eating, they were drinking, they were marrying, they were being given in marriage, *until the day* that Noah entered the ark, and the flood came and destroyed them all. (Luke 17:27 NASB, emphasis mine)

> The rain fell upon the earth for forty days and forty nights. *On the very same day Noah and Shem and Ham and Japheth, the sons of Noah, and Noah's wife and the three wives of his sons with them, entered the ark*. (Gen. 7:12–13 NASB)

In chapter two: "Hidden Treasure (Ultimate Proof of Rapture Timing)," we saw how 96% of the church has believed that the event in Matthew 24:31 is the *physical* second coming of Jesus. The same 96% of the church have believed that fire and brimstone falls at the *physical* second coming (and at Armageddon). Could they be wrong about this as well? That will be our thesis. In order to investigate that thesis, we must understand the term the *day of the Lord*.

THE DAY OF THE LORD

Most Christians, regardless of which rapture timing theory they support, have believed that the term the "day of the Lord" applies to this *day of judgment* when fire falls from heaven. This day is also called the *wrath of God*. Certainly, many Old Testament passages indicate that it is:

> Near is the great *day of the Lord*, near and coming very quickly; listen, *the day of the Lord!* In it the warrior cries out bitterly. *A day of wrath is that day*, a day of trouble and distress, a day of destruction and desolation, a day of darkness and gloom, a day of clouds and thick darkness . . . On the *day of the Lord's wrath*; and all the earth will be *devoured in the fire* of His jealousy. (Zeph. 1:14–15, 18 NASB, emphasis mine)

This passage from Zephaniah indicates that the day of the Lord is all these things.

The day of the Lord has a dual purpose; however, it is not just *punishment* for the wicked, but *protection* of the righteous as well. These dual purposes are summed up in the following verse from Paul's second letter to the Thessalonians:

> For after all it is only just for God *to repay with affliction those*
> *who afflict you,* and to *give relief to you* who are afflicted *and to*
> *us as well* when the Lord *Jesus will be **revealed** from heaven*
> *with His mighty angels in flaming fire.* (2 Thess. 1:6–8 NASB,
> emphasis mine)

The dual purpose of the day of the Lord is a key insight. Jesus will be
revealed from heaven on that day with his mighty angels in flaming fire—
this is a further explanation of Jesus's description in Matthew 24:27–31. The
sign of the Son of Man from this passage in Matthew is his shekinah glory
(called "lightning" in Matthew). It is called "flaming fire" in 2
Thessalonians 1.

Both *pretribulation rapture* supporters and *post-tribulation rapture*
supporters are currently confused about the day Jesus is *revealed*. Some
claim that day is the physical second coming; others claim it occurs prior to
the Seventieth Week. We will now show how both concepts are impossible.
Jesus is *revealed* on the day of the Lord, which occurs after the sixth seal.

In regard to the relief of the saints, we see from 2 Thessalonians
1:6–8 that this salvation occurs on the day when Jesus is *revealed*.
Some *pretribulation rapture* supporters think that this passage refers to the
relief of "tribulation saints" (those that come to faith during the so-called
tribulation), except that Paul slips in a short phrase "and to us." Paul
indicates that he and his companions will receive relief on that same day in
the future as well! How is that possible? Paul and his companions are now
dead. The Thessalonians are also now dead. It is only possible *if the*
resurrection also occurs on the day of the Lord (at the revealing of Jesus)!
These are incredibly significant points.

61

It should be noted that this passage single-handedly destroys the *pretribulation rapture* theory's silent rapture concept. It proves the resurrection (and by extension the rapture) happens on the day Jesus is *revealed*. It is not a silent rapture. Our relief occurs on the day of the Lord after the great tribulation in a *harpazo* that is visible and, in fact, in "flaming fire" (the flaming fire of Jesus's shekinah glory).

This passage also destroys the *pretribulation rapture's* prized theory of "imminence" (that no prophecies need to take place before the rapture takes place). If there are prophecies that must take place prior to the day of the Lord (there are) and if the day of the Lord and the rapture happen on the same day (they do), then these prophecies must precede the rapture as well. We discuss this point in much greater detail in chapter six: "The Backfire Effect (*Pre-Tribulation Rapture* Arguments)." All this supports the timing of the *prewrath rapture.*

FIERY JUDGMENT

Second Thessalonians 1:6–8 also clearly shows that the wicked will be afflicted on the day that Jesus is *revealed*. Jesus also explains the dual nature of this day in Luke 17:29–30, as we have already seen. Jesus is telling us that on the *same day* he is *revealed* and *saves* the righteous (pictured by Lot), punishment will be poured out on the wicked that involves fire and brimstone. This passage poses an enormous problem for both *post-tribulation rapture* and *pretribulation rapture* theories, but the reason why is not well understood. Exponents of these theories claim the day that fire and brimstone falls is the physical second coming. But, it should be noted, not one single passage in all of Scripture depicts fire falling during Jesus's physical second coming or at Armageddon. This news is probably more shocking to you than the evidence we presented in chapter two: "Hidden

Treasure (Ultimate Proof of Rapture Timing)" that Matthew 24:30–31 is not the physical second coming.

In Revelation are twenty-five references to fire. Most of these are used as descriptive of an item such as "eyes of fire" or "lake of fire." There are seven clear references to actual fire. They are assembled in the following graphic:

Fire Reference	Explanation	Possible to be "fire and brimstone" that falls on day Jesus is revealed?
Rev. 8:5, 7, 8	Fire that falls at first trumpet	YES, the fire falls from heaven
Rev. 9:17–18	Fire comes from the mouths of horses at sixth trumpet	NO, fire comes from horses on earth
Rev. 11:5	Fire comes from mouths of two witnesses	NO, fire comes from two witnesses
Rev. 13:13	Fire falls at command of False Prophet	NO, fire is Satan's doing, not God's
Rev. 14:10	Fire and brimstone torments those that worship the beast	NO, timing of fire not mentioned, it may be the fire of the first trumpet
Rev. 17:16, 18:8	Fire falls on the harlot at the command of the beast	NO, fire is Satan's doing, not God's
Rev. 20:9	Fire falls on the wicked at the end of the millennial kingdom	NO, fire does not fall during the Seventieth Week

Figure 14: Fire from Heaven

> **Fiery judgment is a "time marker" and occurs on the same day as the salvation of the righteous. The Rapture precedes the fiery judgment.**

But as we can clearly see, there is only one mention of fire in Revelation that can be the fire that rains upon the wicked at the parousia of Jesus—at the first trumpet judgment. Conspicuously missing in this chart is fire falling at Armageddon. Interestingly, for some of our *pretribulation rapture* brethren, there are no indications of fire falling immediately prior to the Seventieth Week as well.

Let's examine the first trumpet judgment and see why this might be a perfect fit for the start of the fiery judgment of God, God's wrath:

> The first sounded, and there came *hail and fire*, mixed with *blood*, and they were thrown to the earth; and a third of the earth was burned up, and a third of the trees were *burned up*, and all the green grass was *burned up*. (Rev. 8:7 NASB, clarification and emphasis mine)

In both chapter two: "Hidden Treasure (Ultimate Proof of Rapture Timing)" and chapter three: "Moving Pictures (Explicit Rapture Depiction in Revelation)," we learned that the *prewrath rapture* occurs sometime after the sixth seal. In Matthew 24:30–31 and Revelation 6:17, we see that Jesus is *revealed* at that same time and the tribes of the earth mourn. A "half an hour" after the seventh seal, an angel will blow the first trumpet and the fire will fall. It is entirely possible (and likely) that the rapture and the opening of the seventh seal happen on the same day, per other biblical examples of rescue and God's wrath on the same day. This would place the fiery

64

judgment that follows on the *same day as the rapture and the **revealing** of Jesus*. This is consistent with Luke 17, 2 Thessalonians 1, and the *prewrath rapture*, but it is not consistent with either a *pretribulation rapture* position or a *post-tribulation rapture* position, which require fire to fall at Armageddon and the physical second coming. However, nowhere in Scripture is there a picture of fire falling on the last day of the Seventieth Week or at Armageddon (or at the beginning of the Seventieth Week)! *This is a prophecy insight that nearly the entire church has missed!*

In the following graphic, we illustrate this important rapture proof:

NO FIRE FALLS PRE-TRIB   **FIRE FALLS PRE-WRATH**   **NO FIRE FALLS POST TRIB**

Figure 15: Fire Falling from Heaven (Only on the Day of the Lord)

OTHER VERSES OF FIERY JUDGMENTS

We have shown that there are no mentions of fire falling at the physical second coming in Revelation. "But surely," you may ask, "aren't there other references to fire falling on the last day elsewhere in Scripture?" It has been suggested that the reference to fire and brimstone in Ezekiel 38 *may* be the fire at Armageddon. But close inspection shows this reference is actually a reference to the first trumpet judgment. Notice the *same* mention of fire, hail, and blood!

> With pestilence and with **blood** I will enter into judgment with him; and I will rain on him and on his troops, and on the many peoples who are with him, a torrential rain, with **hailstones, fire and brimstone**. (Ezek. 38:22 NASB, emphasis mine)

> The first sounded [*first trumpet*], and there came **hail and fire**, mixed with **blood**, and they were thrown to the earth; and a third of the earth was burned up, and a third of the trees were burned up, and all the green grass was burned up. (Rev. 8:7 NASB, clarification and emphasis mine)

Psalm 18 depicts a dramatic fiery judgment as well. But, as in the previous example, it actually is a reference to the *hail and fire* of the first trumpet judgment:

> He bowed the heavens also, and came down with thick darkness under His feet. He rode upon a cherub and flew; and He sped upon the wings of the wind. He made darkness His hiding place, His canopy around Him, darkness of waters, thick clouds of the skies. From the brightness before Him passed His thick clouds, **hailstones and coals of fire**. The Lord also thundered in the heavens, and the Most High uttered His voice, **hailstones and coals of fire**. He sent out His arrows, and scattered them and lightning flashes in abundance, and routed them. Then the channels of water appeared, and the foundations of the world

> were laid bare at your rebuke, O Lord, at the blast of the breath
> of your nostrils. He sent from on high, **He took me**; *He drew me*
> *out of many waters. He delivered me from my strong enemy.*
> (Psalm 18:9–17 NASB, emphasis mine)

The reference to the channels of water and lightning is reminiscent of Ezekiel 38 as well. The final portion of the passage, "He took me," is a direct reference to the rapture. Although it doesn't use the exact Greek word *harpazo*, the language is similar.

A final passage that is sometimes associated with a fiery judgment is from Zechariah:

> Now this will be the plague with which the Lord will strike all
> the peoples who have gone to war against Jerusalem; their flesh
> will rot while they stand on their feet, and their eyes will rot in
> their sockets, and their tongue will rot in their mouth. (Zech.
> 14:12 NASB)

Clearly, this is a picture of Armageddon, but not of a fiery judgment at all. Hence, there is no evidence of fire falling from heaven at the end of the Seventieth Week, which is the position of both the *pretrib. rapture* and *post-trib. rapture* theories. Once again, the *prewrath rapture* position is affirmed.

SUMMARY

A google search of the Internet reveals that "fire falling at Armageddon" is not a topic that receives any attention. The reason, of course, is there is not a single verse in Scripture that clearly identifies *fire* as falling at the physical second coming of Jesus. Because *fire and brimstone* is clearly associated with the *same day* as Jesus's relief of the righteous (the rapture), this is a serious concern for both traditional rapture theories. If this event depicted in Luke 17 and 2 Thessalonians 1 (where relief of the righteous and fire and brimstone occur on the same day) is not the *prewrath rapture* and the *first trumpet judgment*, what day is this event? Both traditional rapture camps are completely mute on this point.

In the next chapter, we will learn about the history of the *prewrath rapture*, and begin to unpack some of the proofs of its major proponents.

Chapter Five

WHATEVER IS TRUE

(Other *Prewrath Rapture* Proofs)

"Finally, brethren, whatever is true, whatever is honorable, whatever is right, whatever is pure, whatever is lovely, whatever is of good repute, if there is any excellence and if anything worthy of praise, dwell on these things." (Phil. 4:8 NASB)

The president of the United States was a lame duck, and his term was almost over. His party had suffered a crushing defeat in the last election. Not only would the presidency be turned over to the rival party, but Congress would be as well. The American people had spoken, and the policies of this president were soon to be overturned. So in desperation, a plan was hatched: overrule the will of the people and stack the courts against the new party.

This certainly sounds as fresh as today's headlines, but this account references an event that occurred during the early years of the American Republic. The second president, John Adams, was to be replaced by Thomas Jefferson and his Republican-Democratic Party. With less than two weeks remaining before the new officeholders assumed their positions, the Federalist-controlled Congress doubled the number of district courts and circuit courts throughout the nation. Additionally, the number of Supreme Court justices was reduced. This final act was to take place upon the next vacancy of the high court, effectively taking the next Supreme Court nomination out of the hands of the incoming president.

69

After assuming office, Thomas Jefferson ordered the new secretary of state to not issue any of the new judges' commissions, and terminated the Supreme Court session scheduled for 1802 so the Supreme Court could not rule on the new law! If we think politics in the twenty-first century is a crooked business, these events of the nineteenth century dwarf even the twisted self-centeredness of our current times.

The Supreme Court eventually took up the issue, and in one of the most famous decisions of the early court, Marbury v. Madison, 1803, the court ruled it had a right of "judicial review" for acts of Congress. Chief Justice John Marshall wrote the famous, unanimous decision:

> It is emphatically the province and duty of the Judicial Department [the judicial branch] to say what the law is . . . *the Constitution is superior to any ordinary act of the Legislature, the Constitution, and not such ordinary act, must govern the case to which they both apply.* —John Marshall (emphasis mine)[27]

In this decision, the court ruled that the Constitution of the United States should be the final arbiter of law. Any law made by Congress that did not conform to the Constitution could be determined to be unconstitutional. This was the point that the Supreme Court began its long history of monitoring all the actions of government.

In the same way that the Constitution governs (or should govern) the laws of the United States, the Bible governs all matters of faith. Up to this point, this book has been a model of a court case using that standard of judgment—using the Bible as our final authority. Three witnesses (Matthew 24, Revelation 4–9, and Revelation 8:5–8) came forward to present their

70

evidence that the rapture will be *prewrath*. These witnesses were cross-examined by the *pretribulation rapture* theory and the *post-tribulation rapture* theory and were found to be solid and factual. This chapter represents the fourth witness. Finally, in the next section (Section Three: Objections), the two alternative rapture theories will present a number of witnesses in their defense. All of those witnesses' arguments will face cross-examination. At the conclusion we will come to the verdict and hopefully say, "Rapture: case closed."

THE HISTORY OF THE *PREWRATH RAPTURE*

Presently, the *prewrath rapture* is the preferred rapture theory of less than 5% of Christians worldwide, and many misunderstandings about this theory abound. This chapter will examine the theory in greater detail. The *prewrath rapture* position is not a new theory of rapture timing (it dates back to the early church and the original intention of Jesus's teachings), although the formal written presentation is recent. The official presentation of the concept was first considered by Robert Van Kampen and Marvin Rosenthal, and the first published book about the *prewrath rapture* was Marvin Rosenthal's *The Pre-Wrath Rapture of the Church.* Van Kampen followed this work with his own books: *The Sign* and *The Rapture Question Answered: Plain and Simple.*

The most complete writing on the scriptural anchorage of the *prewrath rapture* is Alan Kurschner's recent book, *Antichrist Before the Day of the Lord.*

The primary proof texts for a *prewrath rapture* found in chapters three through five are unique to this book, but many of the proofs found in this chapter are from the work of the other rapture experts mentioned. You will find this additional information edifying. I thank all three gentlemen

(Rosenthal, Van Kampen, and Kurschner) for their profuse contributions to my own understanding of the Word of God related to the rapture.

PLAIN AND SIMPLE

The late Robert Van Kampen began formulating the theological ideas that led to the *prewrath rapture* theory in the mid-1980s. At his dining room table, he diligently searched for the rapture answer and came to realize that the sign in the sun, moon, and stars found in Matthew 24:29 was the key to uncovering the timing of the rapture. This same sign is found in Isaiah, Joel, Ezekiel, Matthew, Mark, Luke, Acts, and Revelation. He grasped that the implications of this sign:

> . . . made the biblical truths of both pretribulationalism and posttribulationalism come together perfectly, without contradiction, inconsistency, or unreconciled passages.[28] — Robert Van Kampen

Within just a few hours of uncovering all the various biblical references to the sign in the sun, moon, and stars, Van Kampen realized that this sign preceded the day of the Lord—the day when the righteous are saved and the wicked punished with fire during the wrath of God. He understood the street fight we described in chapter one: "Solving the Cold Case" and saw the *prewrath rapture* was the solution. Van Kampen and Marvin Rosenthal then began to actively debate this theory, arriving at a common understanding that is memorialized in their books.

Van Kampen and Rosenthal focused on the day of the Lord and demonstrated how it *cannot* simultaneously include the exaltation of God and Satan and the Antichrist:

> The loftiness of man shall be bowed down, and the haughtiness
> of men shall be brought low; *The Lord alone will be exalted in
> that day*. (Isa. 2:17 NKJV, emphasis mine)

> That Day will not come unless the falling away comes first, and
> the man of sin is revealed, the son of perdition, who opposes and
> *exalts himself above all that is called God* or that is worshiped,
> so that he sits as God in the temple of God, showing himself that
> he is God. (2 Thess. 2:3–4 NKJV, emphasis mine)

Obviously if God alone is exalted during the day of the Lord, the Antichrist
cannot also be exalted during that same day! This precludes both a
pretribulation rapture and a *post-tribulation rapture*. Both camps assume
that Antichrist is exalted right up until the physical second coming. These
passages prove that is not accurate.[29] The exaltation of Antichrist and God
are mutually exclusive. Satan is exalted during the great tribulation, and God
is exalted during the day of the Lord.

OTHER REASONS MATTHEW 24:30–31 *IS* THE RAPTURE

Understanding that Matthew 24:30–31 is the rapture and not the physical
second coming of Jesus is critical to establishing the *prewrath rapture* over
the *pretribulation rapture* and *post-tribulation rapture*. In chapters two and
three we presented numerous proofs that Matt. 24:30–31 is the rapture. Alan
Kurschner provides several other reasons that this passage depicts the
rapture as well. First, Mr. Kurschner argues that contrary to *pretribulation
rapture* supporters' claims, Jesus does in fact use rapture language in the
Olivet Discourse. We will discuss these "rapture" terms in greater detail in
future sections and chapters. In the next section we will discuss the Greek

word *episunago* (meaning "gather together"). This Greek word is found in Matthew 24:30–31 and the noun form of it is also used in 2 Thessalonians 2:1, a passage which is nearly universally associated with the rapture. (Interestingly, Dr. Thomas Ice of the Pre-Trib. Research Center attributes the one use in 2 Thessalonians 2:1 to the rapture, but rejects it in Matthew 24:30–31.)[30] In chapter seven: "Center of the Universe (*Post-Tribulation Rapture* Arguments)," we will discuss the Greek word *paralambano* (meaning "taken"). Mr. Kurschner points out that this word is also used in the near universally accepted rapture passage found in John's gospel:[31]

> In My Father's house are many dwelling places; if it were not so, I would have told you; for I go to prepare a place for you. If I go and prepare a place for you, I will come again and *receive* [Gk. *paralambano*] you to myself, that where I am, there you may be also. (John 14:2–3 NASB, clarification and emphasis mine)

Notice how the subtle difference in English translation ("receive" versus "take") has led the church to miss this obvious rapture-related meaning of *paralambano* ("take") in the Olivet Discourse (Matt. 24:40–41).

Second, Mr. Kurschner suggests that Paul (in 1 Thessalonians 4:16–17) and the Olivet Discourse are both discussing the initiation of the parousia of Jesus. It is well accepted that 1 Thessalonians 4:16–17 is depicting the beginning of the parousia (the resurrection and rapture). Mr. Kurschner argues that the Olivet Discourse depicts this same initial phase of the parousia as well. Both passages explicitly refer to this event as Jesus's arrival or coming (parousia). The Olivet Discourse mentions a specific sign (lightning from the east to the west) that accompanies the parousia. A specific sign only makes sense for the initiation of the event. The Olivet Discourse also features a number of illustrations and parables that instruct believers to be *watchful*. Again, this only makes sense for believers to be *watchful* at the beginning of the parousia,[32] *not* prior to the second coming.

Third, Mr. Kurschner points out that the first six seals progress during Revelation 6 without pause, but then a "conspicuous pause" occurs in Revelation 7 prior to the opening of the seventh seal. In chapter three: "Moving Pictures (Explicit Rapture Depiction in Revelation)," we have already discussed how this interlude (Rev. 7) demonstrates how God protects his chosen. The Jewish remnant is sealed and the Christians are raptured. In that chapter, we demonstrated conclusively how the elect move from not being in heaven in the cel depicted in Revelation 5 to being in heaven in the next cel depicted in Revelation 7.

Mr. Kurschner adds to this evidence we have presented. He shows how the language about angels in Revelation 7:1 ("angels standing at the *four corners of the earth* holding back the *four winds* of the earth") is strikingly similar to Jesus's language in the Olivet Discourse ("[His angels] will gather the elect from the *four winds*, from one end of heaven to the other").

Additionally, he demonstrates that the language of Revelation 7:14 and Matthew 24:21–22, 29 both mention that the elect come *out of* the *great tribulation*:[33]

These are the ones who come out of the *great tribulation*. (Rev. 7:14 NASB, emphasis mine)

For then there will be a *great tribulation*, such as has not occurred since the beginning of the world until now, nor ever

75

will. Unless those days had been cut short, no life would have been saved; but for the sake of the elect those days (the *great tribulation*) will be cut short . . . But immediately *after the tribulation of those days* the sun will be darkened, and the moon will not give its light. (Matt. 24:21–22, 29 NASB, emphasis mine)

THE GATHERING TOGETHER

In Matt. 24:31, the elect are gathered together by angels. In chapters two—four, we discovered that this gathering together is the rapture. The resurrected saints and those that have survived the great tribulation are "gathered together" to meet the Lord in the air. Van Kampen provides a word study of the Greek word *episunago* which is translated "gather together" in Matt. 24:31 (also found in Luke 17:37 and the noun-form of it is found in 2 Thess. 2:1). Van Kampen points out that the root word *sunago* also means "gather together." The Greek prefix *epi* adds the additional meaning of "up" or 'upon." This gives direction to the "gathering together." The elect are gathered "up" (to meet Jesus in the air just as in 1 Thess. 4:16-17.) This adds significant evidence that these two passages (Matt. 24:31 and 1 Thess. 4:16-17) are describing the same event.[34]

Naturally, this is not the opinion of the *pretribulation rapture* theorists, because in their minds the rapture had already taken place. Their estimation of what the "gathering together" represents may be best summarized by Dr. Thomas Ice, Director of the Pre-Trib. Research Center:

Apparently as our Lord descends, He will then send out His angelic company to gather in the Jewish, believing remnant that He will rescue from the danger of all the world's armies

76

who have gathered by the anti-Christ in an attack upon Israel
and Jerusalem . . . so our Lord sends out his angels to gather
His elect (saved Jews at the end of the tribulation) from around
the world and bring them to Jerusalem. — Dr. Thomas Ice[35]

Dr. Ice ignores Mark's account of the Rapture that is parallel to Matt. 24:31,
but this account adds an interesting and often overlooked detail that only
further supports it as a rapture text not as a gathering of the Jewish remnant:

He will send forth the angels, and will gather together His elect
from the four winds, *from the farthest end of the earth **to** the
farthest end of heaven.* (Mark 13:27 NASB, emphasis mine)

This passage clearly shows that the destination of the "gathering together" is
the *farthest end of heaven*. The "gathering together" is not horizontal as Dr.
Ice depicts, "from the farthest end of the earth" to Jerusalem; rather it is
vertical, from the earth to heaven! The prepositions "from/to" in
combination clearly show motion and a *destination*, which is heaven.

Pretribulationalists also have ignored important Old Testament
prophecies that clearly show that the regathering of the Jewish remnant to
Israel after the return of our Lord is by foot and by beasts of burden, not by
angelic hosts.

The time is coming to gather all nations and tongues. And they
shall come and see My glory. I will set a sign among them and
will send survivors from them to the nations: Tarshish, Put,
Lud, Meshech, Tubal and Javan, to the distant coastlands that
have neither heard My fame nor seen My glory. And they will

declare My glory among the nations. Then *they shall bring all your brethren from all the nations* as a grain offering to the Lord, on horses, in chariots, in litters, on mules and on camels, to My holy mountain Jerusalem," says the Lord. (Isa. 66:18-20 NASB, emphasis mine)

When it is obvious that the "gathering together" is into heaven and not a regathering of the Jewish remnant, it becomes apparent that it can be nothing other than the Rapture.

THE ELECT

Although episunago is controversial, the most controversial word in Matthew 24 is "elect." Robert Van Kampen discusses the use of the Greek word *eklektos*, which is translated as "elect" in the following verse. We now know this is the *prewrath rapture*:

And He will send forth His angels with a great trumpet and they will gather together His elect [Gk: *eklektos*] from the four winds, from one end of the sky to the other. (Matt. 24:31 NASB)

Although pretribulationalists claim this word means the Jewish remnant (and not Christians), Van Kampen points out that this Greek Word eklektos is utilized frequently in the New Testament in regard to Christians:[36]

If God is for us, who is against us? He who did not spare His own Son, but delivered Him over for us all, how will He not also with Him freely give us all things? Who will bring a charge against God's elect [eklektos]? (Rom. 8:31–33 NASB)

78

There is no distinction between Greek and Jew, circumcised and uncircumcised, barbarian, Scythian, slave and freeman, but Christ is all, and in all. So, as those who have been chosen [eklektos] of God, holy and beloved, put on a heart of compassion. (Col. 3:11–12 NASB)

Paul, a bond-servant of God and an apostle of Jesus Christ, for the faith of those chosen [eklektos] of God. (Titus 1:1 NASB)

These will wage war against the Lamb, and the Lamb will overcome them, because He is Lord of lords and King of kings, and those who are with Him are the called and chosen (eklektos) and faithful. (Rev. 17:14 NASB)

These passages show that in the New Testament the word eklektos refers to those who have placed their faith in Jesus, and in the case of Titus 1:1 can refer specifically to gentile Christians. So although the Jewish remnant may be predestined to be saved, they won't be until the "fullness of the Gentiles has come in." (Romans 11:25–26). And in Amos 5:18–19, the prophet indicates that Israel will endure the day of the Lord. Israel will not be saved until after the rapture of the elect who are Christians.[37]

John is clear that Jewish remnant and the bond servants of God are separate as well. In Rev. 12:13-17, the remnant ("the woman") is Israel and the "rest of her children" keep the testimony of Jesus. Obviously, the Jewish remnant still isn't saved at that point and doesn't testify about Jesus.[38]

Van Kampen does not mention the *Didache*, a highly regarded Christian document from the first century, as substantiation for the elect being Christians. Although the *Didache* is not part of the canon of Scripture, many believe it may be the oral tradition of the disciples. The document is universally accepted as authentic, and it is referenced in the writing of numerous early church fathers.[39]

The final chapter of the *Didache* is entirely devoted to eschatological issues, but even in earlier chapters, end time references are found. Of greatest interest is the ending of a Eucharistic prayer found in chapter 10, which is an exact quote from Matthew 24:

> Remember, Lord, *your church*, to save her from every evil, and to perfect her in your love, and to *gather her together from the four winds*, the sanctified into your kingdom which you have prepared for her. (*Didache* 10:5, emphasis mine)

> And He will send forth His angels with a great trumpet and *they will gather together His elect from the four winds*. (Matt. 24:31 NASB, emphasis mine)

It is obvious from this early church document that first-century Christians equated "the elect" of Matthew 24:31 with the church and *a prewrath rapture*.

PAUL'S THESSALONIAN LETTERS AND MATTHEW 24

Alan Kurschner has outlined thirty separate parallels between the Olivet Discourse and Paul's two letters to the Thessalonians. A table of these parallels is found in appendix two of *Antichrist Before the Day of the Lord*.[40] Of greatest interest to me are the parallels between the rapture passages, which I have summarized in the graphic on the following page:

Point of Comparison	I&II Thess.	Matt. and Mark
Persecution cut short	II 1:6–7	Matt. 24:22
Parousia follows Antichrist	II 2:8	Matt. 24:30–31
Universal perception	II 1:7–8	Matt. 24:30
Jesus comes on the clouds	I 4:17	Matt. 24:30
Power and glory	II 1:9	Matt. 24:30
Angels	I 4:16, II 1:9	Matt. 24:31
Trumpet call	I 4:16	Matt. 24:31
Gather together	I 4:17, II 2:1	Matt. 24:28,31
Meeting (*apantesis*)	I 4:17	Matt. 25:6
In the air	I 4:17	Mark 13:28
Rapture and wrath on the same day	II 1:6–10	Matt. 24:37–41
"Peace and safety" precedes wrath	I 5:3	Matt. 24:37–41
Be watchful	I 5:6–8	Mark 13:35–37

Figure 16: Comparison of Paul's and Jesus's Rapture Passages

(Based on a Table by Alan Kurschner)

This table shows that the rapture-related passages *alone* contain at least fifteen separate positive comparisons between Paul's I & II Thessalonian references and the Olivet Discourse passages of Matthew and Mark. Obviously these references in Thessalonians (like 1 Thess. 4:16–17) are depicting the same events as found in Matthew 24, both accounts supporting a *prewrath rapture.*

THE "END"

Marvin Rosenthal has presented an incredibly insightful teaching about "the end of the age."[41] This topic was initiated by the question the disciples asked that inspired the Olivet Discourse:

> As He was sitting on the Mount of Olives, the disciples came to Him privately, saying, "Tell us, when will these things happen, and what will be *the sign of your coming (Gk: parousia), and of the end of the age?*" (Matt. 24:3 NASB, emphasis mine)

Rosenthal points out the *end of the age* is not the end of the world, but rather the end of the current dominion of man and Satan that will transition at the rapture into the judgment of the wicked (day of the Lord). He also points out it is directly associated with Jesus's coming (parousia). In fact, the disciples' question clearly demonstrates they occur at the same time. Earlier in Matthew, we learn the terms "end of the age" and "the harvest" are also equivalent. "*The harvest is the end of the age*; and the reapers are angels" (Matt. 13:39 NASB, emphasis mine). This creates enormous problems for the *pretribulation rapture* supporters, as they must claim the harvest of the righteous occurs prior to the beginning of the Seventieth Week and still harmonize this supposition with the facts given in Matt. 24.

Matthew's gospel indicates that all these other events below *precede* the "end of the age" (and thus the harvest) and obviously are in reference to the disciples' question that launched the Olivet Discourse:

> You will be hearing of wars and rumors of wars. See that you are not frightened, for those things must take place, but that is not yet *the end*. (Matt. 24:6 NASB, emphasis mine)

82

But the one who endures to *the end*, he will be saved. (Matt. 24:13 NASB, emphasis mine)

This gospel of the kingdom shall be preached in the whole world as a testimony to all the nations, and then *the end* will come. (Matt. 24:14 NASB, emphasis mine)

Teaching them to observe all that I commanded you; and lo, I am with you always, even to the *end of the age*." (Matt. 28:20 NASB, emphasis mine)

Rosenthal points out that in Matthew 24:6, the second sign of Jesus's coming (which is also the second seal of Revelation 6) occurs prior to the end. Of greatest interest to me, however, is that Jesus promises to be with those who receive the Great Commission until *the end* (Matt. 28:20) and that being saved requires enduring until *the end*—when the *harvest occurs at the rapture*. This is not consistent with a *pretribulation rapture,* but is, once again, consistent with the *prewrath rapture* position.

WEDDING GARMENTS

In chapter three (see pages 54-55), we have already discussed the white garments given to the souls beneath the alter (Rev. 6:9-11) which are later worn by the vast multitude (Rev. 7:9). In that chapter, we also mentioned that a white garment was worn by the High Priest in ancient Israel on Yom Kippur to allow him to enter the presence of God. Toward the end of Revelation these garments worn in Rev. 7:9 are defined for us:

Then I heard something like the voice of a *great multitude* and
like the sound of many waters and like the sound of mighty
peals of thunder, saying, "Hallelujah! For the Lord our God,
the Almighty, reigns. Let us rejoice and be glad and give the
glory to Him, for the marriage of the Lamb has come and
His bride has made herself ready." It was given to her to clothe
herself in *fine linen, bright and clean*; for the fine linen is
the righteous acts of the saints. (Rev. 19:6-8)

First, the great multitude in this passage is the same group as the vast
multitude in Rev. 7:9. Although the two passages use different English
adjectives, both occurrences use the same Greek adjective *polus* (meaning
many in number) to define them. They're the same group.

Second, we learn that the white garments are the righteous acts of
the saints and the wedding garments of the bride. As we discussed in Rev.
7:14, the righteousness of the multitude comes from washing their garments
in the blood of the lamb and making them white. Some might also consider
the white garments symbolic of the of the resurrection bodies of the saints
while others might consider them symbolic of the eternal presence of the
saints before God. I consider them all of these things.

These white garments appear numerous times in Revelation. If we
examine them, the timing of the rapture becomes apparent. The graphic on
the following page displays the use of white garments by the saints.

How the white garments are utilized	Reference in Revelation
Promised to the saints	Rev. 3:4, Rev. 3:18
Given to the saints	Rev. 6:9-11
Washed in the blood of the lamb	Rev. 7:14
Put on by the saints	Rev. 19:8
Worn in heaven by the saints	Rev. 7:9
Worn back to earth by the saints	Rev. 19:14

Figure 17: Wedding Garments

This graphic presents a complete picture of the use of the white garments by the saints, from the promising of the garments until they wear them. A popular phrase in American culture is "follow the money," which means that if we follow the trail of money in a scandal, it will help us conclude who was involved in the scandal. In the same way if we follow the white garments in Revelation, we will find the proper timing of the rapture.

Looking at Figure 17, most would conclude that the rapture occurs the moment that the Bride of Christ is in heaven and has put on her wedding garments— immediately before the events of Rev. 7:9. As you probably recall, this is the exact moment we theorized the Rapture occurs in chapter three: "Moving Pictures": after the sixth seal, after great tribulation, after Jesus manifests himself before the entire world, and yet before the trumpet and bowl judgments. The wearing of white garments in Revelation support a *prewrath rapture.*

WHY THE RAPTURE CASE IS STILL UNRESOLVED

At this point, with so much evidence in favor of the *prewrath rapture*, one might wonder why the case is still not closed. *Why hasn't the church found a definitive biblical answer to the rapture dilemma?*

The late Dr. John Walvoord, past-president of Dallas Theological Seminary and perhaps the most well-known spokesman on rapture timing, recognized the reason the debate still lingers:

> Neither posttribulationalism nor pretribulationalism is an explicit teaching of the Scriptures. The Bible does not, in so many words, state either. —Dr. John Walvoord[42]

Now what Dr. Walvoord and most exponents of the two major rapture positions (*pretribulation* and *post-tribulation*) have not considered is that *both* main positions on the rapture are partially correct and partially mistaken. This explains why they are not explicitly found in Scripture and why the unresolved case would result in a no-decision street fight, which is *exactly* what has happened! Fans of both positions "cheer" when their side presents an argument that is factual, but ignore the factual arguments of the other side. Consider the Twitter war that is raging. Isn't this precisely what you see?

> **Both main rapture positions are *equally correct* about a portion of their arguments and *equally incorrect* about the other half of their arguments.**

This "half correct and half mistaken" perception of both main rapture positions has created a challenging situation. It is hard to surrender a position when you realize that a good number of the contentions of your "side" are correct or certainly *seem* correct. Rather than looking for a position that is *completely* biblically correct (with all Scripture in agreement without contradiction—essential for biblical truth), the tendency is to try and find work-arounds for those areas where one is mistaken but wishes to retain one's position.

Another reason for this inconclusive case is that the two sides are primarily arguing against each other. If one only considers two positions that are both in error, it is impossible to find the truth. We propose that truth is the *prewrath rapture* that both sides of this argument tend to ignore.

The result of this inconclusive case is that more Protestant pastors currently believe that the rapture isn't a literal event or are confused about its timing than believe in any one single rapture theory.[43]

SUMMARY

It is apparent that if the *prewrath rapture* is "true," it will be supported by numerous eschatological passages in Scripture, without contradictions between them. The groundbreaking work of Rosenthal, Van Kampen, and Kurschner has provided analysis of a number of these passages that uniquely and powerfully support the primary new rapture-timing proofs provided in chapters two through four (and nine). The scriptural evidence has been presented—without contradictions—and the verdict should be unanimous: the *prewrath rapture* is the "rapture answer." Indeed, the new evidence has cracked the cold case open. The rapture case should be closed!

The reader will need to evaluate the evidence provided in this book and come to his/her own conclusion. We would like to think that biblical truth wins. We pray that the Holy Spirit will lead all of us to understand and accept his biblical truth. Hopefully, all of us will now be willing to end the street fight and help prepare the church for turbulent times of the days ahead.

My experience has shown, however, that even after presenting what seems like irrefutable evidence in a court case, the other party likes to divert attention away from the main argument into sideline arguments. In the next section, "Part Three: The Objections," we will discuss many of these sideline arguments—first from a *pretribulation rapture* perspective in chapter six: "The Backfire Effect (*Pretribulation Rapture* Arguments)" and then from a *post-tribulation rapture* perspective in chapter seven: "Center of the Universe (*Post-Tribulation Rapture* Arguments"). You can evaluate the reliability of these counterarguments used by proponents of the *pretrib.* and *post-trib. rapture* positions. Compare the teachings to Scripture, and then you be the judge.

.

PART THREE:

THE OBJECTIONS

Chapter Six

THE BACKFIRE EFFECT

(*Pretribulation Rapture* Arguments)

They spoke, saying to Him, "Tell us by what authority you are doing these things, or who is the one who gave you this authority?" (Luke 20:2)

H ave you ever noticed that facts do not win arguments? Look at the quote above. Jesus, the Creator of all things who spoke nothing but truth, was not believed by the religious leaders of his day. Why should you or I expect to be believed by those we discuss matters with, even if we quote the very words of Jesus?

Dartmouth investigators Brendan Nyhan and Jason Reifler wrote a paper about what they term the "backfire effect." Not only did they discover that facts don't win arguments, but they found that in the process of debate, your discussion opponents often become more intense in their own beliefs, not less so.[44] The researchers also noted that when viewing an independent news source that gives two sides of an argument, the listener almost invariably agrees with their own preconceived ideas and rejects ideas counter to them, regardless of the merits of the arguments. Additionally, the researchers noticed that even if irrefutable evidence is presented, if the presenter is not viewed as an "omniscient source," the listener rejects the overwhelming evidence.[45]

So I realize that at this point in the book, you might not be convinced by the "rapture answer." Despite the fact there were no adequate responses given to refute the arguments presented, our minds instinctively

91

reflex back to older lines of reasoning we have relied on. The instinctive reaction is to not accept the new information, but rather to say, "Yes, but what about this proof or that proof." I call these "yes, but . . ." arguments. It is human nature to reject new arguments and to concentrate on all previous proofs one has depended on.

This is especially true in relation to the rapture case because both predominant rapture theories are half right and half wrong. Both popular rapture positions—*pretribulation rapture* and *post-tribulation rapture*—contain elements of truth as well as elements that are mistaken. This makes surrendering these positions difficult.

In this chapter, we will examine some of those older lines of reasoning *pretribulation rapture* advocates may be relying on. In the next chapter, we will do the same with arguments the *post-tribulation rapture* supporters usually trust. Hopefully, by the end of these two chapters you will see the hollowness of many of these arguments.

Before we begin to discuss pretribulationalism, we need to remember that it is an inferred position. By that we mean that a pretribulation rapture is never depicted in the Scriptures; it is "assumed" by its followers. Even one of the greatest voices of pretribulationalism, Dr. Richard Mayhue (past dean of The Master's Seminary), saw the hollowness of many of the *pretribulation rapture* arguments:

> Perhaps the position of pretribulationalism is correct, although its proof at times has been logically invalid or at least unconvincing. —Dr. Richard Mayhue[46]

92

This statement exposes an incredibly important issue. If a theological position is not specifically mentioned in Scripture, the burden of proof falls on the proponents of that theory.

> **It is incumbent on *pretribulation rapture* proponents to prove their theory correct.**

Pretribulationalism cannot be the "assumed" correct rapture position. Rather, because the proponents of this theory cannot demonstrate a rapture occurring ***prior*** to the Seventieth Week in Scripture, **they must both categorically prove their position and prove the rapture isn't prewrath**.

In this chapter, we contrast the most popular proofs for the *pretribulation rapture* with the *prewrath rapture*, the position taught by Jesus in the Olivet Discourse and in Revelation as we have discussed. Before we contrast these theories, I need to mention that the *pretrib.* and *prewrath* positions share a lot of similarities:

- Both present the rapture and the *physical* second coming as separate events (although the *prewrath rapture* considers them as *two subparts* of a single, longer event: the parousia, or arrival or coming of Jesus);
- Both believe the rapture physically removes believers from the earth prior to the *wrath of God*; and
- Both believe the saints are taken into heaven for the time the *wrath of God* takes place on earth.

Beyond the similarities, the two positions also have distinct differences, outlined in the graphic on the following page:

Aspect	Pretribulation Rapture	Prewrath Rapture
Wrath of God	The full seven years of the Seventieth Week includes the seals, trumpets, and bowls.	Occurs after the great tribulation and the sixth seal; includes only the trumpets and the bowls.
The Antichrist	Believers do not face the Antichrist.	Believers do face the Antichrist.
Rapture	A silent rapture occurs before the Seventieth Week begins.	After the great tribulation and after the sixth seal when every eye shall see him.
Imminence	Imminent (no prophecies must precede the rapture)	Not imminent (prophecies must precede the rapture)

Figure 18: *Pretribulation* and *Prewrath Rapture* Comparisons

These are the salient differences between the positions. However, this may surprise you—a number of the favorite arguments used by the *pretribulation rapture* supporters are somewhat in harmony with the *prewrath rapture* position. For instance, advocates of the *pretribulation rapture* are considered dispensationalists, believing that God has separated biblical history into defined periods, or dispensations, and that he has *separate plans* for the church and for the unsaved Jews. They believe we are in what they call the "Church Age" and that God will redeem unsaved Israel separately during the Seventieth Week. Although *prewrath rapture* exponents are not dispensationalists, they do believe in a distinct salvation for believers (at the rapture) and, separately, for the remnant of apostate Jews who come to faith when "they . . . look upon me, the one they have pierced [Jesus]" (Zech. 12:10).

Keep You from the Hour of Trial

Pretribulation rapture supporters look at Revelation 3:10 as a lynchpin of support for their rapture position, with their assumption of the rapture being before the whole Seventieth Week:

> Because you have kept the word of my perseverance, I also will *keep you from* the hour of testing, that hour which is about to come upon the whole world, to test those who dwell on the earth. (Rev. 3:10 NASB, emphasis mine)

Pretribulation rapture supporters may be surprised to learn that many *prewrath rapture* supporters (myself included) also strongly believe this verse confirms the rapture. Both groups believe the "hour of testing" relates to the great tribulation. However, the groups differ on the implications of several Greek words, implications that determine the meaning of the passage.

The translation of the two Greek words *tereso ek* in combination has led to most of the misunderstanding of this passage. The traditional English translation of these two words in the passage above, "will keep you from," could mean to remove one thing from another. And this is exactly how the *pretribulation rapture* supporters have interpreted them. They have assumed this passage is saying Jesus will remove believers from the great tribulation. This is an unfortunate translation. *Tereso*, which is translated "keep" in the passage above is better rendered "will guard" or "will observe."

Robert Van Kampen had shown the tiny Greek word *ek* in Revelation 3:10 that is translated "from" actually means "from out of the middle of." He had also stated the Greek preposition *apo* would be used if the verse was saying Jesus would keep his saints away from danger entirely.

95

Van Kampen suggested *Tereso ek* implies they will be first protected or guarded and then delivered from the midst of danger:[47] This usage is parallel to Jesus's statement in John 17:15 where he doesn't desire to take his followers "out of the world," but rather to protect them from (*tereso ek*) the evil one. This translation of tereso ek is also supported by Greek luminaries such as Aune, Osborne, and Beale[48]

As a result of this view of tereso ek, many pretribulationalists re-examined their position on this verse. Dr. Michael Svigel, Chairman for Dallas Theological Seminary's Department of Theology, has admitted that Rev. 3:10 cannot be used as a proof text for a *pretribulation rapture.*[49]

By itself, the preposition *ek* cannot be used proof for a *prewrath* rapture either. Greek grammar is complex and there is a great deal of overlap between the meanings of the prepositions *ek* and *apo.*[50] As in many aspects of the Greek text, context—not grammar—determines the meaning of a passage. And in that context, there is support for a *prewrath* rapture.

The preposition ek is also famously found in Revelation 7, "These are the ones who come *out of* [*ek*] the great tribulation" (Rev. 7:14 NASB, emphasis mine).

> **If the "hour of testing" is the same as the great tribulation (*pretribulation rapture* proponents say it is) then Rev. 3:10 and Rev. 7:14 are parallel verses and speak of the *same* event: the coming out of the middle of (*ek*) the great tribulation.**

Rev. 3:10 is the promise to the saints that they will be guarded and come out of the middle of the great tribulation. Rev. 7:14 depicts the saints after they have come out. The parallel uses of *ek* in John 17:15 above and in Rev. 7:14 both dramatically support a *prewrath* interpretation of Rev. 3:10.

Finally, pretribulational theory also ignores the fact that Revelation 3:10 is a *conditional* statement. And in context, this conditional statement gives the verse its meaning. Marvin Rosenthal has pointed out that *because* believers have kept the "word of Jesus's perseverance," they will be "guarded." Rosenthal shows in three examples how this Greek word "perseverance" [hypomones] is associated with the great tribulation:[51]

> But you will be betrayed even by parents and brothers and relatives and friends, and they will put some of you to death, and you will be hated by all because of My name. Yet not a hair of your head will perish. By your *endurance* [hypomones] you will gain your lives [lit. souls]. (Luke 21:16–19 NASB, clarification and emphasis mine)

> If anyone is destined for captivity, to captivity he goes; if anyone kills with the sword, with the sword he must be killed. *Here is the perseverance* [hypomones] and the faith of the saints. (Rev. 13:10 NASB, emphasis mine)

> If anyone worships the beast and his image, and receives a mark on his forehead or on his hand, he also will drink of the wine of the wrath of God, which is mixed in full strength in the cup of His anger; and he will be tormented with fire and brimstone in the presence of the holy angels and in the presence of the Lamb. . . Here is the *perseverance* [hypomones] of the saints who keep the commandments of God and their faith in Jesus. (Rev. 14:9– 10, 12 NASB, emphasis mine)

So it is doubtful Rev. 3:10 is associated with a *pretribulation rapture* because endurance [hypomones] *through* the great tribulation (not committing apostasy) most likely is the *conditional aspect* that first guards the saints then removes them "from out of the middle of" the trial. The condition that Jesus establishes in order for saints to be "guarded from out of the middle of" the hour of trial is endurance. If this verse was truly demonstrating a pretribulational rescue of the saints *before* the test, "faith" be the conditional requirement. Endurance is required *during* the test.

Before we begin looking at some of the *pretribulation rapture* exponents' other favorite theories, I want to remind you that in chapters two through five, we have already conclusively proven the *prewrath rapture* from the Scriptures. You may have a "yes, but . . ." response to this evidence, so in this chapter: "The Backfire Effect (*Pre-Tribulation Rapture* Arguments)" we are exploring all the arguments that you may be familiar with that have traditionally supported a *pretribulation rapture*. After reviewing these and finding out that they truly don't support it, perhaps you will be open to the proofs you have already witnessed.

THE WRATH OF GOD CONSIDERATIONS

As we have stated repeatedly in this book, both the *pretribulation rapture* and the *prewrath rapture* theories believe that God will physically *harpazo* his children from the earth before he pours out his wrath. The main difference between these two theories is *when* this wrath takes place. The *pretribulation rapture* supporters believe God's wrath is poured out during the entire seven years of the *Seventieth Week of Daniel*. The *prewrath rapture* theory holds that God's wrath only entails the trumpet and bowl judgments that occur at the end of that period. In this section we will examine what the Bible says about these conflicting positions.

The strongly held position of *pretribulation rapture* exponents is that the entire Seventieth Week (or what they call the Tribulation) is the wrath of God. In chapter four: "Synchronized Fireworks (Same-Day Salvation and Wrath)," we learned that the church overwhelmingly considers the day of the Lord to be equivalent to the wrath of God. The following "timing" verses show the day of the Lord is absolutely an event that happens *during* the Seventieth Week, not at its inception:

> Behold, I am going to send you Elijah the prophet *before* the coming of the great and terrible *day of the Lord*. (Mal. 4:5 NASB, emphasis mine)

> The sun will be turned to darkness and the moon into blood *before* the great and awesome *day of the Lord* comes. (Joel 2:31 NASB, emphasis mine)

> Behold, *the day of the Lord is coming*, cruel with fury and burning anger to make the land a desolation; and He will exterminate its sinners from it. For the stars of heaven and their constellations will not flash forth their light; the sun will be dark when it rises and the moon will not shed its light. (Isa. 13:9–10 NASB, emphasis mine)

> Be silent before the Lord God [Rev. 8:1] for the *day of the Lord* is near. (Zeph. 1:7 NASB, emphasis mine)

> You not be quickly shaken from your composure or be disturbed either by a spirit or a message or a letter as if from us, to the

effect that the *day of the Lord* has come. Let no one in any way deceive you for it will not come unless the *apostasy* comes first and the man of lawlessness is revealed. (2 Thess. 2:2–3 NASB, emphasis mine)

Immediately after the tribulation of those days, the sun will be darkened, and the moon will not give its light, and the stars will fall for the sky, and the powers of the heavens will be shaken. (Matt. 24:29 NASB, emphasis mine)

From these timing verses, we can see that a number of prophetic events precede the day of the Lord (God's wrath): the coming of Elijah, the celestial earthly disturbance and silence in heaven, the apostasy, and the revealing of the Antichrist.

The prophet Joel is extremely clear about the timing of the day of the Lord in Joel 2:30–31. Joel states that it occurs *after* the celestial earthly disturbance. It is significant that the Hebrew word translated "wonders" in Joel 2:30–31 is the same Hebrew word used in relation to the plagues and judgments of Egypt. The sun darkening and moon turning to blood are not simple eclipses, but rather events of the magnitude of the Egyptian judgments during the Exodus. At one time, many *pretribulation rapture* exponents believed the event in Joel was not the celestial earthly disturbance pictured in Matthew 24:29 and Revelation 6:12 because of its implications. But Joel repeats himself a few verses later, "For the *day of the Lord is near* in the valley of decision. The sun and moon grow dark and the stars lose their brightness" (Joel 3:14–15 NASB, emphasis mine). Once it is understood that the celestial earthly disturbance pictured in Joel 2:30–31, Isaiah 13:9–10, Matthew 24:29, and Revelation 6:12–17 are all the same event, it also becomes clear that it occurs *after* the great tribulation (Matt. 24:29).

This analysis has provided us with two timing markers. The celestial earthly disturbance occurs *after* the great tribulation and *before* the day of the Lord. Using simple rules of logic, we can safely say that the day of the Lord also occurs after the great tribulation.

Zephaniah also gives us a timing indicator for the day of the Lord in Zephaniah 1:7. The prophet tells us there will be silence before God prior to the day of the Lord. This silence occurs upon the opening of the seventh seal: "When the Lamb broke the *seventh seal*, there was silence in heaven for about half an hour" (Rev. 8:1 NASB, emphasis mine). This perfectly conforms to the *prewrath rapture* theory that holds that the day of the Lord includes the wrath of God and occurs *after* the seventh seal.

During a 2015 videotaped debate between Alan Kurschner (a *prewrath rapture* expert) and Dr. Thomas Ice (executive director of the Pre-Trib. Research Center and *pretribulation rapture*'s most prominent expert), Dr. Ice conceded that Joel 2:30–31, Matthew 24:29, and Revelation 6:12 all refer to the same event, which occurs toward the end of what he calls "the tribulation" period. By extension then, he admitted that the day of the Lord is not the entire seven-year tribulation period because Joel clearly states that the celestial earthly disturbance comes *before* the day of the Lord.[52] This was an incredible but scripturally necessary confession. The extent of this confession is magnified by the prominence of Dr. Ice. He is the author of over thirty books and hundreds of articles, and speaks routinely on the rapture. He may be the most prominent expert on the rapture today, coming from a *pretrib. rapture* perspective. If the day of the Lord truly is the wrath of God, then on the stand, Dr. Ice admitted that it is not the entire Seventieth Week of Daniel.

Marvin Rosenthal has shown how all of these timing indicators in the above passages also present another quandary for the *pretribulation rapture* position. If the *day of the Lord* and the rapture happen on the same day (at the beginning of the Seventieth Week as most of them claim), all of these timing markers would then be prophecies that must be fulfilled *prior* to the rapture and thus destroy this theory's prized theory of imminence (that no prophecies need to be fulfilled prior to the rapture).[53]

Dr. Ice's confession also presents other problems because numerous Scriptures show that salvation of the righteous is reserved for the day of the Lord as well:

Who will also confirm you to the end, blameless in the *day of our Lord* Jesus Christ. (1 Cor. 1:8 NASB, emphasis mine)

So that his spirit may be saved in the *day of the Lord* Jesus. (1 Cor. 5:5 NASB, emphasis mine)

In the future there is laid up for me the crown of righteousness which the Lord, the righteous Judge, will award to me *on that day*; and not only to me, but also to all who have loved *his appearing*. (2 Tim. 4:8 NASB, emphasis mine)

Despite this confession about the day of the Lord by Dr. Ice, *pretribulation rapture* theory still supports the concept that the entire seven-year Seventieth Week is God's wrath. Dr. David Reagan of Lion and Lamb Ministries comments:

When the prophet Habakkuk complained about God doing nothing about the evil of the southern nation of Judah, the Lord revealed that He was going to pour out His wrath on that nation through Babylon [Hab. 1:6]. And when the Lord was finished with Babylon, He raised up the Medes and Persians to conquer the Babylonian Empire, referring to the conquering army as "My consecrated ones" [Isa. 13:3]. During Daniel's 70 Weeks of Years, *much of the wrath of God will be executed through the Antichrist, but it is still the wrath of God.*"[54] —Dr. Reagan, Lion and Lamb Ministries

Dr. Reagan, host of the television program *Christ in Prophecy*, has written twelve books, is an ordained minister, and has made an incredible forty pilgrimages to Israel. In this comment, he presents a theory that God's wrath was poured out on Israel through Babylon. He presents *zero* biblical support in his comment, however, that the coming *wrath of God* is the *entire Seventieth Week of Daniel*! God's Word says that he does nothing without first revealing it through his prophets (Amos 3:7). Dr. Reagan and other *pretribulation rapture* supporters must present *biblical* evidence and not simply make assumptions, which is exactly what Dr. Reagan has done in this comment. Antichrist *will* wrathfully attack Christians and Jews, but God's Word never explicitly states that it is God's wrath. Throughout history hundreds of millions have been killed in all sorts of atrocities and persecutions. Were these other mass murders God's wrath, too? Without an explicit confirmation in the Word of the Lord, we must not say that they were. We must not assume.

ARE THE SEALS GOD'S WRATH?

Pretribulation rapture exponents claim that all seven seals are part of the wrath of God. In fact, their theory hinges on this assumption. It is interesting that they take this position because in Revelation 6 (the chapter where the seals are presented), several passages clearly demonstrate the seals are *not* the wrath of God.

Upon the opening of the fifth seal (the fifth of seven seals), the souls of martyrs are seen under the altar. We discussed these souls in chapter three: "Moving Pictures (Explicit Rapture Depiction in Revelation)." In that chapter, we indicated that these martyrs have *not yet* been resurrected or received immortal "resurrection bodies." These martyrs cry out:

> How long, O Lord, holy and true, *will you refrain from judging and avenging our blood* on those who dwell on the earth? (Rev. 6:10 NASB, emphasis mine)

From this statement, it is obvious that at that point (the fifth seal) the Lord had not yet judged or avenged (poured out his wrath). How can someone claim the first five seals are God's judgments when the text *explicitly* says God was *refraining* from judgment and refraining from wrath?

> **This verse (Rev. 6:10) proves the fifth seal is not God's wrath and *it precludes all of the first five seals from being considered God's wrath* as well.**

This short fifth seal discussion between the martyrs and Jesus is incredibly revealing and of astonishing importance in the rapture timing case.

At the sixth seal, the celestial earthly disturbance occurs. After this event, the unrighteous hide in caves and have this to say:

> They said to the mountains and to the rocks, "Fall on us and hide us from the presence of Him who sits on the throne, and from the *wrath of the Lamb*; *for the great day of their wrath has come,* and who is able to stand?" (Rev. 6:16–17 NASB, emphasis mine)

It is only at this point in the progression of the seals (*after* the sixth seal) that the "great day" (the day of the Lord) and the wrath of God is indicated to "[have] come." We clearly demonstrated in chapter three: "Moving Pictures (Explicit Rapture Depiction in Revelation)" that Jesus is revealed at that point, and after that the rapture occurs.

Given how important this doctrine is for the *pretribulation rapture*, it is surprising how little this issue is discussed in the literature of this theory's supporters. Most of the discussions are not biblically based, but rather are *opinions*. The reason is that the Bible does not explicitly define the seals as God's wrath! An example of one of these opinions is found in George Zeller's article, "Pre-Wrath Confusion": "To say that a judgment [like the fourth seal] which reduces the world's population by a fourth has nothing to do with the wrath of God is incredulous."[55]

In response, a large percentage of those killed at that time (the great tribulation) will be Christians. So we must ask, "Is God's wrath primarily poured out on the Christians who come to faith during this period?" We also must ask, "At what level of tragedy does a mass killing become the wrath of God?" Does the death of fifty million babies to abortion qualify?[56] Does the death of 270 million to Islamic jihad qualify?[57] One can see what a slippery slope such human opinions can be. It is better that we depend on what the Bible actually teaches.

For this reason, a few *pretribulation rapture* exponents have attempted to biblically prove that the seals are the wrath of God. In the rapture debate between Alan Kurschner and Dr. Ice referenced above, Dr. Ice attempted to do just this. As we indicated in the previous section, after the celestial earthly disturbance (sixth seal), the unrighteous say, "Fall on us and hide us from the presence of Him who sits on the throne, and from the wrath of the Lamb; for the great day of their wrath has *come*" (Rev. 6:16–17 NASB, emphasis mine). This is an explicit reference to the timing of God's wrath (*after* the sixth seal). In that debate, Dr. Ice claimed that because the four living creatures also say the word, "come" in Revelation 6:1, 3, 5, and 7, this use of the word "come" in Revelation 6:17 refers back to these statements by the living creatures and makes the entire passage about the seals God's wrath.[58]

First, the use of "come" in Revelation 6:17 is in the aorist tense. Aorist is usually timeless (not denoting the timing of the verb), but it can express the ingressive use, which indicates the beginning of an action. An aorist ingressive use of the verb "come" is seen in a statement of Jesus's upon the arrival of Judas to the garden of Gethsemane:

Then He came the third time, and said to them, "Are you still sleeping and resting? It is enough; the hour *has come* [aorist]; behold, the Son of Man is being betrayed into the hands of sinners. Get up, let us be going; behold, the one who betrays Me is at hand!" (Mark 14:41–42 NASB, clarification and emphasis mine)

106

Clearly this aorist use of "come" marks the beginning of Jesus's passion, just as the phrase "the great day of their wrath has come" marks the beginning of the day of the Lord and God's wrath.

Second, "come" is an incredibly common word, occurring 637 times in the New Testament. To claim this as a reference to the timing of God's wrath requires more substantiation that Dr. Ice offers. For instance, the use of the Greek word translated "come" in Rev. 6:1, 3, 5, and 7 is in the present-imperative-passive tense and implies a desire for someone or something to come. Throughout the first four seals, the living creatures still desire for something or someone to come. That someone may be Jesus not the horsemen, and it may be a reference to Revelation 22 where this *exact use and tense* is quoted. In both Revelation 6 and Revelation 22, this desire is mentioned *four times*. In that second passage, the Spirit, the bride, the one who hears, and John all say "come," just as the four living creatures did in Revelation 6. But they are all calling out for *Jesus* to "come:" Maranatha!

> The Spirit and the bride *say, "Come."* And let the one who hears say, *"Come."* . . . He who testifies to these things says, "Yes, I am coming quickly." Amen. *Come, Lord Jesus*. (Rev. 22:17, 20 NASB, emphasis mine)

In addition to Dr. Ice's comments, several other *pretribulation rapture* theorists have attempted to present reasons that God's wrath begins with the First Seal. They claim Jesus is causing the events that follow the seals. Dr. Mark Hitchcock summarizes this concept:

> The seal judgments which are opened at the beginning of the tribulation are brought forth not by man or Satan, but by the

Lamb Himself, the Lord Jesus Christ (Rev. 6:1). They are messianic judgments. Jesus opens the seals and an angel calls each of the four horsemen to ride across the earth in judgment.[59]

—Dr. Mark Hitchcock

Dr. Hitchcock is an attorney, the author of twenty books, a senior pastor, and adjunct faculty for the Dallas Theological Seminary. As he rightly observes, the events that follow the seals are obviously associated with Jesus's breaking of each seal. It is also obvious that the all-powerful Son of God is *permitting* those events. However, it is not at all obvious that Jesus is *causing* the events. Dr. Hitchcock assumes it. The sense of the passage can also be that the events are *reactions* by Satan and Antichrist to the seven-sealed scroll being opened. These events could be directed by Satan to test the inhabitants of the world. This is similar to what we read in Job:

> Satan answered the Lord, "Does Job fear God for nothing? Have You not made a hedge about him and his house and all that he has, on every side? You have blessed the work of his hands, and his possessions have increased in the land. But put forth Your hand now and touch all that he has; he will surely curse You to Your face." Then the Lord said to Satan, "Behold, *all that he has is in your power.*" (Job 1:9–12 NASB; emphasis mine)

Satan was given God's *permission* to test Job. God may also give Satan the authority to test the inhabitants of the world during the seals. In Revelation 6:8, we see that "authority" will be given to death and hades over a quarter of the earth. Who gives them this authority? God does.

We can easily resolve which answer is correct because we have already proven the first four seals are the work of Satan not God. At the opening of the fifth seal we are told that God has not yet begun to judge or avenge. Revelation 6:10 ends the argument on whether the first five seals are God's wrath; they are not. Many *pretribulation rapture* supporters are aware that the statement by the martyrs at the fifth seal creates enormous difficulties for their position. Interestingly, in the videotaped debate between Alan Kurschner and Dr. Thomas Ice, Dr. Ice *excludes* the fifth seal from what he claims is the wrath of God.[60]

Although it is not required to prove this point, there is further evidence that the seals are not the wrath of God. In chapter two, Dr. Hitchcock himself is quoted as saying the events of Matt. 24 are parallel to those of Rev. 6. The first set of parallel events are found in Matt. 24:4-5 and Rev. 6:1-2 (the First Seal). These verses describe deception by false messiahs. Later in the Olivet Discourse, Jesus expands on this deception to say, "For false Christs and false prophets will arise and will show great signs and wonders, so as to mislead, if possible, even the elect" (Matt. 24:24 NASB). John further clarifies that the False Prophet is responsible for many of these great signs, "And he deceives those who dwell on the earth because of the signs which it was given him to perform" (Rev. 13:14 NASB). This isn't God's doing. He does not deceive or tempt the elect to commit apostasy, "Let no one say when he is tempted, 'I am being tempted by God'; for God cannot be tempted by evil, and He Himself does not tempt anyone" (James 1:13 NASB). God cannot cause the temptation to sin initiated by the first seal, so *the first seal cannot be part of God's wrath.*

Followers of the *pretribulation rapture* are aware that if the wrath of God does not begin until *after* the sixth seal, the rationale for their theory is totally destroyed. Given the overwhelming biblical evidence that the wrath of God does not begin until this later point, it isn't surprising that most *pretribulation rapture* commentators have attempted to prove their point by means of their *opinions* rather than trying to prove it biblically.

1 THESSALONIANS 5

Pretribulation rapture supporter Dr. Renald Showers makes a different argument about the beginning of the *day of the Lord* based on 1 Thessalonians 5.

> For you yourselves know full well that *the day of the Lord will come just like a thief in the night.* While *they are saying, "Peace and safety!" then destruction will come upon them* suddenly *like labor pains upon a woman with child*, and they will not escape. *But you, brethren, are not in darkness, that the day would overtake you like a thief.* (1 Thess. 5:2–4 NASB, emphasis mine)

This passage is one of Dr. Showers's main areas of contention with the *prewrath rapture*. He actually makes *three separate arguments* from this short passage. Let's examine his arguments, and I will point out where I differ from his positions.

First, he argues that if the day of the Lord occurs after the sixth seal is opened, how can it come as a thief in the night to the unrighteous? Obviously, the celestial earthly disturbance will be an event of world-shaking proportions.[61]

Dr. Showers, of course, misses the fact that the day of Lord may begin with the celestial earthly disturbance. It may be the event that catches the unrighteous by surprise (as a thief). This may be immediately followed by the resurrection and rapture and then the pouring out of the wrath of God. In chapter four: "Synchronized Fireworks (Same-Day Salvation and Wrath)," we learned that the day of the Lord is a day of both salvation for the righteous and punishment for the wicked. The celestial earthly disturbance may also occur on this day.

Second, Dr. Showers argues that the world can only say, "Peace and safety" (1 Thess. 5:3) prior to the beginning of the Seventieth Week. He claims that after the start of that period of time there will be no peace or safety.

As with so many pretrib. arguments, this one is based on an assumption—that there can only be "peace and safety" before the beginning of the Seventieth Week. Although there are many possible ways there could be peace and safety during the 70th week, the Book of Revelation describes a time immediately *before a resurrection* when the world will be in wild celebration over what *it* defines as "peace and safety." After 1,260 days, the beast will kill God's "two witnesses" who have testified about God to the unrepentant and brought plagues upon the earth. Here is how Revelation describes the celebration that follows:

> And those who dwell on the earth will rejoice over them and celebrate; and they will send gifts to one another, because these two prophets tormented those who dwell on the earth. (Rev. 11:10 NASB)

The inhabitants of the earth will say "peace and safety" once these witnesses are dead. But three and a half days later, the witnesses will be raised to life. Although the timing of this resurrection is unclear, it may be *the* resurrection on the *day of the Lord* (Rev. 11: 11–12). If this is correct, at the moment that

111

the world rejoices over its safety, sudden destruction of the day of the Lord will come upon them just as the Bible foretold.

Third, Dr. Showers argues that this same verse: "Destruction will come upon them suddenly like *labor pains upon a woman with child*" is in reference to Jesus's beginning of the birth pangs (Matt. 24:4–8), which involve the first three of the seals. Dr. Showers claims the day of the Lord must begin at the breaking of the first seal for this reason.

Dr. Showers completely misses Jesus's intention in Matthew 24:8 when our Lord states the first three seals are the *beginning* birth pangs, not intense labor. Any woman who has experienced childbirth knows the difference between these prelabor contractions and intense labor. That was Jesus's point. The first three seals are prelabor contractions, the beginning of birth pangs.

To prove this idea, the first sign of Jesus's coming parousia (equivalent to the first seal) is deception by false messiahs. This hardly qualifies as *sudden* destruction, as graphically portrayed in a passage from Isaiah to which both Jesus *and* Paul were both referring:

> Wail, for the day of the Lord is near! It will come as destruction from the Almighty. Therefore all hands will fall limp, and every man's heart will melt. They will be terrified; pains and anguish will take hold of them. *They will writhe like a woman in labor*. (Isa. 13:6–8 NASB, emphasis mine)

The very next verses in Isaiah clearly show the timing of these labor pains and the *sudden* destruction come after the celestial earthly disturbance and the sixth seal, just as we have predicted!

112

Behold, the day of the Lord is coming, cruel, with fury and burning anger, to make the land a desolation; and He will exterminate its sinners from it. For *the stars of heaven and their constellations will not flash forth their light; the sun will be dark when it rises and the moon will not shed its light.* (Isa. 13:9–10 NASB, emphasis mine)

The Word of the Lord is completely true and completely consistent. From Genesis to Revelation, all passages point to a *prewrath rapture.* Enthusiasts of the *pretribulation rapture* may try to use a passage like 1 Thessalonians 5:2–4 to prove their theory, but these passages only reinforce the correct timing of the rapture. All rapture verses point to a *prewrath rapture.*

THE BLESSED HOPE

In the preceding sections, we have discussed at length when the wrath of God takes place and when it doesn't. From these discussions, it is clear that the entire Seventieth Week of Daniel is *not* the wrath of God.

Many *pretribulation rapture* supporters, however, still claim that God would never permit his children to endure any part of the Seventieth Week of Daniel. Pastor Billy Crone of "Get A Life Ministries" has this to say about being present in what he calls the seven-year tribulation:

That's not good news, that's not a blessed hope, that's bad news. —Pastor Billy Crone[62]

Pastor Crone is obviously referring to Titus 2:13: "Looking for the blessed hope and the appearing of the glory of our great God and Savior, Christ Jesus." His statement implies that for the appearing of Jesus to truly be a blessed hope or good news, Christians will need to avoid the great tribulation, admittedly the "greatest" time of tribulation since the creation. This statement by Pastor Crone, which echoes the sentiments of nearly all *pretribulation rapture* theorists, however, overlooks several great truths.

First, our "hope" is not in earthly comfort, safety, or possessions. Our hope is in Jesus, and his glorious return is a blessed hope no matter what struggles or persecution intervenes between now and then. Even enduring the great tribulation will not lessen our blessed hope by even the slightest amount.

Second, God did not promise to insulate us from suffering or persecution (tribulation). In fact, he promised us that in this world, we *will* endure tribulation (John. 16:33). He even stated that "*Blessed* are those who have been persecuted for the sake of righteousness" (Matt. 5:10 NASB).

Many are currently enduring tribulations equal to what will occur in the great tribulation at the hands of Islamic jihadists. Do these believers not have a blessed hope because they endure persecution, torture, and death?

Third, the term great tribulation is misconstrued. The Greek word translated "great" in Matthew 24:21 is *megas*, which means "large or widespread." It does not mean "worse or more painful." By using this term, Jesus was telling us that the tribulation will be more widespread than ever before. It is hard to imagine worse persecution than what some believers are currently enduring in the Middle East, but it is easy to imagine that type of persecution being more widespread.

This *pretribulation rapture* belief that Christians should expect to be kept away from persecution is in direct contrast with the teachings of the

New Testament that repeatedly tell us to expect to suffer for the cause of Christ. If you have believed this teaching, please consider the example of Jesus and the disciples who, with one exception, died a martyr's death. Should we aspire to be different from them or emulate them?

OTHER CONSIDERATIONS:

WILL THE CHURCH FACE THE ANTICHRIST?

In Paul's second letter to the Thessalonians, there is an overt statement that the rapture does not occur until after the Antichrist is revealed at the midpoint of the Seventieth Week of Daniel.

> With regard to the coming [parousia] of our Lord Jesus Christ [the rapture] and our gathering together to Him, that you not be quickly shaken from your composure or be disturbed either by a spirit or a message or a letter as if from us, to the effect that the *day of the Lord* has come. Let no one in any way deceive you, for *it will not come unless the apostasy* [Gk. *apostasia*, meaning "defection from the faith"] *comes first, and the man of lawlessness is revealed*, the son of destruction, who opposes and exalts himself above every so-called god or object of worship, so that he takes his seat in the temple of God, displaying himself as being God. (2 Thess. 2:1–4 NASB, clarification and emphasis mine)

First, this passage clearly associates the parousia of Jesus and the rapture with the day of the Lord. Second, it demonstrates that two events must occur prior to the rapture: 1) the great apostasy and 2) the revealing of Antichrist at the *midpoint* of the Seventieth Week. Just as in the previous sections, when the explicit meaning of the verse is obvious (and contrary to the *pretribulation rapture* theory), attempts have been made to explain away the clear implications. In this case, *pretribulation rapture* adherents have focused on the Greek word *apostasia*. Dr. Stanley Ellisen explains this theory's opinion of the meaning of this word:

> Grammatically speaking, the word "apostasy" means "departure" (from the verb *aphistemi*). Since the word is never used elsewhere in the New Testament without a qualifier (e.g., "departure from Moses," Acts 21:12 (sic. actually Acts 21:21); cf. "to depart from the faith," 1 Tim. 4:1; Heb. 3:12), by itself it means simply "departure." It can refer to either a religious (or political) defection or to a physical departure (the rapture). Preceded by the article, it designates a specific departure of which Paul had previously instructed them." —Dr. Stanley Ellisen[63]

The late Dr. Ellisen was a noted and beloved faculty member of Western Seminary and the author of many books on a wide variety of Christian subjects. His comment here sounds very academic and believable, except that "departure" is not what the word apostasia means. *Strong's Concordance* defines apostasia as defection, rebellion, or revolt.[64] This usage is well established. In the New Testament, this word only appears one other time (Acts 21:21) and refers to a religious apostasy from Moses. In the Greek Septuagint, the word is used three times to refer to religious apostasies (Josh. 22:22; Jer. 2:19; 2 Chron. 29:19). Josephus used this word to describe a revolt from the Romans.[65]

116

It should even be questioned whether the word apostasia has *ever* meant what Dr. Ellisen claims! In the previously mentioned debate between Kurschner and Ice, Dr. Ice was asked if he was aware of another *single* use of apostasia in the Bible or *all of Greek literature* where it meant "physical departure." He answered that he was not. (He claimed that Dr. H. Wayne House *was* able to produce an example.[66] My analysis of Dr. House's writings on this Greek word, however, did not demonstrate this example.[67]) Another *pretribulation rapture* scholar, Dr. Paul Feinberg, honestly admits that none of the 355 uses of apostasia in all of Greek literature during a three-hundred-year period from the second century BC to the first century AD mean what some *pretribulation rapture* experts claim it does![68] Rather, it is obvious it should be defined in 2 Thessalonians 2:3 as it is in Acts 21:21 and the Septuagint Old Testament as a defection or rebellion from the faith.

What event was Paul referring to? He uses the definitive article and terms this event "the" apostasy. In Matthew 24:10, Jesus prophesied a great falling away from the faith after the great tribulation begins. Based on this true meaning of apostasia, the rapture must occur *after* this apostasy and after the Antichrist is revealed at the *midpoint* of Daniel's Seventieth Week.

I hope you are beginning to see that a pattern is developing. The explicit meaning of multiple Bible passages strongly implies that the harpazo is a *prewrath rapture*. Because of this, exponents of the other rapture theories have developed work-arounds to support their beliefs, *work-arounds that are not based on sound biblical exegesis*. This reinforces the backfire effect discussed at the beginning of this chapter. That theory states that arguing a position may intensify one's loyalty to a position even if facts presented dismiss it as false. This is, unfortunately, often the case.

IS THE OLIVET DISCOURSE (MATTHEW 24) FOR THE UNSAVED JEWS OR FOR CHRISTIANS?

Continuing in this pattern of creating work-arounds to obscure the clear meaning of Scripture, *pretribulation rapture* proponents have claimed that Jesus only intended Matthew 24–25 for the those practicing Judaism because he delivered it to his chosen Jewish apostles.

We alluded to this proof and its "elaborate set of evidence" in chapter two. Prior to looking at this evidence, we must state initially that saying a portion of the New Testament doesn't apply to the church is an outlandish statement. In the great commission (Matt. 28:20), Jesus appointed us to teach *all* that he commanded. "All that he commanded" includes Matt. 24. So the burden of proof for this bizarre statement falls squarely on the shoulders of the proponents of this theory.

Don Mills, a program director for the Christian Satellite Network and author of numerous articles, summarizes the sentiments from the *pretribulation rapture* camp: "It's a sad fact that many people who read the Olivet Discourse in Matthew 24 will make the assumption that this is referring to the church at the close of this age."[69] The reason for this assumption, of course, is that it's the clear reading of Scripture! All of the New Testament is meant for the church and not those practicing Judaism who reject Jesus and the New Testament. How would they even access this material if it were meant for them?

First, let's examine whether Mr. Mills's logic that the Olivet Discourse was given to "Jewish" disciples is accurate. Peter was a Jew, but was he "unsaved" at the point Jesus gave the Olivet Discourse? Most take it for granted that he was, but the answer is not that easy. In Matthew 16 we read:

118

Simon Peter answered, "You are the Christ, the Son of the living God." And Jesus said to him, "Blessed are you, Simon Barjona, because flesh and blood did not reveal this to you, but My Father who is in heaven. I also say to you that you are Peter [meaning "stone"], and upon this rock [meaning "bedrock"] I will build My church." (Matt. 16:16–18 NASB, clarification mine)

Was this a confession of faith by Peter? It was, and Jesus calls the Holy Spirit–inspired confession the bedrock upon which he would build his church. It can easily be argued that Peter may have been a Christian from that moment on.

Some argue he was not a Christian yet because he did not believe in Christ's resurrection from the dead (Rom. 10:9) and had not yet received the baptism of the Holy Spirit. This unclear nuance of understanding of what constitutes being a Christian, however, only highlights that the disciples might not have been Christians for the *entire period* of the Gospels. All of the material in the Gospels was given to Jewish men.

Mr. Mills misses the obvious problem in logic that all the material in the four Gospels was given prior to the official formation of the church on Pentecost. It was all only for unsaved Jews or all of it was meant for the church. We can't pick and choose and say, "This applies to the church, but this other passage only applies to those who are currently unsaved." If we are to claim that Matthew 24 was not meant for the church, then essential doctrines like the Sermon on the Mount (Matt. 5–7), the Great Commission (Matt. 28:18–20), and Upper Room Discourse (John 13–17) must also not apply to the church. Obviously, no one believes that. Yet, that is the logical problem that *pretribulation rapture* supporters face.

Mr. Mills's second point about why Matthew 24 is exclusively for those practicing Judaism is that certain Jewish-related elements are found in the Olivet Discourse:

> Then those who are in *Judea* must flee to the mountain . . . But pray that your flight will not be in the winter, or on a *Sabbath*. (Matt. 24:16, 20 NASB, emphasis mine)

Mr. Mills contends that "Judea" and "Sabbath" are exclusively Jewish and thus the entire discourse relates solely to the Jews. Obviously this is stretching reality beyond the breaking point. Judea will be the epicenter of the beginning of the great tribulation. The Antichrist sits in the temple of God and displays himself to be God in Jerusalem. Jerusalem and Judea then will be the first to feel the effects of his decree to kill those who will not worship him. Christians and Jews (not solely Jews) are instructed by Jesus to flee this area. If this date were a Sabbath, all travel would be hindered by the observant Jews blocking and restricting egress out of the area. "Judea" and "Sabbath" are mentioned for practical reasons, just as winter is, not because of their relation to Judaism.

The final point Mr. Mills makes is in regard to the words "gather together" in Matthew 24:31. He contends this term is used in relation to the gathering of all Jews back to Israel at the end of the Seventieth Week as depicted in Isaiah 11:10–12, Deuteronomy 30:3–6, Nehemiah 1:8–9, Zechariah 2:6–13, and Psalm 147:2. This belies a misunderstanding of what event is depicted in Matthew 24:31. As we discussed at length in chapter five, it is the rapture during which the living and resurrected believers in Jesus are gathered together. In that previous chapter, we explained that the gathering of the Jewish remnant will take place by foot, by beast of burden (Isa. 66:18-20), and even by boat (Isa. 60:9) not by means of angels.

The first-century church understood that Matthew 24:31 was the rapture and believed that Matthew 24 was meant exclusively for the church. In chapter five, we examined an ancient first-century church document known as the *Didache*,[70] which substantiates this position. This document clearly references the Olivet Discourse as found in the Book of Matthew with numerous quotes and similar passages. Debate rages whether the *Didache* was based on Matthew or whether it was based on an oral tradition of the teaching of the apostles.[71] The *Didache* is a simple document and doesn't include any reference to heretical teaching or persecution, features common in the epistles. For this reason, many scholars, including myself, favor an early date for composition of the *Didache*, perhaps only a few years after the resurrection of Jesus. Regardless of its composition date, however, it is universally acknowledged as reflecting the opinion of the first-century church in regard to the return of Jesus. And based on the numerous quotes of Matthew within it, it was their opinion that the gospel of Matthew (and especially Matthew 24) was for the church.

There are still additional reasons that the Olivet Discourse applies to the church. As mentioned in chapter five, Alan Kurschner has documented thirty parallel similarities between Matt. 24 and the books of 1 and 2 Thess. Figure 16 demonstrates fifteen similarities in regard to the rapture event alone. Pretribulation rapture supporters universally agree that 1 and 2 Thess. are meant for the church, so by extension so is Matt. 24 upon which these books were based.

In chapter five, we also presented a proof of Marvin Rosenthal's that the great commission promises that Jesus will be with his followers until the "end of the age." Matt. 24 clearly shows this event, the end of the

121

age, follows numerous actions in Matt. 24: wars and rumors of war, the preaching of the gospel to all nations, and enduring till the end. Since the end of age is the harvest of the righteous, by extension, Matt. 24 must precede this harvest.

It is quite interesting that Mr. Mills and other *pretribulation rapture* supporters ignore this following passage from the Olivet Discourse:

> Then they will deliver you to tribulation, and will kill you, and you will be hated by all nations *because of my name*. (Matt. 24:9 NASB, emphasis mine)

Jews who currently reject Jesus are not hated because of Jesus's name. In order to be able to apply this verse to these Jews, *pretribulation rapture* supporters must claim that this passage refers to the mythical 144,000 Jewish evangelists who they claim come to faith near the beginning of the Seventieth Week. They believe that Revelation 7:1–8 refers to these mythical evangelists. After the supposed *pretribulation rapture*, supporters of this theory assume these evangelists will discover Matthew 24 and use it as a guidebook for the Seventieth Week. This definitely qualifies as a work-around to attempt to maintain viability of the *pretribulation rapture* position when, in fact, supportive biblical evidence is lacking.

Now God does seal twelve thousand from each of the tribes of Israel (except Dan) to protect them from the pouring out of his wrath, but the passage (Rev. 7:1–8) doesn't say they come to faith in Jesus at that point or become evangelists. Additionally, this chronologically takes place after the sixth seal, after the great tribulation, and after the rapture not at the beginning of the 70th Week.

It is also quite interesting that Jesus makes the following statement in the Olivet Discourse that *pretribulation rapture* protagonists associate with the imminence of the rapture:

> But of that day and hour no one knows, not even the angels of heaven, nor the Son, but the Father alone. (Matt. 24:36 NASB)

How can a passage of Scripture that *supposedly is only for the unbelieving Jews* contain a verse about the imminence of the rapture *that the unbelieving Jews will not participate in*? Think about it! This is the ultimate in circular reasoning. And what I find most fascinating of all is that if Jesus mentions the rapture here in Matthew 24:36, why isn't it given as a sign of his coming when the disciples ask him for a sign? Even if the rapture were a silent one as the *pretribulation rapture* theory proposes, the disappearance of hundreds of millions of people (the church) would be an event of immense proportions to the Jews who were not raptured. It would be a sign.

For all these reasons (and many more), we must reject the *pretribulation rapture* theory's proposal that the Olivet Discourse is only for the Jews.

IS THE CHURCH PRESENT IN REVELATION AFTER CHAPTER 3?

Another somewhat strange but frequent proof for the *pretribulation rapture* is that the church is not mentioned in the Book of Revelation after the letters to the seven churches (Rev. 2–3). Associated with this proof is the belief that Revelation 4:1 is a picture of the rapture. That verse calls for John to "come up here" (to heaven), as if that is a symbol of the rapture. Robert Gromacki of the Pre-Trib. Research Center explains it this way:

> Where is the church during the seven-year Tribulation, as outlined in Revelation 4–19? If posttribulationism were correct, you would expect to see the church mentioned as being on earth during this time. However, that is not the picture one sees in Revelation 4–19. This writer demonstrates through investigating many of the details of Revelation 4–19 that the church is pictured in heaven with Christ, having been raptured before the Tribulation began. —Robert Gromacki[72]

Dr. Gromacki was a distinguished professor of the Bible and Greek at Cedarville University for more than forty years. His *New Testament Survey* is utilized as a textbook in colleges and seminaries throughout the United States. Despite his lavish credentials, I find it interesting that some will argue about what the Bible doesn't say and ignore what it clearly teaches!

In the Book of Revelation, the Greek word *ekklesia*, which is translated "church" is *only* associated with the *names* of the seven churches (for example, the *church* in Ephesus, the *church* in Philadelphia, etc.) or specifically references all seven churches as a group. In Revelation, the universal church isn't mentioned at all by using that word. However, believers *are* mentioned in Revelation and referred to as "bond servants" and "saints," and these references are found throughout the book.

This argument by *pretribulation rapture* enthusiasts is akin to reading a newspaper article about "The First Baptist Church" where the only mention of the word church is found in the first paragraph in regard to the name of the church: The First Baptist Church. In subsequent paragraphs, the newspaper reporter mentions "parishioners, members, and Baptists." It would be terribly wrong to read this article and claim the church disbanded after the first paragraph because the word church didn't appear in it after that point. This ignores the obvious intention of the writer that the parishioners, members, and Baptists *are* the church! Yet this is exactly what this *pretribulation rapture* argument does; it places emphasis on the specific names of seven churches and ignores all the references to the members of the church.

The word church (*ekklesia*) is not commonly used in the New Testament to refer to the universal church. For instance, it is not found in 1 Thessalonians 4:16–17, the most famous rapture passage of all. Does this mean the church is not raptured? Obviously, it does not. The word church is completely absent from the books of Mark, Luke, John, 2 Timothy, Titus, 1 Peter, 2 Peter, 1 John, 2 John, and Jude. Do these entire books of the Bible not apply to the church?

Finally, the word church is absent in the one location in Revelation where we would *most* expect to find it: before the throne in heaven in Revelation 4–5. Not only is the word church absent in these chapters in Revelation, so are all mentions of saints or bond servants. As we mentioned in chapter three, *pretribulation rapture* theory has had to "invent" ways that the church is present in that heavenly scene to justify its contention that the rapture occurs in Revelation 4:1.

Another reason that the word ekklesia is not mentioned in the later chapters of Revelation may be that many who attend church are not raptured or saved! In the Olivet Discourse, Jesus clearly teaches that many will fall away and the love of *most* will grow cold. This is the apostasy. Only those who "endure till the end" will be saved. This is not the entire body currently attending church and calling themselves "Christians." Those who will be saved are the bond servants of the Lord.

The Book of Revelation liberally uses the terms bond servant and saint to refer to *believers*. Both terms are regularly found throughout most of the book, as we will see. Marvin Rosenthal has mentioned, however, that these terms are interestingly absent in the chapters that depict the trumpet and bowl judgments (Rev. 8:6–11:15; Rev. 16). This is entirely consistent with a *prewrath rapture*.[73] The church is, of course, absent from earth during the trumpet and bowl judgments, being the wrath of God, and this is what is reflected in Revelation.

The term bond servant is used of members of the church in Thyatira (Rev. 2:20) and in terms of the martyrs who die at the hand of the harlot (Rev. 19:2). Revelation 1:1 tells us Revelation was given to these bond servants as well. Revelation also makes reference to John and Moses being bond servants (Rev. 1:1; Rev. 15:3). This implies that the bond servants are not simply members of the universal church, but perhaps the most faithful of Jesus's servants.

Revelation refers to the word saints twelve times between Revelation 1 and Revelation 19 (the physical second coming). The Antichrist makes war with the saints (Rev. 13:7), and we are told that captivity and death by the sword will require perseverance and faith of the saints (Rev. 13:10), as will avoiding the mark of the beast (Rev. 14:11–12).

Are some of these saints and bond servants those who come to faith in Jesus *after* the beginning of the Seventieth Week, as we are told by *pretribulation rapture* proponents (so-called "tribulation saints")? Yes, undoubtedly some are, but the following passage indicates "the saints" are more than Tribulation Saints; they are the complete Bride of Christ:

> "Let us rejoice and be glad and give the glory to Him, for the marriage of the Lamb has come and His bride has made herself ready." It was given to her to clothe herself in fine linen, bright

and clean; for the fine linen is the righteous acts of the *saints*.
(Rev. 19:7–8 NASB, emphasis mine)

If the word "saints" in Revelation chapters 4-19 only refers to Tribulation Saints, then only their righteous acts would adorn the "bride of Christ." Obviously no one believes that; therefore the term "saints" in Revelation must include more than "Tribulation Saints."

DOES THE RAPTURE "SYMBOLICALLY" OCCUR IN REVELATION 4:1?

Pretribulationalist, Dr. Michael Svigel, is a department chairman and distinguished professor of Theology at Dallas Theological Seminary. He has admitted that contrary to many pretrib. claims, the Rapture is not symbolically depicted in Rev. 4:1 when John is told to "come up here.[74]" Marvin Rosenthal has pointed out that claiming this "symbolic" rapture is akin to Origen's allegorical thinking[75] rather than sound exegesis.

In addition to the testimony of these outstanding scholars, common sense should dictate that this is not a depiction of the rapture. Daniel, Isaiah, and Ezekiel were all also given visions of the throne of God in heaven (and Paul was actually "caught up" into heaven). John's non-bodily personage ("in the spirit") in heaven is no more symbolic than that of the Old Testament saints or Paul when they saw the Lord.

Rather, Revelation 4:1 is a transitional passage *from* the warnings of the letters to the seven churches in Revelation 2–3 *into* the vision of John before the throne of God, which occupies much of the remainder of the book. As we proved decisively in chapter three: "Moving Pictures (Explicit Rapture Depiction in Revelation)," the raptured saints are represented by an actual vast multitude in resurrection bodies before the throne in Revelation 7:9, not by a single man, John.

DOES THE RAPTURE "SYMBOLICALLY" OCCUR IN REV. 12?

Twenty years ago, pretribulationalists had several places in Revelation where they believed that a *pretribulation rapture* was mentioned. In this chapter, we have already shown that Rev. 3:10 and Rev. 4:1 do not reflect that timing. But, it is a valid assumption that Revelation will describe the Rapture if there is one. (We have already shown this occurs prior to Rev. 7:9). In desperation, therefore, many pretribulationalists have looked to Rev. 12:5 as that last possible mention of their rapture timing.

> And she gave birth to a son, a male child, who is to rule all the nations with a rod of iron; and her child was caught up (Gk: *harpazo*) to God and to His throne. (Rev. 12:5 NASB)

The traditional interpretations of this verse suggest that it refers to the birth and ascension of Jesus during his earthly life and ministry. Recent propositions, however, have suggested that the reference to "a son, a male" is symbolic of both Jesus *and* the church. In this way, pretribulationalists suggest the entire passage has a dual meaning in relation to Jesus's earthly life and to a *pretribulation rapture*.

Dr. Michael Svigel has proposed that a symbolic double meaning of this verse should be considered for three reasons[76]:

- All the symbols in the prophecy are corporate; the woman is Israel, the "son, a male" is the church, and the dragon is Satan and all of his evil world empires.
- Rev. 12:5 is a reference to Isa. 66:6-9 which depicts the birth of all of Spiritual Israel.
- *Harpazo* is a poor word choice for the ascension of Jesus

We will examine all of these points individually and argue that only Jesus uniquely fulfills "a son, a male" in Rev. 12:5.

Dr. Svigel asserts that "a son, a male" symbolizes the church as well as Jesus because all the symbols in Rev. 12:5 depict individuals *and* corporate groups. First, he asserts the "woman" is both Mary and Spiritual Israel, and I agree with him wholeheartedly. Second, he also asserts that the "dragon" is both Satan and the evil world empires that have comprised the heads and horns of the dragon. I don't agree with him.

First, Rev. 12:9 uniquely identifies the dragon as "the serpent of old who is called the devil and Satan." Satan has controlled the evil world empires depicted by his heads and horns but by no means are they "the dragon." Rev. 12 clearly identifies the dragon as a single spiritual being, the devil, who has evil angels under his control. They will be thrown out of heaven after their war with Michael. The evil world empires will not be thrown down and they don't control evil angels. They are not "the dragon."

Dr. Svigel also suggests the birth that is recorded in Rev. 12:5 is a reference to Isa. 66:7, and that since the "son" referred to there is corporate, we can extend that corporate imagery to Rev. 12:5

> *Before she travailed*, she brought forth; before her pain came, she gave birth to a boy. (Isa. 66:7 NASB, emphasis mine)

It should be obvious to all that these two births are not the same. The birth in Isa. 66:7 takes place *before* the woman travails, but Rev. 12's birth is one during travail and pain. The actual Septuagint reference for the birth of "a son, a male" in Rev. 12: 5 is found earlier in Isaiah:

And as a woman in travail draws nigh to be delivered, and cries
out in her pain; *so have we been to thy beloved*. We have
conceived, O Lord, because of thy fear, and have been in pain,
and *have brought forth the breath (Gk: pneuma) of thy
salvation*. (Isa. 26:17-18 LXX, emphasis mine)

This is the passage John was referring to in Rev. 12. The woman cries out in
pain and is in travail. Please notice who is born as a result of this birth: "thy
beloved" and "the spirit (pneuma) of the thy salvation." This is Jesus. He is
God's beloved and the spirit of salvation. John is telegraphing that Israel
(who is talking in this verse) will be as a woman in labor. They will bring
forth the Messiah, God's beloved, and the spirit (pneuma) of salvation. Isa.
66:7 and the birth without labor is considered the rebirth of Israel in 1948 by
many scholars; something totally different than what is depicted in Rev. 12.

In regard to the words "son" and "male," they are not references to
Isa. 66. The word "son" in Rev. 12:5 is drawn from Psalm 2. It is the first
time Jesus is referred to as the Son of God in the Bible:

But as for Me, I have installed My King upon Zion, My holy
mountain. I will surely tell of the decree of the Lord: He said to
Me, '*You are My Son*, today I have begotten You. Ask of Me,
and I will surely give the nations as Your inheritance, And the
very ends of the earth as Your possession. *You shall break
them with a rod of iron*, you shall shatter them like
earthenware.' (Psalm 2:6-9 NASB, emphasis mine)

This Psalm was identified with Jesus in Acts 4:25-28, so the traditional
interpretation is absolutely appropriate that Jesus is the Son. Also notice

130

Psalm 2 is the source of John's quote regarding the "rod of iron." It is unquestionably apparent that John drew the term "son" from Psalm 2, a singular and non-corporate reference.

The term "a male" is also drawn from a singular, non-corporate reference which appears to be the nativity narrative from Luke in which both "son" and "male" are found:

> And she gave birth to her *firstborn son* . . . "Every *firstborn male* that opens the womb shall be called holy to the Lord" (Luke 2:7, 23 NASB, emphasis mine)

Clearly, the Scriptural evidence shows that "a son, a male" is drawn from singular not corporate references. Some might argue that despite the lack of evidence for corporate references in Rev. 12:5, the church is Jesus's Body, and as such, the harpazo mentioned in this verse can be thought to include all of Jesus's Body "symbolically." The logic of this reasoning breaks down quickly. Although the Body is the church, Jesus is the Head of the Body. Both would "snatched up" together, and no one is suggesting that Jesus is part of a harpazo just prior to the seven-year Tribulation. Jesus is the unique Son of God, pure and simple.

HARPAZO AND THE ASCENSION

Rev. 12:5 mentions a harpazo, a snatching up, of "a son, a male." Traditional theory has claimed this is the ascension of Jesus. Dr. Svigel claims that harpazo is a poor choice of words for the ascension. He even includes a table which shows all the various translated meanings of harpazo in the Septuagint and the New Testament to support his point.[77] Unfortunately, Dr. Svigel misapplies a very, very important use of harpazo found in Hosea. It is one of the most misunderstood passages in the Bible. Because of this, I will insert the definition "snatched up" in place of Brenton's translation of harpazo in the Septuagint. The result of this substitution is amazing:

> Wherefore I am as a panther to Ephraim, and as *a lion to the house of Judah*: and *I will [snatch up myself]*, and go away; and I will take, and there shall be none to deliver. I will go and return to my place, until they are brought to naught, and then shall they seek my face. (Hosea 5:14-15 LXX, emphasis mine)

Look at this passage! It is the source reference for John's mention of the "Lion from the Tribe of Judah" found in Rev. 5:5. Notice that it also clearly references Jesus as being "snatched up" (harpazo) although he does it to himself (future middle indicative). He "snatches himself up." This passage further claims that after this snatching up, Jesus will return to "his place" (heaven) until the Jewish remnant are brought to nothing by the Antichrist. Then the Jewish remnant shall seek Jesus's face. This is a very clear eschatological summary of the ascension. So harpazo is undoubtedly a word that can and *should* be associated with Jesus's ascension, contrary to Dr. Svigel's assertion.

WHAT ABOUT THE BIRTH AND THE DRAGON?

The supposed rapture of Rev. 12:5 occurs in the greater vision of Rev. 12:1-5. There are events that take place in that context which further cause us to question its validity as a rapture passage:

> And the dragon stood before the woman who was about to give
> birth, so that when she gave birth he might devour her child.
> (Rev. 12:4 NASB)

Dr. Svigel does not discuss this verse in the framework of his theory, but it is very relevant. He does not explain what the "birth" of the Son is by Spiritual Israel or why Satan is waiting for that moment to devour the Son after his birth. Why is Spiritual Israel the mother? If this is a symbol of the resurrection or the metamorphosis into resurrection bodies, why isn't Jesus pictured as causing this? And why is Satan waiting for this to happen?

However, Rev. 12:4 makes perfect sense in the context of the nativity narrative of Jesus. Herod attempted to kill Jesus immediately after his birth. But in order to take the enormous leap to say this passage symbolizes the rapture of the church, one must fill in all the blank spaces. Rev. 12:4 is a huge blank space in Dr. Svigel's theory.

Although Dr. Svigel wishes us to believe that "the Son" is a symbol for the church, a very real and tangible mention of Christians is found later in this chapter:

> So the dragon was enraged with the woman, and went off to
> make war with the rest of her children, who keep the
> commandments of God and hold to the testimony of Jesus.
> (Rev. 12:17 NASB)

Dr. Svigel argues that these are the mythical Tribulation Saints of the *pretribulation rapture* theory. If they are, they will be great heroes of the faith:

> And they overcame him (Satan) because of the blood of the
> Lamb and because of the word of their *testimony*, and they did
> not love their life even when faced with death. (Rev. 12:11
> NASB, clarification and emphasis mine)

Both verse 17 and verse 11 mention this testimony; the testimony that overcomes Satan! In fact, testimony is a key ingredient of the end times. It is mentioned nine times in Revelation and one time in each version of the Olivet Discourse (Matt., Mark, Luke). If the pretribulation rapture is true, why does God take his saints from the earth and give the job of testimony to the "Tribulation saints" during the greatest need for testimony in history? Is the current church inadequate for the job?

It also doesn't answer why God would choose an oblique symbol for the church in verse 5 and only a few verses later specifically mention Christians in literal terms in verse 17. In conclusion, the *pretribulation rapture* is not depicted in Rev. 12.

TEN VIRGINS AND A JEWISH WEDDING

Many *pretribulation rapture* proponents also look to the customs surrounding Jewish weddings as proof of a *pretribulation rapture*. They point to traditions that seem to indicate that the groom and bride spent seven days in the bridal chamber (*chuppah*) after the groom took his bride home. It is alleged that this represents the seven years that they propose the church will spend in heaven after the rapture.

There are many problems with this position. First, Jewish wedding traditions are not found in the Bible so we can't claim them as "biblical" evidence. Second, this assumption allegorizes the seven-day celebration into seven years. Seven days can also be interpreted as the seven days of the

Feast of Tabernacles, which would be a satisfactory *Jewish* solution. In Revelation 19:7–8, we are given the most explicit mention of the marriage of the Lamb in Scripture:

> "Let us rejoice and be glad and give the glory to Him, for the *marriage of the Lamb* has come and His bride has made herself ready." It was given to her to clothe herself in fine linen, bright and clean; for the fine linen is the righteous acts of the saints. (Rev. 19:7–8 NASB, clarification and emphasis mine)

Notice that the wearing of white garments is the time marker for this wedding as we discussed at length in chapter five. These white garments are given to the saints after the fifth seal (Rev. 6:9–11) and the vast multitude of raptured saints wear them after the sixth seal (Rev. 7:9–17). In fact, not only does the multitude wear white, God covers them with his *chuppah* ("tabernacle" as seen in Rev. 7:16). In addition, the vast multitude waves palm branches (Rev. 7:9), which are a sign of the Feast of Tabernacles (Lev. 23:40; Neh. 8:15) as well.

In chapter one: "Solving the Cold Case," we mentioned the parable of the ten virgins. Many *pretribulation rapture* supporters view this parable in an odd manner as referring to the physical second coming of Jesus (not the rapture) and the virgins as being tribulation saints who missed the rapture and remained on earth. These supporters reason that the ten virgins cannot be the bride because there are ten of them. Rather they assume that they are the wedding party, and that Jesus raptured his one and only bride prior to what they call the tribulation. They further assume Jesus and his bride have spent those seven years in the *chuppah*, or bridal chamber, in

135

heaven. They say that in this parable that Jesus has returned to invite these tribulation saints as guests to the wedding feast.

There are numerous insurmountable problems with this theory. First, the wedding feast was seven days (Gen. 29:21–27; Judg. 14:10–18), but it begins with the physical consummation of the marriage and the announcement *to the wedding guests* that it's consummated. This joyous announcement seems meaningless if the guests don't arrive for seven more days! The guests *must* be present from the very inception of the marriage to witness its consummation. Second, Jesus is referred to as a bridegroom in the parable. Seven years after the marriage he would be a husband, not a bridegroom. And of course, in the preceding paragraph, we have shown how the seven-day wedding feast does not equate with seven years.

So who are these virgins? Can all ten be the bride? Jesus's purpose in the parable was to contrast the wise and foolish virgins who represent the millions of churchgoers waiting for the return of Jesus. Ten is the scriptural number of completion, so they are the complete number of those awaiting Jesus's return. Jesus did not talk of one bride in this parable because its purpose was to show *contrast* between the two groups, but all five of the wise virgins *are* part of the bride.

IMMINENCE

We must remember as we embark on looking at this final area that the *prewrath rapture* has already been undeniably demonstrated by Scripture in chapters two through five. The purpose of this chapter six: "The Backfire Effect (*Pre-Tribulation Rapture* Proofs)" is to show the hollowness of all the remaining *pretribulation rapture* arguments.

The holy grail of all *pretribulation rapture* arguments is imminence. Dr. Thomas Ice states:

The fact that Christ could return, but may not soon, at any moment, yet without the necessity of signs preceding His return requires the kind of imminence taught by the pre-trib. position and is a strong support for pre-tribulationism.[78] —Dr. Thomas Ice

By this, Dr. Ice means that if the rapture is to occur during the Seventieth Week of Daniel, it must be preceded by signs and cannot be imminent. The opposite is then also most likely true—if imminence is true, so is the *pretribulation rapture* position true. So, if it can be proved that Jesus's rapture of the saints *must* follow after certain signs during the Seventieth Week of Daniel then the *pretribulation rapture* is, conversely, proven false. Technically, we have already proven this in chapter two: "Hidden Treasure (Ultimate Proof of Rapture Timing)", but we will present different proof texts in this section.

The late Dr. John Walvoord declared, "The exhortation to 'look for the glorious appearing' of Christ to His own (Titus 2:13)' loses its significance if the Tribulation must intervene first. Believers in that case should look for signs."[79] Dr. Walvoord was a theologian, writer, pastor, and the past-president of Dallas Theological Seminary. He is still considered possibly the most prominent voice of dispensationalism in the world. Despite his lofty and exalted position and academic credentials, his statement sounds confusing when viewed side-by-side with Jesus's command to do just that: to "watch!" After all, how else can someone look for the return of Jesus other than by watching for signs of his coming?

Therefore *keep watch* because you do not know when the owner of the house will come back—whether in the evening, or at midnight, or when the rooster crows, or at dawn. If he comes suddenly, do not let him find you sleeping. What I say to you, I say to *everyone*: "*Watch!*" (Mark 13:35–37 NIV, emphasis mine)

The three versions of the Olivet Discourse (Matt. 24–25; Mark 13; and Luke 21) contain over thirty separate commands to be watchful, to see, or to be observant.[80] We have just demonstrated that the Olivet Discourse is *not* just for the Jews, but even if we had not, this verse still commands the church to watch for signs. Jesus clearly said, "What I say to you, I say to *everyone*." The term "everyone" obviously includes the church as well!

As you might expect based on the information previously presented in this chapter, the supporters of the *pretribulation rapture* have tried to create a work-around for this clear teaching of Scripture as well. This time, these supporters have tried to redefine the Greek word translated "watch" (*gregoreo*). This Greek word literally means to "stay awake" and is also translated "be alert" and "be watchful." Don Hooser, a minister and writer from Washington, has this to say about the command, "It is *spiritual watching* coupled with prayer that gives one the strength to survive temptations and difficult situations."[81] Just as in previous sections, at first glance, this definition sounds spiritually sound, and in many non-eschatological Scriptures, *gregoreo* does carry that meaning. But look at this other command of Jesus's:

> Therefore *if you do not wake up [gregoreo], I will come like a thief,* and *you will not know at what hour I will come to you.* (Rev. 3:3 NASB, emphasis mine)

This is an incredible passage. *It single-handedly destroys imminence.* In this passage Jesus says, in essence, that if you don't watch (*gregoreo*) for signs, he will come to you like a thief and you won't know the hour he is coming! This implies the opposite: if we do watch for signs, we *will* know the timing of this coming! This teaching is supported in Paul's first letter to the Thessalonians. Just two verses after 1 Thessalonians 4:16–17 (the Bible's most famous rapture passage), he had this to say:

> Now as to the times and the epochs, brethren, you have no need of anything to be written to you. For you yourselves know full well that the *day of the Lord* will come just like a thief in the night. While *they* are saying, "Peace and safety!" then destruction will come upon them suddenly like labor pains upon a woman with child, and they will not escape. *But you, brethren, are not in darkness, that the day would overtake you like a thief;* for you are all sons of light and sons of day. We are not of night nor of darkness; so then let us not sleep as others do, but let us be alert and sober. (1 Thess. 5:1–6 NASB, emphasis mine)

Paul contrasts two groups. "They" (the unrighteous) will have the *day of the Lord come* upon them as a thief in the night. However, the "brethren" will not be surprised by the day! They won't be surprised by the parousia of Jesus because they are awake and watchful! I must ask, "How does being watchful to avoid temptation alert us as to the timing of the day of the Lord?" Obviously it does not! Only watching for *signs* will alert the church.

Both passages above (Rev. 3; 1 Thess. 5) refer to the term "a thief in the night." Most *pretribulation rapture* supporters assume this idiom implies imminence. These supporters are mostly unaware that like many other terms used by Jesus, this was also a first-century Jewish idiom that meant something different than what we would normally believe it does today. Revelation refers to this idiom:

> Behold, I am coming *as a thief.* Blessed is he who watches, and keeps his garments, lest he walk naked and they see his shame. (Rev. 16:15 NKJV, emphasis mine)

What does the phrase *like a thief* or *as a thief* mean? What's the connection with being naked? To twenty-first century ears this is certainly odd. During Jesus's day, when the Jewish temple was still standing, a priest was commanded to watch the fire on the altar by night so it would not go out. This was a holy fire, and it was essential that it stay lit. Priests took turns keeping watch. The captain of the temple guard patrolling the temple would come upon the priest unexpectedly *as a thief in the night.* When the captain of the guard checked on his rounds, if a priest was found sleeping, the captain would take his torch and set the priest's garment on fire! The priest would be awakened by the fire and would run through the temple tearing off his burning clothing. This was quite an incentive to keep watch![82]

Do you see how perfectly this fits with Jesus's statement in Revelation 16 about keeping your garment and no one seeing your shame? The statement about a thief in the night refers to us being *watchful* for Jesus's return. We are to stay awake! It implies the opposite of imminence.

IMMINENCE AND THE DAY OF THE LORD

As we learned previously in chapter four: "Synchronous Fireworks (Same-Day Salvation and Wrath)," the rapture and wrath of God (day of the Lord) occur on the exact same day. As we have already shown, this is clearly demonstrated by Scripture (Luke 17: 22–30 and 2 Thess. 1:6–8). Because numerous Bible passages indicate events that must precede the day of the Lord (see the previous section "Wrath of God Considerations"), imminence is not possible.

THE HEAD OF THE HOUSE

Pretribulation rapture aficionados also frequently point to this passage from the Olivet Discourse as proof of imminence:

> Therefore be on the alert, for you do not know which day your Lord is coming. But be sure of this, that *if the **head of the house** had known at what time of the night the thief was coming, he would have been on the alert* and would not have allowed his house to be broken into. For this reason you also must be ready; for *the Son of Man is coming at an hour when you do not think He will.* Who then is *the faithful and sensible slave whom his master put **in charge of his household*** to give them their food at the proper time? (Matt. 24:42–45 NASB, emphasis mine)

The first point of contention about this passage is that it is also found in the Olivet Discourse! In a previous section, we discussed how *if* the Olivet

Discourse is exclusively for the Jews (as *pretribulation rapture* theory claims), it makes no sense to discuss issues concerning the rapture which will have already taken place! This is circular reasoning.

Second, we must closely examine this passage to understand what Jesus was truly communicating. Traditional interpretations of this passage assume Jesus is the thief and he breaks into the house of the "strong man," or Satan (Matt. 12:29), and steals the saints in the harpazo. This interpretation fails for a number of reasons. First, the passage claims the "head of the house" could have *avoided* the break-in of the "thief" if he was alert. Obviously, neither Satan nor any other power could stop Jesus by being alert.

Based on this breakdown of the traditional interpretation, we need to look closer at the identity of the characters. We are told about a head of the household, the master, and a thief. Most commentators truncate this passage after Matthew 24:44, but it obviously continues because two of the characters (the master and head of the house) are clearly identified in the next verse (Matt. 24:45). The master is Jesus. Most of the church has claimed Jesus is the "thief" because in many places we are told he comes "like" a thief. But looking at it in the full context (Matt. 24:42–51), Jesus is obviously the master. We are directly told that the head of the house is Jesus's faithful and wise servant. Who then is the thief? It has to be Satan, the thief who comes to kill, steal, and destroy (John 10:10).

This careful exegesis turns the traditional meaning of this passage on its head. Jesus is telling us that if his faithful and wise servants are *alert*, they can stop the break-in of Satan into their churches and homes. The event Jesus is teaching about in this passage is the *apostasy*, not the rapture. Jesus is instructing us to be alert for the signs of his coming because by doing so we can be prepared for the great tribulation and the apostasy that

142

accompanies it. Jesus speaks of his parousia because it happens at the same general period of time (the Seventieth Week of Daniel) as the apostasy.

Jesus's statement in Matthew 24:44 carries an ominous warning for those holding to the *pretribulation rapture* theory, "For this reason you also must be ready; for the Son of Man is coming at an hour *when you do not think He will.*" Jesus is coming at an hour when 96% of the church does not think he will. He is coming in a *prewrath rapture after* the great tribulation and *not before* it, as so many assume! This will require the church to be prepared for the great tribulation and the apostasy.

THAT DAY

This brings us to the most revered passage about imminence:

> But of *that day* and hour no one knows, not even the angels of heaven, nor the Son, but the Father alone. *For the coming of the Son of Man will be just like the days of Noah.* For as in those days before the flood they were eating and drinking, marrying and giving in marriage, *until the day that Noah entered the ark.* (Matt. 24:36–38 NASB, emphasis mine)

In regard to this passage, my friend, Pastor Steve Müller of Faith Baptist church in Gladstone, Australia, has brought to my attention the supreme importance of the words "that day" in Matthew 24:36. Proper interpretation of this verse hinges on these words.

> Grammatically, Jesus's use of the words *"that day"* in Matthew 24:36 must refer back to a day he was just describing in the preceding verses. It *cannot* refer to an unspoken and silent

143

pretrib. rapture that he never mentioned. There can be *no doubt* that *"that day"* is clearly in reference to the events of Matthew 24:29–31: "Immediately *after* the distress [tribulation] of those days"—not before, as the pretribbers would have us believe. — Pastor Steve Müller (emphasis mine)

With this simple observation, Pastor Müller dismantles the *pretribulation rapture* theory's use of this verse. Matthew 24:36 refers to the harpazo of the *prewrath rapture* in Matthew 24:30–31 and not to the imminence of an unspoken *pretribulation rapture*.

Second, if we observe the full context of this passage, we can see that imminence is not even implied. The coming of the Son of Man will be "just like the days of Noah." In this passage, as in the passage we looked at in a previous section (1 Thess. 5), we see a contrast between the righteous (Noah) and the unrighteous. The unrighteous are completely surprised by the flood, but in Genesis we read Noah *was not surprised* because God warned Noah in advance:

> For *after seven more days*, I will send rain on the earth forty days and forty nights; and I will blot out from the face of the land every living thing that I have made. (Gen. 7:4 NASB, emphasis mine)

As Noah prepared the ark, he did not know when God would send the flood. However, there came a point in time when God warned Noah of the approximate timing of the flood ("after seven more days"). This is exactly parallel to the situation the church is in right now. We are preparing for the return of Jesus, and we do not know the timing of his coming. However, when the midpoint of the Seventieth Week of Daniel begins, we will know its approximate timing and "that day will not overtake [us] like a thief" (1 Thess. 5:4 NASB).

One thing can be said with certainty, however: Matthew 24:36 cannot refer to a *pretribulation rapture*.

THE FIRST RESURRECTION

I have exhausted most of the main proofs that *pretribulation rapture* advocates use to support their theory. I would also like to take time to look at a counterargument they make in response to a theory of the *post-tribulation rapture* exponents. In 1 Thessalonians 4:16–17, we learned that the resurrection precedes the rapture, and in Revelation we learn that there are two resurrections: one at the time of the rapture (the first resurrection) and one at the end of the millennial kingdom. In regard to the first resurrection, we are told that it contains those who do not take the mark of the beast.

> Then I saw thrones, and they sat on them, and judgment was given to them. And I saw *the souls of those who had been beheaded because of their testimony of Jesus* and because of the word of God, and *those who had **not** worshiped the beast or his image*, and *had **not** received the mark on their forehead and on their hand*; and they came to life and reigned with Christ for a thousand years. The rest of the dead did not come to life until the thousand years were completed. This is the *first resurrection*. (Rev. 20:4–5 NASB, emphasis mine)

This is a clear and unambiguous Scripture. The first resurrection contains martyrs from the Seventieth Week of Daniel. Todd Strandberg, editor of the *Rapture Ready* Internet wall, expounded on another work-around for this explicit Scripture to justify the *pretribulation rapture*. He claims there is more than one first resurrection:

> One pre-trib writer, explaining this passage, said, "The first did not mean first in time, but rather first in kind." The first resurrection was for God's people; the second will be for the unsaved. A quick way to shoot down the notion that the first resurrection is tied to a specific date, as opposed to a more general time frame, is to take note of the tribulation rapture of the two witnesses. —Todd Strandberg[83]

The first contradiction in the argument Mr. Strandberg makes is that the term first resurrection is singular, not plural as in "first resurrections." It is a singular event. In Paul's first letter to the Corinthians, he indicated *all* would be raptured at the last trumpet.

> Behold, I tell you a mystery; we will not all sleep, but we will *all* be changed, in a moment, in the twinkling of an eye, *at the last trumpet.* (1 Cor. 15:51–52 NASB, emphasis mine)

This completely flies in the face of Mr. Strandberg's argument. In order for *all* to be changed at the last trumpet (a specific singular event), there must be one, singular resurrection.

Second, it is clear the first resurrection takes place *only* at Jesus's coming:

> In Christ all will be made alive. But each in his own order:
> Christ the *first fruits, after that those who are Christ's at his*
> *coming, then comes the end*, when He hands over the kingdom
> to the God and Father, when He has abolished all rule and all
> authority and power. For He must reign until He has put all His
> enemies under His feet. The last enemy that will be abolished is
> death. (1 Cor. 15:22–26 NASB, emphasis mine)

This verse is amazingly specific. It indicates the order of resurrections.

The resurrection of Jesus and the Old Testament saints who rose with him (Matt. 27:52) is called the first fruits resurrection. (This term *first fruits* mimics the first portion of the Hebrew harvest which was divided into three parts. My theory is that the harvest of souls [the resurrection] will be divided into exactly three parts as well.) Here is a brief explanation of the *Three-Part Harvest*:

- *First fruits harvest*: a limited, preliminary harvest which was presented to YHWH as an offering
- *Primary harvest*: the harvest when the majority of the grain was reaped
- *Gleanings harvest*: a final sweep through the fields to reap any remaining grain

In 1 Corinthians 15:22–26, the primary harvest is listed second as "those who are Christ's at his coming." Please pay strict attention to what is mentioned next in order: "the end, when he [Jesus] hands over the kingdom to the God and Father" and abolishes death. This occurs at the very end of the millennial kingdom. ***There are no "extra" resurrections between the primary harvest resurrection that specifically occurs at Jesus's coming*** *and the end of the millennial kingdom.* After Jesus hands over the kingdom at the end of the thousand years, then the second resurrection mentioned in Revelation 20:5 occurs. The second resurrection mimics the gleanings harvest of a three-part Hebrew harvest.

Mr. Strandberg, along with thousands of other *pretribulation rapture* proponents, cite the resurrection of the two witnesses as if it has to be a separate resurrection from the one, singular first resurrection. Let's look at the primary text about the two witnesses:

> I will grant authority to my two witnesses, and *they will prophesy for twelve hundred and sixty days,* clothed in sackcloth . . . When they have finished their testimony, the beast that comes up out of the abyss will make war with them, and overcome them and kill them . . . *But after the three and a half days, the breath of life from God came into them,* and they stood on their feet; and great fear fell upon those who were watching them. And they heard a loud voice from heaven saying to them, "Come up here." *Then they went up into heaven* in the cloud, and their enemies watched them. (Rev. 11:3, 7, 11–12 NASB; emphasis mine)

Although the timing of the resurrection of the witnesses is complex and unclear, all that is scripturally required for them to be resurrected and raptured as part of the first resurrection is that they begin their ministry 1,263 and a half days prior to it. There is nothing in the text that supports that this is a separate resurrection. Later in his article, Mr. Strandberg states that the two witnesses minister during the first half of the Seventieth Week. The only possible hint of that timing for their ministry is the length of their ministry: 1,260 days. But this number of days could be correlated with the first half of the Seventieth Week or second half *or overlap the two halves.*

Others say that their resurrection is associated with the end of the "second woe" which occurs after the sixth trumpet (Rev. 11:14). However, Revelation chapters 10, 11, 12, 13, and 14 are primarily visions which are separate from the chronological story-line of Revelation. These chapters primarily deal with one topic each: the woman (chapter 12), the Beast (chapter 13), and the witnesses (chapter 11). Certainly no one believes all the events of Rev. 12 and 13 occur after the seventh trumpet as they appear in Revelation. Nor do many believe that *all* 1260 days of the witnesses' ministry occur after the sixth trumpet as strict chronological order would dictate. Rev. 11 should not be considered chronological and the witnesses' ministry may occur earlier or later than believed by many.

As we stated previously, the timing of the ministry of the witnesses is complex and somewhat unclear. However, the testimony of 1 Cor. 15:22-26 makes apparent that there are no "extra" resurrections between Jesus's parousia and the end of the millennial kingdom. This should preclude a separate resurrection of the witnesses.

IS THE SEVENTIETH WEEK ONLY FOR THE UNSAVED JEWS?

Finally, some *pretribulation rapture* supporters believe that Daniel's prophecy of the seventy weeks precludes Christians from being able to enter the Seventieth Week. They base this thinking on Daniel 9:24, which only mentions the Jews:

Seventy weeks have been decreed for *your people* and *your holy city.* (Dan. 9:24 NASB emphasis mine)

The church didn't exist until sixty-nine of the weeks had taken place. Also during the Seventieth Week itself, the church will not experience all seven years, as they will be raptured before the end. Jews who have not repented historically faced the first 69 weeks and will face the entire Seventieth Week. In this way, the seventy weeks could *only* be decreed for the unsaved Jews; they will experience all of it. Additionally, the church was a mystery in Daniel's day. Naturally the angel did not specifically mention it, but neither did he preclude it from participating in the Seventieth Week.

The Seventieth Week can also apply to the church because it is grafted into "Spiritual Israel" (Rom. 11:17). This is how many Old Testament prophecies that were given to the Jews also now apply to the church. For example, the New Covenant in Jeremiah 31:31 was given to the House of Israel and the House of Judah. Yet, nearly all Christians easily accept that the new covenant is to apply to them as well.

SUMMARY

In chapters two through five, we definitively proved the *prewrath rapture*. However, because it is human nature to resist new ideas even when presented with facts, this chapter six: "The Backfire Effect (*Pre-Tribulation Rapture* Arguments)" looked at a number of proofs used by the *pretribulation rapture* exponents to support their theory. I hope this detailed examination of these arguments has helped exhaust the value of these proofs in your mind.

One aspect I was not fully aware of prior to writing this book was the widespread use of work-arounds by proponents of this theory to avoid explicit and clear Scriptures that discount their ideas. The graphic on the following page helps visualize the extent of this practice in the *pretribulation rapture* camp:

Work-around	Scripture	Concept
Claim the celestial earthly disturbance in Joel 2:30–31 is not the same as Matt. 24:29 and not the same as Rev. 6:12–17	Joel 2:30–31pters Matt. 24:29 Rev. 6:12–17	The events in these three passages are of an earthshaking nature. They are obviously depicting the same event.
Claim the raptured church are the 24 elders in Rev. 4–8	Rev. 4–8	True raptured church are the vast multitude in Rev. 7:9
Claim the word apostasia means "departure" and is a code word for the rapture	2 Thess. 2:3	Apostasia never means "departure" in Bible or anywhere in Greek literature
Claim the seals are God's wrath	Rev. 6:1–17	At the fifth seal, God states the martyrs will have to wait a little while longer until He pours out his wrath (Rev. 6:10)
Claim 1 Thess. 5:2–4 demonstrates that the day of the Lord occurs prior to the Seventieth Week	1 Thess. 5:2–4 Rev. 11:9–12 Matt. 24:8 Isa. 13:6–10	Three separate proofs show that the death of the two witnesses are the "peace and safety" the world claims, the day of the

Work-around	Scripture	Concept
		Lord comes like a thief via the celestial earthly disturbance, and that the labor pains listed come after the celestial earthly disturbance.
Claim Matt. 24:36 proves the imminence of the rapture	Matt. 24:36	If Matt. 24:36 is about the rapture that the Jews will never see, then why is this verse in a passage that pretribulationalists claim is for the Jews?
Claim that the church isn't present in Revelation after chapter 3	Rev. 2–3	The word "church" only appears in proper names in Revelation; pretribulationalists ignore the dozens of references to "bond servants" and "saints"
Claim the word "watch" only means	Mark 13:35–37	In Rev. 3:3 we see that if we watch,

Work-around	Scripture	Concept
to watch to avoid temptation, not to watch for "signs"		Jesus's coming will not come upon us as a thief in the night
Claim the "first" resurrection really means multiple resurrections of the righteous	Rev. 20:5 1 Cor. 15: 51–52	All the righteous will awake and be changed at the last trumpet, not during multiple resurrections

Figure 19: Pretribulation Rapture Work-arounds

I believe this table provides ample proof of the backfire effect we discussed at the beginning of the chapter, where proponents cling to a belief even in the face of facts to the contrary. It is also proof of the theory we proposed in chapter five: "Whatever Is True (Other *Prewrath Rapture* Proofs)," that the *pretribulation and post-tribulation rapture* theories are half correct and half mistaken. The arguments that proponents of these theories propose that are correct cause them to create work-arounds for the arguments of the other side that are correct rather than reconsidering their own position.

What is truly amazing is that almost *all* of the proofs for the *pretribulation rapture* rely on these work-arounds. In some cases, *pretribulation rapture* theory claims that singular events like the resurrection or the celestial earthly disturbance are actually multiple events. In other instances, it has been claimed that words with obvious meanings like "watch" or "apostasy" mean other things, even if those meanings cannot be found elsewhere in Greek literature. When entire sections of Scripture are deemed to be in contrast with this theory, those sections (Olivet Discourse— Matt. 24) are said to not apply to Christians. If you are still a believer in this concept, look at figure 19: "Pre-Tribulation Work Arounds" once again. Are these proofs worthy of your faith in this theory?

Chapter Seven

CENTER OF THE UNIVERSE

(*Post-Tribulation Rapture* Arguments)

". . . invalidating the word of God by your tradition which you have handed down." (Mark 7:13 NASB)

B ased on our observations, some things seem to *have* to be true. Every morning for nearly six thousand years, mankind has watched the sun rise in the east, travel across the sky, and set in the west in the evening. Six hundred years before the birth of Jesus while the Israelites were in captivity in Babylon, the ancient Greeks began to theorize about the motion of the heavenly bodies. Based on observing eclipses, they correctly deduced that the earth was a sphere—lunar eclipses advanced in the form of a disk which was the earth's round shadow on the moon. In the fourth century, BC, Plato suggested that the earth was a sphere at the center of the universe around which the sun, moon, planets, and stars rotated in circular orbits.[84]

But careful observation of the heavenly bodies proved Plato's theory wrong. Aristotle augmented Plato's theories by adding a series of forty-seven to fifty-five concentric spheres to which all the heavenly bodies were thought to be attached. Planets were attached to multiple spheres, according to Aristotle, to account for their eccentric motions. He theorized the moon touched the earth, which accounted for the dark spots on its surface and the lunar phases.

The Greeks were not willing to consider that the earth moved, however. They rightly predicted the phenomenon of stellar parallax—that if the earth moved, the stars would appear in different positions depending on the earth's position. Since the appearance of the constellations always remained the same, the Greeks dismissed the idea that the earth was moving. The Greeks never considered the extreme distances between the earth and the stars. It wasn't until the 1800s that stellar parallax was proven.[85]

The height of Greek astronomical theories was the Ptolemaic model. Developed in the second century AD by Claudius Ptolemaeus (Ptolemy), it relied on a system of spheres within other spheres within which the planets orbited. The center of the spheres was thought to be slightly off-center, which permitted eccentric motions. Ptolemaeus's system was even able to account for the retrograde motion of the planets. The model was able to track and predict planetary motion so accurately that it stood as the standard astronomical model for over a millennium.[86] Scientists eventually discovered that Ptolemaeus made a serious mistake in assuming that the earth was the center of the solar system rather than the sun. The model which *seemed* to be so correct turned out to be fraught with serious error.

The *post-tribulation rapture* theory is the "Ptolemaic model" of eschatology. The mistaken notion that the coming of Jesus depicted in Matthew 24:30–31 is the *physical* second coming led proponents of this theory to create a complex theological system to account for Jesus's return at the end of the Seventieth Week of Daniel. Just like the Ptolemaic model, this theory endured for centuries, from the writings of the early church fathers until today. However, as knowledge of the Bible increased, challenges to this theory arose. Modifications were made, just as modifications were made to Plato's original theory of astronomy.

But adherents of this *post-tribulation rapture* theory have never been willing to let go of the central premise that Matthew 24:30–31 depicted the *physical* second coming of Jesus, just as the Greeks weren't willing to let go of their theory that the earth was the center of the universe.

In chapter two, we were hopefully able to shatter that premise (that Matthew 24:30–31 depicted the *physical* second coming of Jesus) once and for all. But if you began reading this book as an exponent of the *post-tribulation rapture* theory, you probably have some other "Yes, but . . ." questions of your own.

As we explained in chapter five, we have theorized that both the *pretribulation rapture* position and the *post-tribulation rapture* position are half correct and half mistaken. For example, the *post-tribulation rapture* theory is correct when it suggests that the rapture will occur after great tribulation. Adherents of that theory also agree with most if not all of the counterproofs presented in the previous chapter.

A number of their assumptions are mistaken, however. You personally may have some pet proofs for a *post-tribulation rapture* that you have relied on over many years that prevent you from letting go of this theory. The purpose of this chapter is to help you consider alternatives to those proofs.

THE LAST TRUMPET = THE SEVENTH TRUMPET?

We have already shown from 1 Corinthians that the resurrection and rapture both occur at the last trumpet:

> In a moment, in the twinkling of an eye, at the *last trumpet*; for the trumpet will sound, and the dead will be raised imperishable, and we will be changed. (1 Cor. 15:52 NASB, emphasis mine)

> For the Lord Himself will descend from heaven with a shout, with the voice of *the* archangel and with the *trumpet of God*, and the dead in Christ will rise first. (1 Thess. 4:16 NASB, emphasis mine)

First, the vast majority of *post-tribulation rapture* proponents believe that the seventh trumpet of Revelation is the last trumpet because it the final trumpet mentioned in Revelation. Now that we have established that the rapture which precedes the seventh seal precedes the trumpet judgments as well, we know that this is *impossible*. The importance of establishing the *sequential* order of seals – trumpets – bowls first can now be seen in coming to a correct rapture position.

Second, notice that in 1 Thessalonians 4:16, the last trumpet is referred to as the trumpet of *God*. In Zechariah 9:14, we read, "*God* will blow the trumpet." Yet the seventh trumpet is blown by an *angel* and not by God:

> Then the seventh *angel* sounded [Gk: *splazio*, meaning "sounded his trumpet"]; and there were loud voices in heaven. (Rev. 11:15 NASB; emphasis mine)

Thus the seventh trumpet cannot be the last trumpet because an angel blows it rather than God.

If the "last trumpet" isn't the seventh trumpet of Revelation, what is it? In the first century, the term "last trumpet" was a Jewish idiom that meant a specific trumpet blast on the Feast of Yom Teruah (Feast of the Blowing of Trumpets).[87] It was the final, long blast of the trumpet on that day. Although Christians today rarely celebrate the seven "Feasts of the

Lord" (Heb: mo'edim) and are unfamiliar with the various terms and idioms associated with them, believers in the first century were very familiar with these holidays (Holy days) and idioms like the "last trumpet."

Yom Teruah, which is also known as Rosh Hashanah, is the Feast of the Blowing of Trumpets, including the long, *last trumpet* blast on that day (*tekiah gadolah*, literally "great sound of a trumpet"). Jesus referred to this trumpet blast directly by saying, "And He will send His angels with a *great sound of a trumpet*, and they will gather together His elect from the four winds" (Matt. 24:31 NKJV, emphasis mine). In Jewish thought, there were three trumpet blasts on mo'edim. The *first trumpet* was blown on Pentecost (Shavuot) and *the last trumpet* was blown on Yom Teruah. The *jubilee trumpet* was blown on Yom Kippur of Jubilee years to announce the Jubilee.[88] So when Paul referred to the last trumpet in 1 Cor. 15:52, this may have been a *specific reference* to Yom Teruah and the *tekiah gadolah*.

This analysis would suggest that the rapture might occur on Yom Teruah. It is beyond the scope of this book to examine that issue any further, but it is an intriguing theory.

Returning to our analysis of the last trumpet, author Michael Snyder, in his recent book *The Rapture Verdict* (2016), claims the statement made by the twenty-four elders after the blowing of the seventh trumpet indicates the resurrection and rapture happen at that point.[89]

> You have taken your great power and have begun to reign. And *the nations were enraged, and your wrath came*, and *the time came for the dead to be judged*, and the time to reward your bond-servants the prophets and the saints and those who fear your name, the small and the great, and to destroy those who destroy the earth. (Rev. 11:17–18 NASB, emphasis mine)

The Greek verbs in this passage (have taken, were enraged, came, etc.) are in the aorist indicative and may indicate *past action* which continues. These are not actions happening at that moment as Mr. Snyder claims. Rather, they are a summary list of actions that previously occurred during the final three and a half years of the Seventieth Week. The reference to "the nations were enraged" refers to Psalm 2:1 and the abomination of desolation at the *midpoint* of the Seventieth Week. God then responded with his resurrection and rapture (the judging of the dead and the rewarding of the saints). Then God's wrath began to be poured out. Finally, the seventh trumpet depicts Jesus being crowned king while he and the saints are still in heaven and prior to Armageddon. Hence, the claim made by Mr. Snyder related to his understanding of the timing of the rapture after the seventh trumpet judgment appears to be incorrect.

THE HARVESTS IN REVELATION 14

Nearly all commentators have difficulty in interpreting Revelation because *various sections* of it are not in chronological order. These sections include Rev. 2–3 and Rev. 10–14. This is an incredibly helpful insight, but there isn't universal agreement on these nonsequential passages. Upon study, these sections of Revelation appear to be previews of later sections or flashbacks to previous sections. As we have already indicated, many *post-tribulation rapture* theorists also believe the trumpet and bowl judgments occur randomly throughout the seals (we have already proven this to be false). Other commentators believe that only Revelation 12–13 are nonsequential and that the other portions are sequential. This interpretation would mean that the harvests depicted in Revelation 14 would follow the seventh trumpet and would imply a *post-tribulation rapture*. Author Michael Snyder articulates this position:

160

> Following this incredible series of declarations in Revelation chapter 11, we find an actual physical description of the rapture in chapter 14 [he correctly assumes Revelation 12 and 13 are nonsequential]. —Michael Snyder [90] (clarification mine)

Fortunately, it is quite simple to determine that Revelation 14 is also nonsequential to the main storyline of Revelation, just as Revelation 12–13 are nonsequential. The events in Revelation 14 represent *three separate visions* that occur at various times during the Seventieth Week. The chronological order of these visions is completely jumbled within Revelation 14. In fact, the three visions probably occur in reverse order. In the *first vision* of the Lamb and the 144,000, Jesus is already standing on Mount Zion after his physical second coming. The *second vision*, the vision of the three angels, seems to occur at the beginning of the day of the Lord (although I am not sure of the exact timing of the flight of these angels). And in the *final vision*, the vision of the two harvests, Jesus "reaps" the earth followed by an angel reaping the unrighteous.

The statements made by the angels in the vision of the three angels highlights the nonsequential nature of Revelation 14. The second angel refers to mystery Babylon already having fallen, but this is not actually depicted until Revelation 17. The third angel makes a statement that "blessed are the dead who die in the Lord from now on"; however, the next event in Revelation 14 is the rapture. This warning by the angel seems horribly tardy since the rapture is the next event.

Mr. Snyder also believes all the events of Revelation 19:7–10 involving the marriage of the Lamb occur immediately prior to the *physical* second coming and Armageddon. He believes this also proves a post-tribulation rapture.[91] Contrary to his thinking, however, portions of this passage refer back to an earlier section of Revelation. The text states that the saints in Revelation 19:8 *were* given white garments to wear. This is an event that happened prior to Rev. 19:8. The vast multitude in Revelation 7:9–17 that we discussed in chapter three: "Moving Pictures (Explicit Rapture Depiction in Revelation)" is depicted *already* wearing these garments. Rev. 7:9 is the point that the bride puts on the white garments.

What is the reason that John discusses the fine linen in Revelation 19? Obviously, we cannot say with certainty, but I can take an educated guess. Both Revelation 19:8 and 19:14 refer to the "fine linen, bright (white) and clean" of the saints. This direct reference alerts the reader that the riders of the white horses going to Armageddon are the *same saints* participating in the marriage of the Lamb. Although we can't be sure that was the motive, we can be sure they were not newly raptured immediately prior to Armageddon but were raptured previous to that event.

THE DAYS SHALL BE SHORTENED

One of the greatest misunderstandings of *post-tribulation rapture* enthusiasts (and *pretribulation rapture* enthusiasts) is their thinking that the great tribulation extends through the entire last three and a half years of the Seventieth Week for *both* Christians and Jews. To support this position on the great tribulation, they point to Jesus's words and the verses in Daniel to which he was referring:

> For then there will *be* great distress, unequaled from the
> beginning of the world until now—and *never to be equaled*
> *again.* (Matt. 24:21 NIV, emphasis mine)

> And there will be a time of distress *such as never occurred*
> *since there was a nation until that time* . . . "How long will it

be until the end of these wonders?" I heard the man dressed in linen, who was above the waters of the river, as he raised his right hand and his left toward heaven, and swore by Him who lives forever that it would be for *a time, times, and half a time.* (Dan. 12:1, 6–7 NASB, emphasis mine)

He [Antichrist] will speak out against the Most High and wear down the saints of the Highest One, and he will intend to make alterations in times and in law; and *they will be given into his hand for a time, times, and half a time.* (Dan. 7:25 NASB, clarification and emphasis mine)

It is clear from these passages that the time of unparalleled distress and the time that the unsaved Jews will be given into the hands of Antichrist shall be 1,260 days ("time, times, and half a time"). There is no argument on this point. But will this same time period apply to Christians? Jesus's words do not support this position:

If **those days** had not been *cut short* [Gk: *koloboo*, meaning "shorten, abbreviate, or curtail"], no one would survive, but *for the sake of the elect those days will be shortened.* (Matt. 24:22 NIV, clarification and emphasis mine)

But immediately after *the tribulation of* **those days** the sun will be darkened, and the moon will not give its light. (Matt. 24:29 NASB, emphasis mine)

163

As we have mentioned before, Jesus said there would be great distress after the midpoint of the Seventieth Week. He did not say this tribulation would last the entire second half of the seven-year period. In fact, he said just the opposite! He indicated that "those days" (of great tribulation) would be *cut short for the elect (Christians). Post-tribulation rapture* enthusiast Richard H. Perry argues against this point about the "cutting short" of those days:[92]

> Jesus is saying that if the Antichrist were not stopped at the end of the 3½ years of persecution "no one would survive." In other words, if the *great tribulation* were allowed to continue until its natural conclusion—say another year for example—then, "no one would survive." But, "for the sake of the elect those days will be shortened." Christ will return at the end of the 3½ years, gather the elect and defeat the Antichrist before everyone is killed. Therefore, the *great tribulation* will be stopped at the second coming. —Richard H. Perry

Mr. Perry is author of the *Last Days Mystery* website as well as the book, *Of the Last Days*. His statement, which is echoed by most *post-tribulation rapture* exponents, seems to make sense until you examine it closely. What days was Jesus indicating that he would cut short? The use of the same term "those days" in Matthew 24:29 clearly demonstrates it will be the days of great *tribulation*. We already have seen Antichrist will be given authority to kill, steal, and destroy for a set period of days, months, and years: "time, times, and half a time" (1,260 days).

When Daniel received his vision (Dan. 7) 550 years before Jesus walked this earth, the Antichrist's authority was delineated: 1,260 days. The natural conclusion of the great tribulation (as stated by Mr. Perry) could

164

never exceed those days; it could never be an "extra year." God's Word has decreed *the exact length* of the Antichrist's authority. And "those days" (1,260 days) are precisely the number of days Jesus was referencing when he said they would be cut short (for the elect *and* the elect only). In chapter five, we saw how in the New Testament the "elect" refers to Christians.

Dr. Renald Showers presents a different argument. He claims that the Greek word *koloboo* ("to cut short") is in the aorist indicative tense. Because this tense frequently can refer to past action that continues, he then claims that this shortening of days was a past action of God when He shortened an indefinite great tribulation to only 1,260 days.[93]

Dr. Showers fails to recognize that the use of the Greek aorist indicative is primarily a "timeless" tense, and timing of the verb is dependent on context. In total, there are three verbs in Matt. 24:22. Two are in the aorist indicative and one in the future tense. All three verbs must make sense in a unified whole. The word *koloboo* is in the aorist indicative *as is* the Greek word *sozo* (meaning "to save") in the verse: "Unless those days had been cut short (koloboo), no life would have been saved (sozo)." If the "cutting short" took place long ago in Daniel's day, the physical salvation of the Christians also would have had to have taken place at that time. But this makes no sense. Fortunately, the context of Matt. 24:22 clarifies the future tense meaning of the cutting short: "For the sake of the elect (Christians) those days *will be* cut short." But why would Jesus utilize two different tenses in one verse?

Hebraic prophets frequently used "past tense" in prophetic passages as an idiom to indicate a future action that was *sure* to happen. Numerous passages such as Gen. 6:18, Gen. 15:18, Num. 21:34, and literally dozens of others, utilize this "prophetic perfect" idiom. This usage is common in the New Testament as well, and explains why different passages describe concepts such as our salvation, justification, and glorification as past events, while other passages describe these same concepts as future events[94].

Sometimes, these Hebraic prophets would alternate past tense in the first usage of a verb with another tense (such as future tense) in the very next verse[95]; Psalm 45:7 is an example. This may explain the use of two tenses for "cutting short" in this one verse. Jesus may have been prophesying using this prophetic perfect idiom. This would explain the use of a past-like tense (aorist indicative) and the future tense in *one verse* of Scripture; all the while demonstrating that this passage is a *future* event.

DOES JESUS HAVE A THIRD COMING?

A favorite argument of *post-tribulation rapture* supporters is to claim that a separate rapture and physical second coming implies that Jesus has three comings. Rev. Bill Lee-Warner summarizes the *post-tribulation rapture* approach to this issue:

> Titus 2:13 ["looking for the *blessed hope* and the *appearing of the glory of our great God* and Savior, Christ Jesus"] is often used by pretribulationists to show that there is a difference (of time and objective) between what they refer to as "the rapture" and "the revelation of Christ." The "blessed hope" and the "glorious appearing" are said to be two different events, or in effect, two distinct comings of Christ. For the pretribulationist, the "blessed hope" is seen as the rapture, when Christ comes (secretly) "for" the saints at the beginning of the *Seventieth Week of Daniel* while the "glorious appearing" is seen as Christ's physical return to earth "with" his saints at the end of the *Seventieth Week of Daniel*, for the

final judgment of the world and the setting up of the millennial kingdom on earth. —Rev. Bill Lee-Warner

Rev. Lee-Warner is the editor of the *Sola Scriptura* website, a pastor, writer, and lecturer. After this statement, he then exposes multiple reasons, both grammatical and scriptural, why the *pretribulation rapture* position of three comings of Jesus cannot be correct.[96] I agree with him wholeheartedly! This is probably a shock to most *post-tribulation rapture* supporters who have not taken the time to consider the *prewrath rapture*.

There is only *one second coming* or arrival of Jesus. It takes place at the rapture that occurs after the sixth seal that's pictured in Matthew 24:30–31, and *it extends throughout the wrath of God.* It ends at the physical second coming. The term the "physical second coming" is actually a misnomer; it isn't a coming of Jesus at all. It is the landing portion of his coming to the earth! Let me explain.

The words "second coming" *don't appear in the Scriptures.* Although our culture talks about the second coming, this is not a biblical phrase or concept! The Bible uses four different Greek words to describe the return of Jesus: *erchomai, epiphaneia, apokalypsis*, and *parousia*. All four words frequently are translated "coming," but that is not the true meaning of each of the words. *Erchomai* is the word most closely meaning "coming," but it is used over six hundred times in the New Testament and most often has generic meaning rather than always having a "second coming" meaning. *Epiphaneia* means the visible appearing of a deity. *Apokalypsis* means revelation or revealing. *Parousia* is the word most frequently used to mean "second coming," and it occurs twenty-four times in the New Testament. An examination of the HELPS Word-studies for this Greek word is extremely enlightening:

3952 parousía (from parōn, "be present, arrive to enter into a situation") properly, coming, especially the arrival of the owner who alone can deal with a situation (cf. LS). 3952 (parousía) is a "technical term with reference to the visit of a king or some other official, 'a royal visit'" (Souter)—"hence, in the NT, specifically of the Advent or Parousia of Christ (A–S).[97]

From this study, we ascertain that parousia is a noun, not a verb; in other words it is an event, not an action. We also see it can be a technical term that means "arrival or visit of a king;" specifically in this case the arrival and visit of Jesus to the earth. Visits are usually not a single day.

So in terms of a second coming, the Bible calls it "an appearing," "a revealing," and "the visit or arrival of a king." All three of these meanings imply the first *visual* sighting of Jesus, not necessarily his landing upon the earth. It is my opinion that all of these terms refer to the sighting of Jesus upon the day of the Lord and the rapture.

In appendix A: "Summary of Rapture Timing Theories," we undertook a thorough study of the uses of harpazo in Scripture. I think it would be enlightening and surprising if we undertake a similar study of parousia (the most common "second coming" word) in this section.

In Matthew 24, the disciples specifically ask about this event, the parousia, in connection with the end of the age:

As He was sitting on the Mount of Olives, the disciples came to Him privately, saying, "Tell us, when will these things happen, and what will be the sign of your coming [parousia], and of the end of the age?" (Matt. 24:3 NASB)

168

If there was any doubt of what that event would be, Jesus defined it for the disciples as the rapture only two dozen verses later in that same chapter.

> For just as the lightning comes from the east and flashes even to the west, so will the coming [parousia] of the Son of Man be . . . But immediately after the tribulation of those days the sun will be darkened, and the moon will not give its light, and the stars will fall from the sky, and the powers of the heavens will be shaken. And then the sign of the Son of Man will appear in the sky, and then all the tribes of the earth will mourn, and they will see the Son of Man coming on the clouds of the sky with power and great glory. And He will send forth His angels with a great trumpet and they will gather together His elect from the four winds, from one end of the sky to the other. (Matt. 24:27, 29–31 NASB, emphasis mine)

In 1 Corinthians, parousia is used in connection with the resurrection, which immediately precedes the rapture:

> In Christ all will be made alive. But each in his own order: Christ the first fruits, after that those who are Christ's at His coming [parousia]. (1 Cor. 15:22–23 NASB)

In 1 Thessalonians, parousia is used in connection with the resurrection and the rapture:

> We who are alive and remain until the coming [parousia] of the Lord, will not precede those who have fallen asleep. For the Lord Himself will descend from heaven with a shout, with the

169

voice of the archangel and with the trumpet of God, and the dead in Christ will rise first. Then we who are alive and remain will be caught up together with them in the clouds to meet the Lord in the air, and so we shall always be with the Lord. (1 Thess. 4:15–17 NASB)

In 2 Thessalonians, parousia is used in connection with the rapture:

Now we request you, brethren, with regard to the coming [parousia] of our Lord Jesus Christ and our gathering together to Him. (2 Thess. 2:1 NASB)

Conspicuously missing from this study of parousia is any mention of the word in Revelation 19:11–19, the most definitive biblical passage about what we call the physical second coming (or landing) of Jesus!

From this study, we clearly see that the rapture of Matthew 24:30–31 *is* the initiation of this event: the second coming or parousia of our Lord. It is at his arrival when every eye shall see him (Rev. 1:7). This event begins with the rapture, and as we have seen from a study of the actual Greek words, there is no requirement for Jesus to land at that point.

This is the great mistake of the *post-tribulation rapture* theory. It presupposes that Matthew 24:30–31 is the *physical* second coming— analogous to the ancient Greeks who mistakenly presupposed that the earth was the center of the universe. This assumption is not true, and this further disproves the *post-tribulation rapture* position. Careful examination of both primary rapture texts (Matt. 24:30–31 and 1 Thess. 4:16–17) show that Jesus

170

descends from heaven, but *nowhere in these texts do we see him touching the ground at that point*, which would be the case if the *physical* landing of Jesus upon the earth was pictured.

In summary, Jesus's "second coming" will be a complex series of events. Jesus's "first coming" was not simply a single event; it was not just his birth, but extended throughout his life. In the same way, I propose that his "second coming" is not a simple, single event, but rather it begins with his appearing on the clouds and it extends throughout the Millennial Kingdom and beyond.

THE PAROUSIA IS A SINGLE EVENT

The *post-tribulation rapture* supporters are correct, however, when they point out that there are not three comings of Jesus as suggested *by pretribulation* supporters: one in the first century, a silent rapture (pretribulation), and the physical second coming. Our Lord's return is consistently portrayed in Scripture as a **single event**: the rapture.

> As He was sitting on the Mount of Olives, the disciples came to Him privately, saying, "Tell us, when will these things happen, and what will be *the sign* of your coming, and of the end of the age?" (Matt. 24:3 NASB, emphasis mine)

From the disciples' question, it is clear that there is *one* sign for the parousia which is, therefore, a singular event. That event is defined by Jesus as occurring in Matthew 24:31.

In 1 Thessalonians 4:15 as well (a verse that all *pretribulation rapture* supporters claim is the rapture), we saw that the resurrection and rapture occur at the parousia, which is also seen as a singular, one-time event:

> We who are alive and remain until *the* coming of the Lord, will
> not precede those who have fallen asleep. (1 Thess. 4:15 NASB)

This is reinforced by Paul's words to his protégé Timothy:

> I charge you therefore before God and the Lord Jesus Christ,
> *who will judge the living and the dead at his appearing* and his
> kingdom. (2 Tim. 4:1 NKJV, emphasis mine)

It is clear that the judgment of the dead (resulting in the resurrection) and
the living (resulting in the rapture) happen at the visible appearing of Jesus.
There will be no silent rapture.

A FOURFOLD "LAST DAY" RESURRECTION?

In John 6 we are told four separate times that Jesus will raise the righteous
on the last day. *Post-tribulation rapture* supporters have looked at this
passage and seized it as the *ultimate* vindication of their position. Dr. Gavin
Finley (*End-Time Pilgrim*) states their case this way:

> The Bible repeatedly shows us that the righteous dead will be
> resurrected very late in this age. Too late, in fact, for an early
> special pre-trib or mid-trib rapture to be hitched up with it. For
> example, four times in John 6 Jesus repeats that He will raise
> up/resurrect His people. Furthermore, Jesus states categorically
> that this glorious resurrection was not going to occur until the
> "last day."

172

John 6:39: This is the will of the Father who sent me, that of all He has given Me I should lose nothing, but should raise it up at the *last day*.

John 6:40:And this is the will of Him who sent me, that everyone who sees the Son and believes in Him may have everlasting life; and I will raise him up at the *last day*.

John 6:44: No one can come to me unless the Father who sent Me draws him; and I will raise him up at the *last day*.

John 6:54: Whoever eats my flesh and drinks my blood has eternal life, and I will raise him up at the *last day*.

Is our Lord Jesus trying to get a message to us here? If He saw fit to tell us four times in the one message that He will raise His people up at the "last day" then who would dare contradict Him? And who would dare tamper with the message the Holy Spirit has so clearly laid out for us in the holy Scriptures? —Dr. Gavin Finley[98]

Dr. Finley is an anesthesiologist, a writer, and editor of the *End-Time Pilgrim* website. He certainly presents his argument in a most passionate way. Grieving the Holy Spirit is nothing that any of us wants to undertake, but Dr. Finley must know that his position on these verses is not the only possible interpretation. Dr. Finley's fellow *post-tribulation rapture* supporter, Michael Snyder, asks the question:

Did He [Jesus] mean the last day of the tribulation? Did He mean the last day of this age? Did He mean the last day before He begins to reign? There is certainly a lot of room for debate here." —Michael Snyder[99] (clarification mine)

173

Mr. Snyder asks some good questions. Dr. Finley interprets this passage from his own frame of reference as the literal last day of the Seventieth Week of Daniel, but that is not the only possible interpretation. There are many "last" days.

I, too, interpret this passage from my biblical frame of reference. As demonstrated in chapter two, I'm aware that the resurrection and rapture happen prior to the trumpet and bowl judgments (which are God's wrath) and *cannot* happen on the last day of the Seventieth Week. Based on this perspective, what can "last day" mean?

The apostle Peter informs us that God does not reckon time as humans do.

> But do not forget this one thing, dear friends: with the Lord *a day is like a thousand years*, and *a thousand years are like a day*. The Lord is not slow in keeping his promise, as some understand slowness. Instead he is patient with you, not wanting anyone to perish, but everyone to come to repentance. But *the day of the Lord* will come like a thief. (2 Pet. 3:8–10 NIV, emphasis mine)

In this one short passage, Peter gives us three possible definitions of the word day. First, we see the traditional twenty-four-hour day, "a thousand years are like a day (twenty-four hours)." Second, the passage indicates that to Jesus, a day can be a thousand years (a millennia). Finally, we also see the term "the day of the Lord." From these three definitions, we now have three possibilities for the meaning of the "last day." This concept deserves a much fuller explanation. The passage in 2 Peter exists in the context of a much longer section of Scripture. This section begins in 2 Peter 3:3:

Above all, you must understand that in the *last days* scoffers will come, scoffing and following their own evil desires. They will say, "Where is this 'coming' [parousia] he promised? Ever since our ancestors died, everything goes on as it has since the beginning of creation." *But they deliberately forget that long ago by God's word the heavens came into being and the earth was formed* out of water and by water. (2 Pet. 3:3–5 NIV, emphasis mine)

This section of Scripture from 2 Peter 3 is most fascinating. The first phrase I want to bring to your attention is "last days." This is universally understood to not only mean the days immediately before Jesus's return, but the entire period from the New Testament until today. In Hebrews we read:

But in *these last days* he has spoken to us by his Son (Heb. 1:2 NIV, emphasis mine)

Why the entire period from the resurrection of Jesus until today can be considered "last days" will become apparent as we study 2 Peter 3. This phrase is not the same as "last day," but it is similar. It is my theory that both of these phrases may be referring to the same length of days.

Returning to Peter's teaching, he indicates that scoffers will come who doubt the coming parousia of Jesus. (In the last section, we learned that the parousia is the rapture.) He then makes a strange statement; he blames the doubt of the scoffers on their deliberately forgetting the creation narrative! Commentators have been confused by this verse. Barnes interprets this verse that the scoffers are expecting the world to continue as it currently is. In this they neglect that things were not always this way: there was a creation.[100] This interpretation fails to grasp the verses that follow, however:

> *But do not forget this one thing, dear friends: With the Lord a day is like a thousand years*, and a thousand years are like a day. The Lord is not slow in keeping his promise, as some understand slowness. Instead he is patient with you, not wanting anyone to perish, but everyone to come to repentance. *But the day of the Lord will come like a thief. The heavens will disappear with a roar; the elements will be destroyed by fire*, and the earth and everything done in it will be laid bare. (2 Pet. 3:8–10 NIV, emphasis mine)

Peter stresses the "day is like a thousand years" motif ("do not forget this *one* thing") to explain the importance of remembering the creation narrative. And he links this equivalency to the day of the Lord when the heavens will disappear with a roar and fire will burn the earth. Ancient Hebrew tradition has presumed that each of the *seven days in the Genesis account represent a millennium (one thousand years)*; that the "days of man's rebellion" are six thousand years from creation and the millennial kingdom is the seventh day, the day of rest.[101] Hebrews 4:1–5, which details the "seventh day" being the 1000-year Millennial rest, further confirms this theory.

In this way, the creation account in Genesis 1 functions as prophecy, with the creative acts in each day mirroring the redemptive acts of God done during each consecutive thousand-year period of earth history (assumed six thousand years of biblical earth history). An article on the website www.TheGospelintheEndTimes.com[102] entitled "Is the Creation Narrative a

Prophecy?" gives detailed analysis of this prophecy, the symbolism of the creative acts by God, and the timing of the redemptive acts.

In summary, Peter (in 2 Pet. 3:8–10) refers to this "Creation Prophecy" to remind the "scoffers" that God has a timetable for the parousia of his son: six thousand years from creation. Interesting as that may be, our purposes here concern the meaning of a "day." In this case, it can mean a thousand-year day. When Hebrews 1:2 says that the first-century writer of that book was in the "last days," this likely may have meant that the writer considered himself in the *last few millennia* before the parousia. In the same way, Jesus may likely have been referring to the *last* thousand-year "day" as the timing of the resurrection in the fourfold mention of the "last day" in John 6.

It is also possible this "last day" refers to the day of the Lord. Dr. Finley and Mr. Snyder would probably agree with this idea. However, what few are aware of is that the day of the Lord is not a single day. In three places in Isaiah, the timing of this day is given as a *year*.

> For the Lord has a *day* of vengeance, a *year* of recompense for the cause of Zion. (Isa. 34:8 NASB, emphasis mine)

> To proclaim the favorable *year* of the Lord and the *day* of vengeance of our God. (Isa. 61:2 NASB, emphasis mine)

> For the *day* of vengeance was in my heart, and my *year* of redemption has come. (Isa. 63:4 NASB, emphasis mine)

At this point in our discussion, it should suffice for us to consider that this year long (or even millennia-long) day of the Lord may well have been what

Jesus was referencing in John 6 when he spoke of a last day. The one thing we can be sure of is that he was *not referring to the last day* of the Seventieth Week. Now that we know that Jesus's return (and the resurrection) precedes the trumpet and bowl judgments, which are God's wrath, it cannot be on the last day of the Seventieth Week, as *post-tribulation rapture* supporters expect.

THE BOOK OF JOEL

Author Michael Snyder quotes Joel 2:1–17 in numerous places in his book, *Rapture Verdict*, and claims over and over that this passage depicts the battle of Armageddon (it does not), and that Joel 2:10 depicts Matthew 24:29 (it does).[103]

One must remember that Old Testament revelations of end-time events frequently *appear* to happen in chronological order, when in fact they do not. Daniel's Seventy Weeks is an example with a two-thousand-year gap between the sixty-ninth and Seventieth Weeks. The Book of Joel is another example with three separate references to the celestial earthly disturbance (Joel 2:10, 2:30–31, 3:15–16). Obviously any one separate mention of this event can't be used as a time marker for other events around it.

In support of his thesis, Mr. Snyder made reference to Joel 2:4, "Their appearance is like the appearance of horses," to claim that this army depicted by Joel in chapter 2 are the saints of God coming on white horses. What he failed to realize is that this is a direct quote of Revelation 9:7 and refers to the army of *locusts* that appear at the fifth trumpet. This locust army is also mentioned in Joel's previous chapter, Joel 1. Specifically, in Joel 1:6 he refers to locusts with the "teeth of lions," which is also a direct quote of Revelation 9:8 and the locust army of the fifth trumpet. One must remember that the chapter and verse marking were not there in the original text. Joel chapter 1 and the first part of chapter 2 read more like a continuation of one story—of the locust army invasion. So the first part of this chapter (Joel 2) does not refer to Armageddon but refers to events during the yearlong wrath of God during the day of the Lord, which includes the fifth trumpet.

SEALING OF THE SAINTS

A major problem for the *post-tribulation rapture* theory is that Christians must be on the earth during the entire Seventieth Week, and most probably during the wrath of God which is poured out upon the day of the Lord. This appears to be in direct opposition to 1 Thess. 1:10 and 1 Thess. 5:9. How these saints are protected from God's wrath in the *post-tribulation rapture* position requires some mental gymnastics (work-arounds) to accomplish. Proponents of this rapture theory have three notions on how the saints are protected from God's wrath:

- God selectively lets his wrath fall upon areas where the saints are not located, much as he protected Goshen during the Exodus plagues.
- God's wrath (considered only the bowls by this theory) doesn't begin until after the Seventieth Week ends; other wrath is considered "Satan's wrath."
- God seals the saints and supernaturally protects them.

The first theory, indeed, *sounds* good, but there is absolutely no biblical evidence to support it, so it remains unproven.

The second theory is summarized by the late *post-tribulation rapture* supporter, Ed Tarkowski:

179

Posttribulationism: this doctrine believes God's wrath is poured out immediately *after* the tribulation and, therefore, saints in the tribulation period will not experience that wrath. Saints in the tribulation are persecuted under *Satan's wrath* and fury, so saints suffering God's wrath during the tribulation is not a problem in this doctrine. That wrath is simply not there during the tribulation period, but Satan's is (see Revelation chapters 12 and 13).[104] —Ed Tarkowski (emphasis mine)

Later in his essay, Mr. Tarkowski admits that the day of the Lord and his wrath begins *after* the sixth seal. I agree, the wrath of God begins after the sixth seal. In fact, if you carefully read Mr. Tarkowski's words, you might think he was a *prewrath rapture* supporter. However, the error of the *post-tribulation rapture* position presented by Mr. Tarkowski is that it misinterprets the order of the seals – trumpets – bowls. As we explained in an earlier section of this chapter, these events are sequential and follow one after another. Once this is understood, it is obvious that God's wrath begins with the trumpet and bowl judgments. Since the fifth trumpet is five months long itself, the wrath of God begins at least that long prior to the end of the Seventieth Week.

The third theory utilizes Revelation 7:1–8 for support. The late Frank L. Caw Jr. explains this position on the sealing of the saints:

Contextually-speaking, the *great tribulation* will have just ended, and the unleashing of the *sixth seal* upon the earth will have made people realize that the great day of his wrath is come, i.e., the *day of the Lord*. However, before any Divine judgments are released upon the earth, God will protectively seal any

180

Tribulation Saints who will have managed to escape execution by the Antichrist. Thus, the four angels will be commanded not to harm the earth and the sea until after the protective sealing is completed. Moreover, the Jewish tribulation saints symbolized as 144,000 Jews are mentioned specifically in the passage above to illustrate the fact that the Dispensation of Grace will have just ended at that point in time so that the Dispensation of Law (i.e., Daniel's Seventieth Week) can begin without mixing the two dispensations. Then Revelation 7 concludes its account by portraying the martyred tribulation saints resurrected in heaven just before the *seventh seal* begins.[105] —Frank L. Caw Jr. (emphasis mine)

Mr. Caw, author of *The Ultimate Deception,* took a position that the Christians who survive the persecution of the Antichrist are sealed in Revelation 7:1–8 along with the 144,000 Jews (the remnant). This position is held by many *pretribulation rapture* theorists (like Mr. Caw) and *post-tribulation rapture* theorists. From a post-trib. point of view, this would allow Christians to remain alive until a *post-tribulation rapture* at the end of the Seventieth Week. Let's examine the text of Revelation 7:1–8 to see if this is feasible:

After this I saw four angels standing at the four corners of the earth, holding back the four winds of the earth, so that no wind would blow on the earth or on the sea or on any tree. And I saw another angel ascending from the rising of the sun, having the seal of the living God; and he cried out with a loud voice to the four angels to whom it was granted to harm the earth and the sea, saying, "Do not harm the earth or the sea or the trees until we have sealed the bond-servants of our God on their foreheads." And I heard the number of those who were *sealed*, *one hundred and forty-four thousand* sealed *from every tribe of the sons of Israel*: from the tribe of Judah, twelve thousand were sealed, from the tribe of Reuben twelve thousand, from the tribe of Gad twelve thousand, from the tribe of Asher twelve thousand, from the tribe of Naphtali twelve thousand, from the tribe of Manasseh twelve thousand, from the tribe of Simeon twelve thousand, from the tribe of Levi twelve thousand, from the tribe of Issachar twelve thousand, from the tribe of Zebulun twelve thousand, from the tribe of Joseph twelve thousand, from the tribe of Benjamin, twelve thousand were sealed. (Rev. 7:1–8 NASB, emphasis mine)

First, the text is specific that only 144,000 are sealed. It is also specific that those sealed are from the Hebraic tribes; this is a particularly *Jewish* remnant. There *isn't the slightest indication* that any gentiles are sealed. The purpose of the sealing is also abundantly clear: to protect the sealed Jews prior to the pouring out of God's wrath. The first two trumpet judgments specifically target the land, trees, and sea, and the angels are told to not harm these things until after the sealing.

Are the 144,000 protected by being raptured or do they remain on the earth and endure the Wrath of God? To me, it's unclear. In Rev. 14:4 we are told they are "*first fruits* to God and to the Lamb." Might these newly sealed Jewish men be the first apostate Jews to repent upon seeing Jesus coming on the clouds (Rev. 16:6)? The very next verses in Revelation (Rev. 7:9-17) are part of the "moving picture" of the rapture we learned about in chapter three. Could these be 144,000 new Jewish believers and part of that great multitude? We aren't told.

Some *post-tribulation rapture* proponents also claim that a later verse in Revelation supports a sealing of Christians:

> Then out of the smoke came locusts upon the earth, and power was given them, as the scorpions of the earth have power. They were *told not to hurt the grass of the earth, nor any green thing, nor any tree,* but only the men who do not have the *seal of God on their foreheads.* (Rev. 9:3–4 NASB, emphasis mine)

Again, we see the locusts are not to hurt the *grass or trees* (reference to Revelation 7) or anyone with *the seal of God on their foreheads* (reference to both Revelation 7 and 14). These may be the 144,000 repentant Jews (if they remain on the earth) or may be other later repentant Jews who must face the Wrath of God. There is *no biblical reference to Christians being sealed to protect them from God's wrath.*

The ark is the picture of God's protection from his wrath. Noah and his family were lifted off the earth during the time of the flood. Prior to that time, it is likely Noah endured much tribulation at the hands of wicked men. "Now the earth was corrupt in the sight of God, and the earth was filled with violence. God looked on the earth, and behold, it was corrupt; for all flesh had corrupted their way upon the earth" (Gen. 6:12 NASB). God permitted Noah to endure tribulation, but when it came time for God to pour out his wrath, God lifted Noah above the face of the earth. The ark is a picture of the rapture to come.

LEFT BEHIND OR TAKEN?

Another misconception of those ascribing to the *post-tribulation rapture* theory (and many of the *pretribulation rapture* theory as well) is that the righteous are left behind and the unrighteous are taken (away to judgment) in Matthew 24:40–41. In the words of *post-tribulation rapture* supporter Dr. Michael Brown, "We want to be left behind."[106] Dr. Brown is the host of the "Line of Fire" radio show. As an author and speaker, he has devoted his life to awakening the church. He and I have much in common. But in regard to his statement about being "left behind," is it good advice? Do we want to be left behind?

The quickest, easiest way to determine that Dr. Brown's statement is *not* accurate is to examine the three rapture analogies given by Jesus: Noah, Lot, and the parable of the ten virgins. In each case, the righteous are taken *away from* the judgment and the unrighteous are left behind to *face* immediate judgment. First, in the Noah analogy, Noah and his family are *taken away* from the flood by means of the ark, and we are told by Jesus that it will be just like that at the coming of the Son of Man:

> *Just as it happened in the days of Noah*, so it will be also in the days of the Son of Man: they were eating, they were drinking, they were marrying, they were being given in marriage, until the day that Noah entered the ark, and the flood came and destroyed them all. (Luke 17:26–27 NASB, emphasis mine)

Second, in the Lot analogy, we are again specifically informed that Lot *went out from Sodom* quickly to escape judgment. Once more, we are told it will be *just the same* on the day the Son of Man is revealed. Also notice that on

184

that same day, fire and brimstone rain down from heaven and destroy the wicked who remain in Sodom. We discussed this in detail in chapter four.

> It was the same as happened in the days of Lot: they were eating, they were drinking, they were buying, they were selling, they were planting, they were building; but on the day that *Lot went out from Sodom* it rained fire and brimstone from heaven and destroyed them all. It will be *just the same* on the day that the Son of Man is revealed. (Luke 17:28–30 NASB, emphasis mine)

Third, in the example of the parable of the ten virgins, the wise virgins go "in with" the bridegroom while the foolish are left behind, outside of the wedding feast, and the door was shut.

> And while they were going away to make the purchase, the bridegroom came, and those who were ready went in with him to the wedding feast; and *the door was shut.* Later the other virgins also came, saying, "Lord, lord, open up for us." But he answered, "Truly I say to you, I do not know you." (Matt. 25:10–12 NASB, emphasis mine).

Finally, these analogies match perfectly with the depiction of the parousia in Matthew 24:31 where the angels *gather together the elect* and the elect are the ones *taken.*

> And He will send forth His angels with a great trumpet and they will *gather together His elect* from the four winds, from one end of the sky to the other. (Matt. 24:31 NASB, emphasis mine)

These three analogies and the parousia of Matthew 24:31 present Jesus's clear teaching. But as we discussed previously in regard to *pretribulation rapture* theory, when the clear teaching of Scripture seems contrary to one's opinion, it is common to see Greek words redefined in the attempted usage of work-arounds. In regard to this issue of "taken or left behind," the Greek words in Matthew 24:40: *paralambano* ("to take from" or "to take to") and *aphiemi* ("to release" or "send away") have been called into question. Because one meaning of *aphiemi* can be "to forgive," *post-tribulation rapture* theorists argue that those left behind are the church; that they are "forgiven" (*aphiemi*).

However, close examination shows this is *not* the case. *Paralambano*, the word used for those taken, conveys an intimate receiving to oneself—which will certainly be the case at the rapture. In Matthew 1:20, this word is used when Joseph is instructed to take Mary as his wife. It is also frequently used when one takes a companion with them. *Aphiemi* reflects the opposite of both of these ideas. In 1 Corinthians 7:13 it is used when a woman *divorces* her husband. It is also used when one desires to no longer travel with a companion and leaves them behind. When *aphiemi* is used in combination with *paralambano*, these opposite (antonym) meanings are obvious and the appropriate translation.

VULTURES AND A BODY

Because the meaning of "taken" and "left" are misunderstood by many in both the *pretribulation rapture* and *post-tribulation rapture* camps, several of Jesus's seminal teachings on the rapture have been grossly misinterpreted. One of these is the beautiful but brief illustration of the vultures and the body. Jesus taught this illustration on at least two separate occasions, both of which involve his parousia.

For just as the lightning comes from the east and flashes even to the west, so will the coming [parousia] of the Son of Man be. Wherever the corpse [Gk: *ptoma*, meaning "dead body"] is, there the vultures [Gk: *aetoi*, meaning "eagles"] will gather [Gk: *sunago*, meaning "gather together"]. (Matt. 24:27–28 NASB)

Two men will be in the field; one will be taken and the other will be left. And answering they [his disciples] said to Him, "Where, Lord?" And He said to them, "Where the body [Gk: *soma*, meaning "living body") is, there also the vultures [Gk: *aetoi*, meaning "eagles"] will be gathered [Gk: *episunago*, meaning "gather together"]." (Luke 17:36–37 NASB, clarification mine)

Pastor Jim McClarty of Florida summarizes the primary position of both *pretribulation rapture* and *post-tribulation rapture* camps on their mistaken view of this illustration:

Jesus was not referring to those "taken to be with the Lord at the rapture when He comes." He was speaking of a gathering of people to the place where the carrion birds would eat their flesh. We see that prophecy fulfilled in Revelation 19 (Rev. 19:17–18, where birds eat the flesh of those who die at Armageddon).[107] — Pastor Jim McClarty, (clarification mine)

Again, as we have repeatedly seen in other applications, a mistaken understanding of Greek words is behind the misinterpretation. The primary misunderstood word is *aetoi* which means eagles (not vultures)! Now an eagle can be a carrion bird as well as a carnivore, but this passage may not be talking about birds at all! In the Bible, the term "eagle" is commonly associated with heavenly beings. Sometimes, the heavenly being has the form of an eagle. In Ezek. 1:10 and Ezek. 10:14 each of the cherubim have four faces; one of which is an eagle's face. In Rev. 4:7, one of the living creatures is like a flying eagle. Prior to the three woes (the fifth, sixth, and seventh trumpets) an "eagle" messenger speaks!

> I heard an eagle flying in midheaven, saying with a loud voice,
> "Woe, woe, woe to those who dwell on the earth, because of
> the remaining blasts of the trumpet of the three angels who are
> about to sound!" (Rev. 8:13 NASB, emphasis mine)

Sometimes God's agents are given the attributes of an eagle. God's people are frequently delivered by eagles' wings as can be seen in Rev. 12:14, Exo. 19:4, and Isa. 40:31. God's agents are frequently said to be like eagles as can be seen in Jer. 48:40 and Jer. 4:13; and in the Song of Moses, God himself is likened to an eagle in Deut. 32:11. Obviously, "eagle" is a very common biblical term associated with divine beings.

It is not surprising that in the setting of a parable, Jesus might use *aetoi* as a symbol for angels. Once this likely meaning of eagle is understood, Jesus's short illustration jumps to life.

A second misconstrued word is translated "gather" in Luke 17:37. The Greek word is *episunago* which means "gather together upwards." We have already studied this great "rapture" word in chapter five.

Earlier, on the same day that he delivered the Olivet Discourse (in Matt. 24), Jesus utilized this same word, *episunago*, and combined it with the bird motif. In a probable reference to Deut. 32:11, he attributed the qualities of a bird (or eagle) to himself.

188

Jerusalem, Jerusalem, who kills the prophets and stones those
who are sent to her! How often I wanted to *gather* your
children *together* (episunago) the way a hen *gathers*
(episunago) her chicks under her wings, and you were
unwilling. (Matt. 23:37 NASB, emphasis mine)

Then later on that very same day, when describing the rapture in parable
form (Matt. 24:28), Jesus referred to "gathering together" and eagles a
second time. Finally, literally seconds after speaking the parable, Jesus
mentioned "gathering together" a third time in Matt. 24:31. That time, he
made it clear that angels will do the gathering.

This word, episunago (or its noun form), is used in these other
Rapture passages which we have already examined several times, where it is
believers who are gathered together upwards:

And He will send forth His angels with a great trumpet and
they will gather together (episunago) His elect from the four
winds, from one end of the sky to the other. (Matt. 24:31
NASB, emphasis mine)

Now we request you, brethren, with regard to the coming
(parousia) of our Lord Jesus Christ and our gathering together
(episunagoge) to Him (2 Thess. 2:1 NASB, emphasis mine)

In Matthew's version of the parable, the word translated "gather" is *sunago*
which also means "gather together." (It is missing the prefix *epi* which
means "above" found in the Luke 17 version.) In both instances the words
used by Jesus, episunago ("gather together upwards") and sunago ("gather

189

together"), do not mean to simply gather. Rather they imply gathering something together. The way our English Bibles are translated, one would think the aetoi were gathering as in a flock. That is not the meaning.

Finally, two other Greek words are misconstrued in the traditional interpretation of the parable. The illustration in Luke uses the Greek word for living body *(soma)* and the Matthew version uses the Greek word for dead body *(ptoma)*. The word "body" does not only mean a "corpse."

Once the correct meanings of all the Greek words are understood, the crystal-clear connotation that Jesus had in mind for this illustration becomes apparent. ***Jesus's angels will gather together the dead saints (Resurrection) and the living saints (Rapture)!*** This passage has absolutely nothing to do with Armageddon. The fact that both the *pretribulation rapture* exponents and *post-tribulation rapture* exponents misinterpret Matt. 24:30-31 as the physical Second Coming only intensifies the misunderstanding of the illustration of the vultures and the body and a possible link between it and Armageddon.

Now that we have looked at the sense of the words Jesus spoke, let's look at the context to see if our interpretation is true. If we look at the illustration in context in Matthew, we see it concerns the parousia (which we now know as the rapture). Only three verses later (Matt. 24:30-31), Jesus explains this same event in clear, concrete terms (not as a parable). Once viewed in this way, it is so easy to see that Jesus was clarifying his parable for the disciples. If the word sunago in verse 28 was properly translated in the English, the two uses of the same term "gather together" in such close proximity would help readers properly interpret the parable. Unfortunately, this is not the case.

If we look at the illustration in context in Luke, it also helps explain the issue of "taken" and "left:"

190

Two men will be in the field; one will be taken and the other will be left. And answering they (his disciples) said to Him, "Where, Lord?" And He said to them, "Where the body (Gk: soma, meaning "living body") is, there also the vultures (Gk: aetoi, meaning "eagles") will be gathered (Gk: episunago, meaning "gather together")." (Luke 17:36-37 NASB, clarification and emphasis mine)

When the disciples ask "Where, Lord?" there are two possible meanings to their question: 1) where are they taken? or 2) where is this going to happen? Jesus immediately acknowledged the disciples question, "Where, Lord?" by saying, "Where the (living) body is . . ." Jesus answers the second question! He tells the disciples where this event is going to happen. He does not say where they are taken. We now understand that it is the righteous that are taken, and of course, this would be the primary concern of the disciples. They would be disturbed that perhaps they had to be in Jerusalem to be taken. Jesus calmed their fears by saying in essence, "Wherever the living body (of Christ—the church!) is, there the angels will gather them together."

You may have wondered about the illustration used on the cover of this book. I'm sure it seemed a strange work of art to employ for a book on the rapture—birds flying around in the lightning. Look at it again. Can you now see it is a tongue in cheek depiction of this illustration of the vultures and the body as depicted in Matt. 24:27–28? The sign of the Son of Man (lightning) will appear, and Jesus will send his *aetoi* (angels rather than vultures) to rapture the saints!

191

DO THE SAINTS RISE AND THEN IMMEDIATELY
DESCEND DURING THE RAPTURE?

A pattern has been established. Most misunderstandings of rapture timing stem from an avoidance of what the text literally says or from a mistranslation of one or more of the Greek words in the passage. Another example of a misunderstanding of this nature is voiced by Dr. Craig Keener on page 352 of his commentary on Matthew:

> We can especially expect the term parousia (which bears many possible meanings) to convey the image of a royal appearance when writers conjoin the term with a *quasi-technical expression apantesis*, "meeting," as in 1 Thess. 4:17.[108] —Dr. Craig Keener (emphasis mine)

Dr. Keener is a professor of New Testament at Asbury Theological Seminary. He is the author of fifteen books, innumerable articles, and is a noted international speaker. In his commentary, Keener quotes Best, Marshal, Bruce, and Milligan on the use of this word apantesis. The interpretation of all of these learned men is that this word "meeting" signifies a technical term used in the Greek for the greeting of a royal dignitary and then escorting him back to one's own city. (Notice Dr. Keener is only willing to claim it is a *quasi-technical* term.) By this, all these esteemed individuals imply that the use of this word in 1 Thessalonians 4:17 implies that after meeting Jesus in the air, the saints and Jesus then immediately return to the earth. As in all the other examples where we have looked at misapplied words, this usage sounds logical—except for one problem, it simply isn't true! Professor of New Testament and Greek (Messiah College) and *Post Tribulation Rapture* expert Michael Cosby explicitly states that "apantesis was not a technical (term) and that all the elements of Hellenistic receptions are missing from 1 Thess. 4:14–17."[109] The author stated that he began his research to *strengthen* previous research in this area, but ended up realizing the traditional *post-tribulation rapture* position on this word was mistaken! This rejection of the theory by a leading *post-tribulation rapture* supporter certainly speaks volumes, and Michael Cosby deserves to be commended for his honesty.

This word, apantesis, is used one other time in Scripture in relation to the return of Jesus (in the parable of the ten virgins). As can be plainly seen, the bridegroom (Jesus) and the wise virgins *do not* return to the virgins' home, but rather continue on to the wedding feast:

> Then the kingdom of heaven will be comparable to ten virgins, who took their lamps and went out to meet [apantesis] the bridegroom . . . the bridegroom came, and those who were ready *went in with him* to the wedding feast. (Matt. 25:1, 10 NASB)

On his website, Alan Kurschner also points out four separate Scriptures that specifically demonstrate that believers are ushered into heaven after the rapture (2 Cor. 4:14; John 14:2–3; Rev. 7:13–15; and Isa. 26:19–21).[110] Additionally, as we pointed out in chapter five, Mark 13:27 clearly delineates the destination of the rapture. It is very clear from this abundance of evidence that the destination of the rapture is heaven—not an immediate return to the earth.

JESUS'S STAINED ROBES

In Rev. 19:13, we observe that Jesus's robes are dipped in blood *prior* to his returning to earth on a white horse to fight Armageddon. *Post-tribulation rapture* (and *pretribulation rapture*) experts must claim that this blood is Jesus's own. From their point of view, it can't be the blood of the unrighteous because he has not returned to earth yet. But they miss the direct and obvious reference this phrase was drawn from:

> I have trodden the wine trough alone, and from the peoples
> there was no man with me. I also trod them in my anger and
> trampled them in my wrath; and their lifeblood is sprinkled on
> my garments, and I stained all my raiment. (Isa. 63:3 NASB)

In Rev. 19:15, John reiterates that Jesus treads the winepress of the Wrath of God. How did Jesus stain his garments prior to Armageddon? During the Wrath of God which immediately follows the *prewrath rapture*.

POST-TRIBULATION RAPTURE WORK-AROUNDS

In chapter six, we learned that the *pretribulation rapture* exponents have developed a number of work-arounds to justify their theory in light of numerous clear Scriptures to the contrary. In this chapter, we have seen that *post-tribulation rapture* exponents have done the same thing. The *post-tribulation rapture* work-arounds are presented in the graphic beginning on the following page:

Work-around	Scripture	Concept
Claim the seals – trumpets – bowls are not sequential	Rev. 6, 8–9, 16	These events (seals – trumpets – bowls) are presented sequentially in Revelation, and numerous proofs abound that they are consecutive
Claim the seventh trumpet is the last trumpet	Rev. 11:15	The seventh trumpet is blown by an angel (not God) and it is clear that as of the sixth bowl, the physical second coming has not yet occurred
Claim the phrase "those days shall be shortened" means that an infinite great tribulation will be shortened to 3 1/2 years	Matt. 24:22	Ignore that "those days" refer to the 1,260 days of the "times of the Gentiles"
Claim that a *prewrath rapture* teaches three comings of Christ		The arrival (parousia) of Christ is clearly defined as

Work-around	Scripture	Concept
		beginning at the rapture and is an extended event through the physical second coming (landing) of Jesus
Some claim that saints avoid the wrath of God during the Seventieth Week by God selectively avoiding them while pouring it out on others		There is no Scripture to substantiate this claim
Claim the wrath of God doesn't begin until after the Seventieth Week	Rev. 6:17	The wrath of God clearly begins after the sixth seal
Claim the saints are sealed to protect them from the wrath of God	Rev. 7:1–8	Only the Jewish remnant is sealed to protect them from the wrath of God
Claim the righteous are left behind and the wicked are taken	Luke 17:26–30 Matt. 25:1–13	In Jesus's analogies of the rapture, Noah, Lot, and the wise virgins are all

Work-around	Scripture	Concept
		"taken" to safety and the wicked left behind
Claim the illustration of the vultures and the body refers to Armageddon	Matt. 24:28	Mistranslation of three Greek words *aetoi, episunago,* and *soma* leads them to misunderstand that this illustration is actually about the rapture
Claim apantesis indicates that Jesus and the righteous descend back to earth immediately after the rapture	1 Thess. 4:17	Scriptural evidence (Matt. 25:1–13) indicates that apantesis does not require a return to the earth

Figure 20: Post-Tribulation Rapture Work-arounds

SUMMARY

The *post-tribulation rapture* theory is one of the oldest of the three rapture-timing theories, dating back to the days of the early church. To their credit, the early church understood that believers would undergo much tribulation. But just as the ancient Greeks relied on their traditions about the earth being the center of the universe despite the mounting evidence that it wasn't, so, too, have many in the church continued to hang on to the *post-tribulation*

197

rapture by manipulating the meanings of clear readings of Scripture that show the rapture does not occur at the very end of the Seventieth Week.

In chapters two through five, we established convincing evidence that the *prewrath rapture* is the rapture timing answer. In chapter six: "The Backfire Effect (*Pre-Tribulation Rapture* Arguments)" and chapter seven: "Center of the Universe (*Post-Tribulation Rapture* Arguments)," we demonstrated the error in all the major arguments of both the *pretribulation rapture* and *post-tribulation rapture* camps. You are probably surprised. I am sure you may now doubt some of the strongly held rapture beliefs you held before reading these chapters. We are in a search for truth, so I would hope that would be the case.

In Part Four: "Application," we will reach the most important chapter of the book. Chapter eight: "Brethren, What Shall We Do?" will address the question, "How can individuals and churches overcome the trials ahead?" It is vital that we understand those concepts in the days ahead.

PART FOUR:

APPLICATION

Chapter Eight

BRETHREN, WHAT SHALL WE DO?

"Now when they heard this, they were pierced to the heart, and said to Peter and the rest of the apostles, 'Brethren, what shall we do?'" (Acts 2:37 NASB)

The evidence contained in this book for a *prewrath rapture* is overwhelming, if not conclusive. Considering that 96% of Christians currently favor another view of the rapture, I'm sure this material has been shocking to you to say the least. At this point, you have probably begun working through the stages that humans go through to accept a new idea. Those predictable stages are contained in the acronym SARA:

S – Surprise or shock

A – Anger

R – Rejection

A – Acceptance

All of us go through this pattern of stages. Emotionally, I was sitting where you are only ten years ago. You see, I used to hold a *pretribulation rapture* position. In fact, as a young Christian, I was never taught there were any other alternatives. After being presented with convincing evidence for the *prewrath rapture*, I remember the initial shock of realizing this basic foundation of my "faith" was gone. (True faith, of course, is only found in the person of Jesus.) But, I had placed faith in the *pretribulation rapture* to protect me and my family. It was comforting to think that we would not face persecution of a level that frequently leads to martyrdom.

Then, I remember being angry, angry that I was losing what I thought was my blessed hope. Perhaps you are angry at me right now. I also remember the rejection phase, scrambling to discover that one proof that could restore my faith in pretribulationalism. I remember searching for proof after proof, only to be disappointed. At that time, when I had reached the end of my rope and let go, I remember the acceptance phase. According to Dr. Barbara Annis, an expert on gender intelligence, men come into this acceptance phase quicker than women do. Men tend to say, "If I can't change it, I might as well move on and solve the problem this has created." Women, however, tend to stay stuck in the rejection phase for a much longer time.[111]

Whichever adjustment phase you are in, this chapter is devoted to action steps we need to take as individuals, families, and churches. You may be ready for this chapter or you may not. If you are not ready to read on and begin to think about the implications of what we've learned, I understand. You may want to set this book aside until you are ready to say, "Brethren, what shall we do?" You also may decide to reread this book for a second exposure to the scriptural evidence presented.

However, eventually planning for the future is necessary. As a worldwide body of believers, we are woefully unprepared for what we will face in the near future. None of us know that day, but we can all see that the season of Jesus's return is fast approaching. His grace has granted us this short period to prepare, but we are not to waste this precious time. We should be about our Master's business. The courage to face the future will stem from knowing we are preparing God's flock with Jesus right by our side. "Teaching them to observe *all* that I commanded you; and lo, I am with you always, even to the end of the age" (Matt. 28:20 NASB, emphasis mine). That preparation should especially include "the end of the age."

SCARING SEEKERS OUT OF OUR PEWS

How do we approach this preparation?

At the beginning of this book, we discussed concern that if we mention issues like martyrdom and persecution, we will scare seekers out of our pews. So before we begin to discuss how to ready our churches for these events, we need to spend some time discussing this valid concern. If we explain what lies ahead, many seekers *and* many current church attenders will find a venue where these topics are avoided.

However, it is this author's opinion that we should not ignore teaching about these topics regardless of whether some in our pews choose to leave our churches. I realize this is radical thinking, but our Lord himself did not mince words in terms of what it would take to become his follower. Consistently throughout his ministry, Jesus advised those listening to his teaching to "count the cost" (Luke 14:28) before becoming a disciple. Part of that cost would be that "in this world we will have tribulation" (John 16:33). He also stated the world will hate us and that we should "know that it has hated me [Jesus] before it hated you" (John 15:18). Regarding martyrdom, Jesus was clear that those who attempt to "save their life will lose it" (Luke 9:24). In all these ways, Jesus was abundantly clear that suffering for the cause of his kingdom is a fundamental component of being a Christian. Not only did Jesus say to expect persecution, he stated that "blessed are you when men hate you" (Luke 6:22).

During his earthly ministry, Jesus valued the depth of devotion of his followers, not the sheer number of them. Although we don't want a single seeker to leave our churches, some who aren't truly believers will do so. In John 6, Jesus delivered a teaching that most of his followers found hard to accept. For this reason many left him—never to walk with him again:

> *For Jesus knew from the beginning who they were who did not believe* . . . as a result of this many of His disciples withdrew and were not walking with Him anymore. So Jesus said to the twelve, "You do not want to go away also, do you?" Simon Peter answered Him, "Lord, to whom shall we go? You have words of eternal life. We have believed and have come to know that you are the Holy One of God." (John 6:64, 66–69 NASB, emphasis mine)

Those who truly believe in and love Jesus will not leave. In fact, knowing that you may face persecution and martyrdom helps one devalue the things of this world and value Jesus's kingdom even more. Although preparing our churches for what is to come may cause some to switch to a church that avoids this teaching, the vibrancy of true belief that permeates the remaining "remnant" congregation may lead to an explosion of evangelism. We are responsible to teach the truth in love. The Holy Spirit is responsible for the growth of our churches.

"ALL WE NEED IS LOVE"

Our love for Jesus is always the primary matter to settle before any other issue. It is no coincidence that loving the Lord our God is the first and greatest commandment. In the letter to the church of Ephesus, Jesus had this to say:

> But I have this against you, that you have left your *first love*. Therefore remember from where you have fallen, and repent and do the deeds you did at first. (Rev. 2:4–5 NASB, emphasis mine)

We all must do a self-assessment of our relationship to our Lord; all other preparation springs from our love for Jesus. The Greek word *agapao* (*agape*) means loving what we place first in our lives, what totally consumes us and drives us. This is the type of love God expects. Things that we agapao may include careers, family, money, comfort, houses, or self.

Do you love (agapao) God? Most of us would automatically say, "Yes, of course!" But, how often do we put his will and his desires above our own? Are we consumed and driven by what he desires for our life and not what we want? Is our own happiness more important than what *God desires* for our lives? We all must be brutally honest when we answer these questions. No one will be able to overcome the Seventieth Week of Daniel without the infilling of the Holy Spirit and a sold-out devotion to Jesus.

How do we develop this type of love? First, all relationships arise from time spent with the person. Nothing will substitute for reading Scriptures, fasting and praying, and working alongside our Master serving his children. We must first have a relationship with Jesus.

But a relationship with our Lord is not the same as agapao love for God. Agapao love means a loss of self, a setting aside all our own thoughts, emotions, and desires that are contrary to God's will. Agapao means denying yourself and taking up your cross.

> He was saying to them all, "If anyone wishes to come after Me, he must deny himself, and take up his cross daily and follow

205

Me. *For whoever wishes to save his life will lose it, but whoever loses his life for My sake, he is the one who will save it.*" (Luke 9:23–24 NASB, emphasis mine)

We are all familiar with the above passage; the one who tries to save his life will lose it. In church-world, we think of this in relation to serving our church families, giving our tithes, etc. We also think of this in terms of our lives within our own families, sacrificially loving our spouses and children. All of these things are wonderful. However, the days are coming when self-denial for the sake of Jesus will take on a different, more intense character.

In the times that are coming upon the world, there will be powerful pressure to deny Jesus; it is the essence of apostasy. The only defense against this enormous pressure to commit apostasy will be agapao love for our Lord. Jesus's restoration of Peter after his denial explains how this works.

PETER'S AGAPAO LOVE (A CASE STUDY)

Most Christians know that Peter denied Jesus three times on the night he was betrayed. After Jesus's resurrection, he restored Peter in a passage where he asked him three times whether Peter loved him. Let's look at the specific passage:

So when they had finished breakfast, *Jesus said to Simon Peter*, "*Simon, son of John*, do you love [Gk: agapao] me more than these?" He said to Him, "Yes, Lord; you know that I love [Gk: *philo*] you." He said to him, "Tend My lambs." He said to him again a second time, "Simon, son of John, do you love [Gk: agapao] me?" He said to Him, "Yes, Lord; you know that I love

[Gk: philo] you." He said to him, "Shepherd My sheep." He said to him the third time, "Simon, son of John, do you love [Gk: philo] me?" Peter was grieved because He said to him the third time, "Do you love [Gk: philo] me?" And he said to Him, "Lord, You know all things; you know that I love [Gk: philo] you." Jesus said to him, "Tend My sheep." (John 21:15–17 NASB)

This is a very interesting portion of Scripture. Notice that John refers to Peter as Simon Peter, whereas Jesus only refers to him as Simon. In some ways, this contrast of names shows Jesus may have been trying to say that Peter had regressed to a level that he was at before Jesus gave him the name Peter ("Rock"). (This naming of Peter was the result of Peter's confession of Jesus as Messiah [Matt. 16:16–18.]) Peter's later denial resulted in the removal of the name. Denial of Jesus is apostasy. Peter had a long road to climb to restoration.

Second, Jesus asked Simon Peter if he loved him more than "these." The phrasing is a bit ambiguous and could mean Peter's profession (fishing), or Jesus could be asking if Peter still thought he loved him (Jesus) more than the other disciples did. On the night he betrayed Jesus, Peter had bragged that even though all the others would reject Jesus, he would not (Matt. 26:33). I rather like this second meaning because it would mean that Jesus was reminding Peter of his past failing (as he restores him). He also showed it was a failure of *love*. After each of Jesus's questions, he asked Peter to demonstrate his love by "feeding" (spiritually nourishing) Jesus's followers (the lambs). Chapter one is based on this principle.

Also notice the Greek words translated "love" give this passage an incredibly different meaning in the Greek as opposed to the English. The words that Jesus used for the first two occurrences of "love" are more intense (agapao) than Peter's (philo). As we have seen, agapao can be thought of as godly love, while philo can be thought of as brotherly love. The first two times Jesus asked Peter if he loved him, Jesus used agapao, but Peter only replied that he loved Jesus with a brotherly love. Most likely, he was embarrassed by his failure and didn't want to claim the higher level of love Jesus was asking. Finally, on the third question, Jesus lowered the standard of love he asked about. This third time he asked Peter if he loved him like a brother. Peter became angry at this lowering of the standard and told Jesus, "You know I love you like a brother." Philo love is given to those you know and like and who like you in return. But maybe Peter got angry because he remembered Matthew 5:46 where Jesus said, "If you love those who love you, what reward will you get? Are not even the tax collectors doing that?" Jesus then explained to Peter that he was going to need a higher standard of love if he was not going to fall away again.

> "Truly, truly, I say to you, when you were younger, you used to gird yourself and walk wherever you wished; but when you grow old, you will stretch out your hands and someone else will gird you, and bring you where you do not wish to go." Now this He said, signifying by what kind of death he would glorify God. And when He had spoken this, He said to him, "Follow Me!" (John 21:18–19 NASB)

In this way, Jesus was telling Peter (and us) that philo love would not be enough. Agapao love was going to be necessary in the future in order for Peter (and us) to overcome and become victorious.

As we know, Peter became a leader of the church, a great evangelist, and a writer of two epistles that bear his name. He also overcame his trial at the end of his life. Tradition tells us that he was crucified upside down on a Roman cross. Jesus does not remove all from the trial; to some he says, "Follow me."

If Peter fell away after spending three and a half years with our Lord, we must beware to arrogantly say (as Peter did) that we would die first before betraying our Lord. Rather, we need to pray that we will all be filled with agapao love for Jesus to the point where we lay our own interests aside. The pressure to commit apostasy during the Seventieth Week will leverage everything: our jobs, homes, food, family, our very lives, etc. If we value anything higher than Jesus, we risk falling into apostasy. Most in the Western church today "love" Jesus. But do they love Jesus more than their spouses and children? Do they love Jesus more than their jobs; or is their love just philo love?

Knowing that we will face the great tribulation is a wonderful blessing! Thinking about that trial helps us focus on our relationship to Jesus and what it will take to overcome the Seventieth Week. This is why the *pretribulation rapture* theory is such a trap; it allows its exponents to believe they can enter the kingdom with less than a sold-out, agapao love for Jesus. It allows them to think they can get by without giving up everything to follow him. **Proper understanding of rapture timing, however, blesses us by allowing us to devalue the things of this world**, which we will only leave behind anyway.

THE SECOND KEY

If the greatest commandment is to love the Lord our God with our heart, soul, mind, and strength, the other half of that greatest commandment is the *second key* to overcoming the Seventieth Week: *love your neighbor as yourself.* The two most powerful expressions of that love will be *evangelism* and *forgiveness.*

Jesus surrendered everything to save the lost:

> Jesus, who, although He existed in the form of God, did not regard equality with God a thing to be grasped, but emptied Himself, taking the form of a bond-servant, and being made in the likeness of men. Being found in appearance as a man, He humbled Himself by becoming obedient to the point of death, even death on a cross. (Phil. 2:5–8 NASB)

We are commanded to have this same attitude—to give up everything we have to accomplish that mission as well. Look at what Jesus had to say in Luke's version of the Olivet Discourse about our testimonies during the Seventieth Week:

> But before all these things, they will lay their hands on you and will persecute you, delivering you to the synagogues [Gk: *synagogas,* meaning "assemblies"] and prisons, bringing you before kings and governors for My name's sake. *It will lead to an opportunity for your testimony.* (Luke 21:12–13 NASB, emphasis mine)

During the Seventieth Week, persecution will lead to testimony. Numerous *pretribulation rapture* theorists have critiqued the *prewrath rapture* by stating that sanctification of the saints is an insufficient reason for them enduring the Seventieth Week. This passage from Luke shows that another purpose of the Seventieth Week is the *testimony* of the saints, not just sanctification. (Although Dan. 11:35 and 12:10 show it's a component). We know that the gospel will be preached in the whole world. One way will be through the persecution and testimony of the saints!

Now this testimony will be twofold. Of course, it will be given to the lost. But that is only one of its targets. Fellow Christians will need to see agapao love modeled before them. The way sold-out Christians live their lives in those days of persecution will encourage those around them to do the same. The prophet Daniel speaks of this:

> Those who have insight will shine brightly like the brightness of the expanse of heaven, and those who lead the many to righteousness, like the stars forever and ever. (Dan. 12:3 NASB)

In 2017 in the Middle East, we are seeing a microcosm of what the worldwide persecutions of those days will be like, as ISIS is committing genocide of Christians in that region. Yet, in the midst of the slaughter, more Muslims have come to Christ in the sixteen years since 9/11 than in the previous fourteen centuries![112] Martyrdom truly is the seed of the church. God uses that testimony to draw people to himself. As strange as it may sound, God can use it as a means of evangelism; of course, those martyred will be richly rewarded by God in the next life.

FORGIVE US OUR DEBTS AS WE FORGIVE

Forgiveness will also be a means of testimony. Horrific things will be done by the forces of the Antichrist. We are still commanded to forgive the way Jesus did as he hung dying on the cross. The testimony of former Nazi concentration camp survivor Corrie ten Boom highlights the power of forgiveness. Her story involves forgiving, years later, one of her Nazi tormentors:

> "I, who had spoken so glibly of forgiveness, fumbled in my pocketbook rather than take that hand [of her tormentor]. He would not remember me, of course—how could he remember one prisoner among those thousands of women? But I remembered him and the leather crop swinging from his belt. It was the first time since my release that I had been face to face with one of my captors and my blood seemed to freeze."
>
> "You mentioned Ravensbrück in your talk," he was saying. "I was a guard in there." No, he did not remember me.
>
> "But since that time," he went on, "I have become a Christian. I know that God has forgiven me for the cruel things I did there, but I would like to hear it from your lips as well. *Fräulein*"— again the hand came out—"will you forgive me?" . . . "And so woodenly, mechanically, I thrust my hand into the one stretched out to me. And as I did, an incredible thing took place. The current started in my shoulder, raced down my arm, sprang into our joined hands. And then this healing warmth seemed to flood my whole being, bringing tears to my eyes."
>
> "I forgive you, brother!" I cried. "With all my heart!" —Corrie ten Boom (clarification mine)[113]

We, too, need to be as willing to practice forgiveness of others, even after horrendous things have happened to us. God understands, and he will help us be more like Jesus.

Apocalyptic Evangelism

The *pretribulation rapture* theory's concept of imminence will disarm the church during this time prior to and including the Seventieth Week. Prophecies fulfilled before your eyes can have an awesome impact on evangelism. If one believes there are no more prophecies to be fulfilled (as with a belief in imminence), they will miss this enormous opportunity.

Apocalyptic evangelism is a form of evangelism that uses *fulfilled prophecy as a basis to prove the claims of Jesus* and the Bible. This technique was most dramatically utilized by Peter in his sermon on the day of Pentecost (Shavuot) as seen in Acts 2:

> This is what was spoken of through the prophet Joel: "And it shall be in the last days," God says, "That *I will pour forth of My Spirit on all mankind; and your sons and your daughters shall prophesy*, and your young men shall see visions, and your old men shall dream dreams; Even on My bondslaves, both men and women, I will in those days pour forth of My Spirit and they shall prophesy. And I will grant wonders in the sky above and signs on the earth below, blood, and fire, and vapor of smoke. The sun will be turned into darkness and the moon into blood, before the great and glorious *day of the Lord* shall come. And it shall be that everyone who calls on the name of the Lord will be saved." (Acts 2:16–21 NASB, emphasis mine)

First, Peter identified the prophecy that the Israelites were seeing fulfilled before their eyes: the pouring out of God's Spirit. Peter also mentioned the supernatural darkening of the sky upon Jesus's crucifixion as "just as you yourselves know" (Acts 2:22). Peter then quoted a second prophecy from Psalm 16, which they would have recognized:

> I saw the Lord always in my presence; For He is at my right hand, so that I will not be shaken. "Therefore my heart was glad and my tongue exulted; Moreover my flesh also will live in hope; Because *You will not abandon my soul to Hades, nor allow Your Holy One to undergo decay.* You have made known to me the ways of life; You will make me full of gladness with Your presence." (Acts 2:25–28 NASB, emphasis mine)

All those in attendance knew the rumors of Jesus having risen from the dead. Peter showed how this prophecy from Psalms could only apply to Jesus and not to its author David. The result of Peter's sermon (and the working of the Holy Spirit through the Word) was that three thousand were saved and baptized on that one day.

Believers will most likely have the opportunity to utilize this technique in the coming years as they see end-time prophecies fulfilled. They will be able to say, "This is what God's Word said would take place." It will be a powerful evangelistic tool; *if* those Christians *believe* that there will be prophecies to fulfill prior to Jesus's return and *recognize* the prophecies when they are being fulfilled before their eyes.

PREPARING THE CHURCH

In addition to preparing themselves for the Seventieth Week, Christians are responsible to help prepare their brothers and sisters in Christ. In the letter to the church of Pergamum, Jesus specifically tells us that he will hold believers *responsible* for the morality and beliefs of others in our churches:

214

I have a few things against you, because you have there some who hold the teaching of Balaam, who kept teaching Balak to put a stumbling block before the sons of Israel, to eat things sacrificed to idols and to commit acts of immorality. (Rev. 2:14 NASB, emphasis mine)

The first aspect of preparing the churches is to awaken as many believers as possible to the biblical truth about rapture timing and the fact that we will face the great tribulation. Unless brothers and sisters are awake, they won't be receptive to other preparatory steps. Distributing as many copies of this book as possible is an excellent first step in that process. A ten-week small group Bible study is also available. If you wish to email me directly regarding how to accomplish this or to arrange a conference or speaking engagement, feel free to contact me at *nelson@thegospelintheendtimes.com*.

In my teaching ministry, I have frequently heard stories similar to the following:

I told the person I was with some things I had learned about the *prewrath rapture*. This person shot down what I said and told me that a *pretrib. rapture* is most likely because the Bible says that "no one knows the day or the hour." – Janae S.

What this *pretribulation rapture* believer espoused to Janae was a sound bite, not a proof; a ten-second dismissal of her idea.

In order to counter a sound bite, it is often helpful to provide a "counter sound bite" to get the other person thinking. Then, I recommend giving them a copy of this book, which does a *complete* job of answering

215

their strongly held beliefs. Examples of answers to sound bites are found in the following graphic:

Sound Bite	Counter Sound Bite
The church isn't found between Revelation 4–19	The word "church" in Revelation only refers to seven *specific* churches by name. It isn't the church universal. However, "Why isn't the church pictured in heaven in Rev. 4–5 at the beginning of the tribulation if it's already raptured?"
Jesus said we can't know the day or hour of his return	Jesus said we couldn't know the day or hour of "that day," which has to refer to a day he referenced in the Olivet Discourse. He did not reference a *pretrib. rapture*, so it cannot be "that day"; it has to refer to Matt. 24:30–31, which describes a different timing of the rapture
Jesus said we will be resurrected on the "last day"	Did you notice Jesus didn't say the last day of "what?" Was it the last day of the millennial kingdom, his return, or Satan's rule? Did you ever notice that in the Olivet Discourse, Jesus gave us the first six seals of Revelation as signs of his coming, but never mentioned the trumpets or bowls? Why was that?

Figure 21: Sound Bites and Counter Sound Bites

My friend, Janae, might apply the following answer to the sound bite she received above from her acquaintance:

> You know, that is exactly what the verse says. But did you ever notice Jesus said we couldn't know the day or hour of "that day." Grammatically, this verse had to be about a day he had just referred to, and because he didn't mention a *pretrib. rapture*, it couldn't be "that day." When I learned that it shocked me because I'd never heard that before. But I've been reading this new book, *Rapture: Case Closed?* that answers most of the questions I ever had about the rapture. May I give you a copy?

PREPARING FOR THE SIGNS OF JESUS'S COMING

We now know that Christians will encounter the *six signs of Jesus's coming* (the first six seals). An excellent second step is to prepare our churches for what Jesus has plainly told us will occur during each sign.

DECEPTION BY FALSE MESSIAHS

The *first sign* that Jesus gave us is that false messiahs will arise:

> See to it that no one misleads you. For many will come in my name, saying, "I am the Christ," and will mislead many . . . Then if anyone says to you, "Behold, here is the Christ," or "There *He is*," do not believe him. For false Christs and false prophets will arise and will show great signs and wonders, so as to mislead, if possible, even the elect. Behold, I have told you in advance. So

if they say to you, "Behold, *He* is in the wilderness," do not go
out, *or*, "Behold, *He* is in the inner rooms," do not believe *them*.
(Matt. 24:4–5, 23–26 NASB, emphasis mine)

Jesus has specifically told us that his parousia will be like lightning from the
east to the west (Matt. 24:27). It will be unmistakable and it will follow the
celestial earthly disturbance, which will also be unmistakable. However,
Jesus warns us that false messiahs and prophets will arise prior to these
events. These false messiahs may claim to be Jesus (they will come in his
name) and will perform great signs and wonders. This will be such a great
deception that only those who are spiritually prepared will be able to resist.
Jesus said the false messiahs will mislead many, and if possible, even the
elect. These signs will not be some magic tricks; they will be demonically
empowered wonders. Those within the church that are attracted to signs and
wonders and are not discerning will be especially vulnerable.

The Muslims expect Jesus to return in the person of Isa (the Muslim
Jesus). If he arises, this *false* Jesus will support the claims of the Mahdi, the
Muslim Messiah. The Jews expect two messiahs: Messiah ben Joseph and
Messiah ben David. Should demonically empowered men arise to fill these
roles prophesied by the heretical Muslim Scriptures and the teaching of the
Jewish rabbis, the deception may be great indeed. We must prepare our
churches for what the true signs will be.

WARS AND CHAOS

The *second sign* is war and chaos. Fear is an overriding emotion. God
anticipates that people will be fearful from the second seal on. That is why
he instructs us, "See that you are not frightened, for those *things must take*

place" (Matt. 24:6 NASB, clarification and emphasis mine). Jesus is telling us that he has all things under his control; that these *things must take place* before the kingdom is ushered in.

Fear of pain and death are at the top of the list of our human fears. In the letter to Smyrna, Jesus lays these fears wide open; he tells us we should anticipate *prison and death*:

> *Do not fear what you are about to suffer.* Behold, the devil is about to cast some of you into *prison*, so that you will be tested, and *you will have tribulation for ten days. Be faithful until death, and I will give you the crown of life . . .* He who *overcomes* will not be hurt by the *second death*. (Rev. 2:10–11 NASB, emphasis mine)

Jesus has let us know these are *things that must take place*. The Seventieth Week of Daniel is not an accident; it is the sovereign will of Jesus. And Jesus has prepared a role for us in it, but in order to assume that role we must not fear:

> But for *the cowardly* and unbelieving and abominable and murderers and immoral persons and sorcerers and idolaters and all liars, their part will be in the *lake that burns with fire and brimstone*, which is the *second death*. (Rev. 21:8, emphasis mine)

Notice that the first category of those who will face the second death are the cowardly. This is incredible! How many Christians in our Western churches are *expecting* to lay their lives down for Jesus and the gospel? How many will be *afraid* and *frozen* from proper action or hide when the time comes to choose life or faithfulness? Jesus expects us to follow his command and *love him more than our own life*. "For whoever wishes to save his life will lose it, but whoever loses his life for My sake, he is the one who will save it" (Luke 9:24 NASB). God expects us to bring his gospel to a dying world regardless of the cost.

During the second sign of Jesus's return, he specifically commands us to not be frightened:

> You will be hearing of wars and rumors of wars. *See that you are not frightened*, for *those things* must take place, but that is not yet the end. For nation will rise against nation, and *kingdom against kingdom*. (Matt. 24:6–7 NASB, emphasis mine)

Jesus warns Christians to not be frightened because events that surround this sign would frighten most people. This fear will drive more unsuspecting people into apostasy, causing them to worship the Antichrist. This is why this warning is so important—we must never worship the Antichrist.

> They worshiped the beast, saying, "Who is like the beast, and who is able to wage war with him?" (Rev. 13:4 NASB, emphasis mine)

Notice that it is the Antichrist's prowess in war that leads many to worship him. Jesus also gives us a hint *where* some of these wars will take place by quoting the phrase "kingdom against kingdom" from Isaiah:

> So *I will incite Egyptians against Egyptians*; and they will each
> fight against his brother and each against his neighbor, city
> against city *and kingdom against kingdom.* (Isa. 19:2 NASB,
> emphasis mine)

In my opinion, this is strong evidence that the war that begins at the second
seal will involve an Egyptian civil war which the Antichrist will join.

FAMINE AND ECONOMIC COLLAPSE

The *third sign* that Jesus gave us is famine and economic collapse. The
church is divided on whether we should prepare for the apocalypse to come.
Some are putting away gold, groceries, and guns and planning to
be survivalists. Others plan to trust that God will provide in days that are
approaching and aren't preparing at all. So, what does Scripture say? Is
there a verse in the New Testament in which Jesus clearly teaches that we
should put food away for the hard times? Does Jesus want Christians to
become preppers? Shockingly, the answer is yes, and there *is* a verse that
supports this idea—Matthew 24:45:

> Who then is the faithful and sensible slave whom his master put
> in charge of his household *to give them their food* at the proper
> time [Gk: *kairos*, meaning "appointed time")? (Matt. 24:45
> NASB, emphasis mine)

As a church, we tend to read past this highly important yet obscure verse
found in Matthew's version of the Olivet Discourse. One day a few years

ago, it struck me that Jesus was giving us a riddle. He is asking *"Who* is this wise and faithful slave?" We have three clues:

- He is a wise slave
- He is put in charge of his master's household
- He provides food for that household at the appointed time

Have you guessed the riddle yet? The answer is Joseph, the wise and faithful slave that Potiphar put in charge of his household (Gen. 39:1–6) and, later, that Pharaoh put in charge of Egypt (Gen. 41:33–57). Joseph provided food for that household, both Hebrews and Egyptians, as well as later, for all of Egypt in the seven-year famine. Once we solve the riddle of this verse, its meaning opens up to us: Jesus wants us to be Joseph for *his* household in the coming "appointed time."

We need to stop and pause. If you are not familiar with this teaching, I am certain your jaw has just dropped. Jesus wants us to be a Joseph for his household? Yes, he does. He doesn't want us to only prepare for our own household, but for *his household*. There is an incredible difference. Christians who are preppers for their own households store up gold, guns, and groceries for themselves. Many plan to escape the hard times and hide in a mountain retreat or a bunker. I call these persons "survivalists." Jesus is calling us to provide for his household: *both the Jewish remnant and the church*. I call the persons who will sacrificially provide for the "least of these" during hard times "revivalists."

Jesus also indicates that he wants us to provide this food at a specific time, and it is critically important to understand what this time is. Joseph stored up food to provide it during the appointed time of the seven-year famine that occurred in the Middle East in those days. In so doing, he saved the lives of his brothers and their families in addition to saving numerous Egyptians. Jesus is calling us to provide his household with food during the coming appointed time. What might that time be? Just a few verses earlier in Jesus's Olivet Discourse, he taught the disciples that there would be famines during the beginning of the birth pangs period (the first three and a half years of the Seventieth Week of Daniel). Might this be the appointed time? I believe it is.

We also know that the False Prophet will institute the mark of the beast during the Seventieth Week:

> He causes all, the small and the great, and the rich and the poor, and the free-men and the slaves, to be given a mark on their right hand or on their forehead, and he provides that no one will be able to buy or to sell, except the one who has *the mark*, either the name of the beast or the number of his name. (Rev. 13:16– 17 NASB, emphasis mine)

Is the mark of the beast directly tied to the famines? Do the False Prophet and Antichrist take advantage of the food shortage to offer a "solution" in the form of a new economic system that provides food? **We know that taking this mark and participating in this economic system leads to eternal damnation. This is important stuff.**

If this scenario is accurate, millions or billions of hungry people might readily take the mark to avoid starvation. What if Christians had food stored up and were able to provide it to some of those in need at this time? Would this stored food be part of the impetus for those needy to reject the mark of the beast and come to faith in Jesus? It is an interesting and intriguing theory. In Jesus's letter to the church at Pergamum, we read:

But I have a few things against you, because you have there *some* who hold the teaching of Balaam, who kept teaching Balak to put a stumbling block before the sons of Israel, *to eat things sacrificed to idols* and to commit *acts of* immorality. (Rev. 2:14 NASB)

First, notice Jesus says there are "some" in the church who hold to false teaching and Jesus holds this against the *entire* church. This clearly teaches Jesus holds us responsible for his entire household. Second, part of the false "teaching of Balaam" was to cause Israel to eat unholy food that was sacrificed to idols. In a modern analogy, might this be food purchased through the mark of the beast? Might prepared Christians be able to help their fellow brothers and sisters resist the mark if they have food to share?

PACK YOUR LUNCH

How will we ever be able to provide food for our entire church, you might ask? You won't be, obviously. But you might be able to "pack your lunch." Jesus's feeding of the five thousand is instructive. The disciples first came to Jesus and recommended he send the crowds away to find food. Jesus then asked the disciples to feed them. The puzzled disciples were only able to find a young boy with a lunch of two fish and five loaves. From this simple lunch, Jesus was able to feed the huge crowd.

The faith of this boy who packed his lunch and willingly gave it to the Master to distribute to help feed the crowd was what Jesus desired to see. From this simple act, the crowd experienced a great miracle. If we "pack our lunch" and willingly give it to others during the appointed time, will Jesus multiply our efforts? I think this well may be the case.

This also brings up the point of solely relying on the provision of God *without effort on our own.* Jesus acted upon the faith of the young boy. The boy packed food because he knew he'd need it. He planned to stay and listen to Jesus as long as he could, and he planned in advance to do so by packing a lunch. He then willingly surrendered all he had. We know there will be famines; Jesus has told us as much. Isn't it presuming upon the Lord to believe he will provide for us without any effort on our parts to contribute to that provision? Yes, Jesus will provide for us, but don't we share in the responsibility to do what we can, and then to rely on him to do what only he can? We observe that pattern repeatedly in Scripture.

When the appointed time comes, there will be many more important issues than our survival. Once the Seventieth Week of Daniel begins, the great countdown to the return of our King will also begin. We will be entering the two-minute warning, to use a football analogy. Strategies we have employed previously will need to be modified.

Revivalist preppers will step out in faith and use the food they have stored up to bolster the faith of those who haven't prepared. In this way, they likely will participate in a great miracle and possibly the salvation of many souls. The "food" they provide will likely be physical food as well as "spiritual" food in terms of the gospel!

Survivalist preppers will horde their food and attempt to survive at all costs. With Jesus only a few years away at that point, does that even make sense? Do you want to spend your last days hiding in a bunker eating beans, or do you want to participate in the great spiritual battle against Satan and the kingdoms of this world that will "prepare the way of the Lord?"

Which prepper will you be?

In the three versions of Jesus's Olivet Discourse in the gospel accounts (Matthew, Mark, and Luke), he instructed us with over thirty commands to be *observant*, to *see*, and to be *watchful*.[114] The reason he instructs us to be watchful is because in the Olivet Discourse he gives us a number of signs. We will only see them if we watch. The most significant sign, the *fourth sign*, is the abomination of desolation that occurs at the midpoint of the Seventieth Week of Daniel:

> Therefore *when you **see** the abomination of desolation* which was spoken of through Daniel the prophet, standing in the holy place (let the reader understand), then those who are in Judea must flee to the mountains. (Matt. 24:15–16 NASB, emphasis mine)

Jesus wants us to be watchful so we can see the signs he has warned us about. These signs form a chronology (Gk. *chronos*) which Paul assumes Christians will understand (1 Thess. 5:1). Paul assumes we will be familiar with the chronology of the end times because it was given to us by Jesus in the Olivet Discourse. Paul expects us to have committed these signs to memory to help ourselves and others.

When believers see this horrible sign of the abomination of desolation set up upon the newly rebuilt temple of God, they can know that the *physical* return of our Savior to the earth is only *forty-two months away*. That is all the time that the Antichrist is given authority. At that point, believers can also know that the resurrection and *prewrath rapture* is earlier than his physical coming. With that little time remaining, what should their strategy be: survivalist or revivalist? Jesus inspired John to quote Jeremiah 15:2 in this passage in Revelation:

> If anyone is *destined for captivity,* to captivity he goes; if anyone kills with the sword, with the sword he must be killed. *Here is the perseverance and the faith of the saints.* (Rev. 13:10 NASB, emphasis mine)

Trying to be a survivalist will be pointless. Many are destined for captivity or death. True faith is shining the light of Jesus even in the midst of persecution. This will be especially important to demonstrate and model before our weaker brothers and sisters.

THE GREAT TRIBULATION

The *fifth sign,* the great tribulation, will be one of the most significant events in world history. It will be *a time of decision.* The *eternal destiny* of much of the world will hang in a balance. Most Christians will be forced to choose between physical death (and spiritual life) or physical life (and spiritual death). This will be a monumental choice. How Christians handle this public decision will have an *eternal impact* on those watching: both unbelievers and those whose faith might be weak. In the letter to Sardis, with application to the church during this time, Jesus addresses this concern:

> Wake up, and *strengthen the things that remain, which were about to die*; for *I have not found your deeds completed in the sight of My God.* So remember what you have received and

heard; and keep it and repent. (Rev. 3:2–3 NASB, emphasis mine)

Jesus's command is to *strengthen the things that were about to die*. This may have a personal application (strengthening our own faith), but it also has a corporate application. By the testimony of our words and deeds (martyrdom), we can strengthen the resolve and faith of those watching, both unbelievers and believers. It will be the greatest time of witness the world has ever seen. Christians may have been through a lot during the first years of the Seventieth Week, but God's Word is telling them that their deeds are not completed. They still need to witness during this most significant time, during the great tribulation. That witness may include *martyrdom*.

This idea of strengthening those who are weak is a direct reference to the book of Hebrews, which teaches on the purpose of suffering, even unto death:

You have not yet *resisted to the point of shedding blood* in your striving against sin; and you have forgotten the exhortation which is addressed to you as sons, "My son, do not regard lightly the *discipline of the Lord*, nor faint when you are reproved by Him; for those whom the Lord loves He disciplines, and He scourges every son whom He receives [direct quote of Prov. 3:7]." . . . *He disciplines us for our good, so that we may share His holiness*. All discipline for the moment seems not to be joyful, but sorrowful; yet to those who have been trained by it, afterwards it yields the peaceful fruit of righteousness.

Therefore, *strengthen the hands that are weak.* (Heb. 12:4–6,
10–12 NASB, clarification and emphasis mine)

God disciplines us so we can become holy as he is holy. It is interesting that
this passage also references resisting to the point of shedding blood, which
occurs during the great tribulation, and *strengthening the weak.*

God's promise of reward to those that suffer is great. "He who
overcomes will thus be *clothed in white garments*; and I will *not erase his
name* from the *book of life,* and *I will confess his name before My Father
and before His angels*" (Rev. 3:5 NASB, emphasis mine). These are the
ones who will participate in the wedding supper of the Lamb. A momentary
trial that is overcome will lead to this greatest of rewards.

In Jesus's letter to the church of Sardis, he wrote these instructions:
"*Wake up and strengthen* the things that remain." Notice, Jesus's command
is to *wake up* first, and then to *strengthen the things that remain* (those who
have not yet committed apostasy). This command to wake up is a reference
to the parable of the ten virgins, which we examined in chapter one:
"Solving the Cold Case." In our previous discussion of this parable, we
mentioned that all ten virgins (the entire church) will be asleep prior to
Jesus's parousia, but a cry will go out at midnight to go out and "meet" the
bridegroom. Midnight is the darkest hour. It is my opinion that the midnight
cry is the abomination of desolation and the beginning of the great
tribulation. It will be impossible for the church to remain asleep at that time.
All ten virgins go out into the world, and all of them light their torches (GK:
lampas), which are symbolic of our testimonies. However, only half of them
have enough oil to keep their torches burning during that dark time. The oil
symbolizes agapao love for Jesus empowered by the Holy Spirit.

229

Unfortunately, those without agapao love will most likely fall away (their lamps go out). Not only might they fall away, but Jesus tells us many will betray their brothers and sisters. In Daniel 11:34, the prophet also tells us during that time "many will join with them [the saints] in hypocrisy," probably for the purpose of betraying them as well. It will be a time of great deceit. Yet, it is the perseverance and faith of the saints to ignore the risks and continue their testimony. Jesus comes and takes those whose lamps are still burning into the wedding feast.

THE CELESTIAL EARTHLY DISTURBANCE

But those days (the days of the great tribulation) will be cut short, most likely by the *sixth sign*, the celestial earthly disturbance. This will be a time of great terror for the unrighteous, but a sign of rejoicing for the saints. Jesus tells us:

> But when these things [the darkening of the sun, etc.] begin to take place, straighten up and lift up your heads, because your redemption is drawing near. (Luke 21:28 NASB, clarification mine)

While the rest of the world is hiding in caves, Christians are to lift their heads because Jesus's parousia has almost come.

The celestial earthly disturbance reminds us dramatically of the rapture, and reminds us that false rapture theories are dangerous. They have the potential to lull the church to sleep; sleeping saints cannot be watchful. The time to wake up is not during the great tribulation when the choice of life and death is set before them. The time to wake up is *now* so that they (we) can help awaken the church.

The Gospel in the End Times Ministries is dedicated to awakening the church. I suggest you to volunteer to join this worthy effort at www.thegospelintheendtimes.com.

> **The time to awaken the church from the error of false rapture theories is now.**

Proper understanding of the rapture and its timing, at the present time, may lead a person to strengthen their faith to evangelize now and to participate in the resurrection and rapture later.

In the recent rapture timing debate between Alan Kurschner and Dr. Thomas Ice, Mr. Kurschner mentioned that if the *pretribulation rapture* position is mistaken, it is a great threat to the church. Dr. Ice responded that if it is mistaken, Christians will still dutifully go to a martyr's death just as saints throughout the ages have done. His position is that the *pretribulation rapture* theory is of no risk to the church, even if it is wrong.[115] I am sure Dr. Ice is correct that *some* Christians will overcome the Seventieth Week despite having no preparation. Jesus, however, states that half of the virgins are foolish and they will be shut out of the wedding feast. My heart breaks for the foolish virgins. Hopefully, now that you are aware of proper rapture timing, yours does as well.

SUMMARY

Even the apostle Peter needed to be reminded that it would take agapao love of Jesus for him to tolerate the trails ahead and overcome them. Peter bragged to Jesus on the night he was betrayed that even if all the other disciples committed apostasy, he would not. That did not turn out so well. After Peter's fall from grace, Jesus asked him if he still thought he loved Jesus "more than these" (the other disciples). We must not be as presumptuous as Peter was. Our love of Jesus and our work in preparation of the church must be our number-one focus. We can summarize this needed preparation in the graphic.

Six Principles of Overcoming
1) Spiritually prepare by loving and trusting Jesus alone and displaying that love to the world.
"Love the Lord your God with all your heart, and with all your soul, and with all your mind, and with all your strength." The second is this, "You shall love your neighbor as yourself." (Mark 12:30–31 NASB)
2) Emotionally prepare for tribulation (imprisonment and martyrdom).
Do not fear what you are about to suffer . . . Be faithful until death, and I will give you the crown of life. (Rev. 2:10 NASB)
3) Prepare now to be "Joseph" to provide food at the "appointed time."
Who then is the faithful and sensible slave whom his master put in charge of his household to give them their food at the proper time? (Matt. 24:45 NASB)
4) Be watchful of the chronologic signs of Jesus's return and use in evangelism.
Keep watching and praying that you may not enter into temptation; the spirit is willing, but the flesh is weak. (Matt. 26:41)

Six Principles of Overcoming
5) Use our response to tribulation as a means of witness to the unsaved and encouragement to the weak in faith.   *He disciplines us for our good, so that we may share His holiness. All discipline for the moment seems not to be joyful, but sorrowful; yet to those who have been trained by it, afterwards it yields the peaceful fruit of righteousness. Therefore, strengthen the hands that are weak. (Heb. 12:10–12 NASB)*
6) Awaken the church from the error of false rapture theories.   *But the Spirit explicitly says that in later times some will fall away from the faith, paying attention to deceitful spirits (1 Tim. 4:1 NASB)*

Figure 22: Six Principles of Overcoming

All of the members of the church need to be involved in this preparation so that each of us can be overcomers in the days ahead, as we watch for the signs Jesus has given us related to his coming. We need to prepare individually and teach this in our churches.

Of course, the first step in preparation is to accept the position on the timing of the rapture which is so clearly taught in Scripture and as presented in this book. Those members of the church alive at the time will go through much tribulation before being rescued by the rapture. May God grant us all wisdom and strength to overcome until he comes again—our blessed hope! Unfortunately, the *pretribulation rapture* theory has the potential to cause believers to assume that something less than a complete sold-out love for Jesus will be enough. But as we have learned, only agapao love will save. As Jesus commanded Peter and the others on the night he was betrayed, "Watch and pray."

As you have considered the evidence in this book you have probably come to the conclusion that the rapture cold case is closed. The church will face the Antichrist prior to being rescued in a *prewrath rapture*. And after reading the suggestions for preparation in this chapter, you may be realizing that you may face your own personal tribulation in coming to grips with what must be done. Many of our readers have spent a career espousing a rapture theory that Christians will be spared from the hard times to come. Now that we know that believers will face the Antichrist, a decision must be made only you can answer:

> **Will you risk your reputation, career, and friendships to save the souls of those under your leadership?**

May God grant you the wisdom, strength, and courage to follow him.

Epilogue for Leaders

> *For though we walk in the flesh, we do not war according to*
> *the flesh, for the weapons of our warfare are not of the flesh,*
> *but divinely powerful for the destruction of fortresses. We are*
> *destroying speculations and every lofty thing raised up against*
> *the knowledge of God, and we are taking every thought captive*
> *to the obedience of Christ. (2 Cor. 10:3–5 NASB)*

Y ou have completed the book. Perhaps you previously believed and taught a different rapture timing theory than what this book presents, and your head might be spinning right now. It is a scary thought to consider that you may have believed something different than what the Bible teaches. You are not alone. The statistics we present in appendix A indicate that 96% of pastors believe in a rapture theory other than the *prewrath rapture*. Nearly every leader who has read this book faces the same dilemma. I personally confronted this crossroad a dozen years ago, so I know that many questions hang in the air for you:

- Is this book correct? Will the rapture be *prewrath*? How can you test this theory?
- If it is, what impact will this knowledge have on your ministry?
- What impact will this knowledge have on your denominational and group affiliations?
- What impact will this knowledge have on your friendships with other leaders?

As strange as it seems, some of these questions are the answers! By that, I mean that you are not alone; you have friends, board members, elders, and denominational leaders with whom you have shared a relationship for many years. They are persons you trust to properly handle the Word of God. These friends are your greatest resource. So don't worry about the impact this new knowledge will have on your ministry just yet until you are absolutely convinced what this book presents is true. Together, you and these friends can decide that issue. "Where there is no guidance the people fall, but in abundance of counselors there is victory" (Prov. 11:14 NASB).

I strongly recommend continuing your journey to truth by sitting down with one or more of your friends and sharing this book with them. The Word of God will stand up to your scrutiny. If you and your group of friends decide that this book has factually presented the biblical case, then together you can begin to address how to change your position on the rapture for each of your respective ministries.

The most important issue to remember in all of this is that the *eternal fate of millions may hang in the balance*. As teachers, Jesus has made us responsible for those souls.

A second aspect to consider is that the truth sets us free. Changing your position on the rapture may seem like a personal tribulation, but after doing an exhaustive examination of Scripture (by working through this book), you will know without a doubt what the true timing of the rapture will be. This is freeing.

Our ministry realizes, however, that you may need additional help in this admittedly difficult process. Feel free to contact us as well. Whatever resources are at our disposal, we will make available for you. After all, what could be more important? Our contact information follows:

The Gospel in the End Times Ministries

www.TheGospelInTheEndTimes.com

nelson@thegospelintheendtimes.com

May God grant you grace and wisdom in your search for truth and in your ministry. May He one day say to you: "Well done, good and faithful slave. You were faithful with a few things, I will put you in charge of many things; enter into the joy of your master" (Matt. 25:21 NASB).

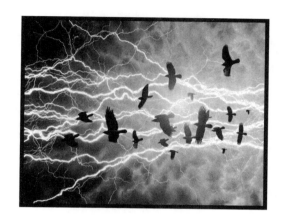

APPENDICES

Appendix A

SUMMARY OF RAPTURE TIMING THEORIES

WHAT IS THE RAPTURE?

I realize that we come from different backgrounds and different understandings of what the rapture is all about. In the next few sections, let me take a moment to unpack the meaning behind some of the terms we used throughout this book. You may already know this—the word "rapture" does not appear in the Bible; other words are used that have the same connotation. The most definitive passage concerning this event is found in Paul's first letter to the Thessalonians:

> For the Lord Himself will descend from heaven with a shout, with the voice of the archangel and with the trumpet of God, and *the dead in Christ will rise first*. Then we who are alive and remain *will be caught up* [Gk: harpazo] together with them *in the clouds to meet the Lord in the air*, and so we shall always be with the Lord. (1 Thess. 4:16–17 NASB, emphasis mine)

We return to this verse many times throughout this book, but for our purposes now, let me point out two important facts. First, the rapture is intimately tied to another event—the resurrection of the dead in Christ, which is one of the essential doctrines of the church. As shown in the above Scripture, these two events cannot be separated. To deny the rapture is to deny the resurrection.

Second, as we pointed out earlier, the word rapture does not appear in the Scriptures. The word used in the Greek New Testament is harpazo, which is translated "caught up." Perhaps we should term the rapture the "catching up." But catching up doesn't adequately convey what this Greek word means. HELPS Word-Studies defines harpazo as:

> *Seize by force*; snatch up, suddenly and decisively—like someone seizing bounty (spoil, a prize); to take by *an open display of force* (i.e. not covertly or secretly).[116]

The word conveys a forcible removal in a public way. Most of us have become familiar with hostage situations and the rescue efforts that frequently accompany them. Most of us have seen reenactments or TV dramas that have portrayed police freeing hostages by an active display of force. This is the core meaning of harpazo, that Jesus will rescue his children forcibly, visibly, and quickly. The harpazo will snatch them up quickly and carry them away from danger.

Third, the direction of the rapture is up and into the clouds. 1 Thess. 4:16-17 doesn't' mention how long believers stay "in the clouds" and where the believers go after this initial upward harpazo, but it cannot be denied that they are taken off the ground and into the clouds.

Finally, the rapture is a *relatively* new concept in Scripture. It was a "mystery" during the Old Testament, and was only revealed to the church in New Testament times.

> Behold, I tell you *a mystery*; we will not all sleep [die], but we will all be changed, in a moment, in the twinkling of an eye, at the last trumpet; for the trumpet will sound, and the dead will be raised imperishable, and *we will be changed.* (1 Cor. 15:51–52 NASB, clarification and emphasis mine)

Paul once again links the raising of the dead (the resurrection) with the rapture (see also 1 Thess. 4:16–17), but in the verses above Paul clearly lets us know this was a newly revealed *mystery*. The resurrection appears several times in the Old Testament (Dan. 12:1–2; Ezek. 37, etc.), but the rapture does not (although individuals such as Enoch were raptured). The reason is that the rapture is solely for those who have placed their faith in Jesus.

RAPTURE TIMING THEORIES

There are *five main theories* about the timing of the rapture. One is that there is no rapture at all. Those who hold to a *no-rapture* position include those who believe in preterism (believe the vast majority of prophecy was fulfilled in AD 70) and amillennialism (believe Jesus will not have a literal one-thousand-year reign on earth, as mentioned in Revelation 20). If you want to learn more about why these positions are mistaken, consider Joel Richardson's masterful book, *When a Jew Rules the World*. However, the scope of *Rapture: Case Closed?* is the rapture, and we have already eliminated the no-rapture theory as a viable position in our discussion in the last section. First Thessalonians 4:16–17 clearly leaves no doubt that the rapture event will occur forcibly, visibly, and quickly snatching up believers into the air to rescue them into the presence of Jesus.

The remaining main theories differ as to the *timing* of this event. They are termed the *pretribulation rapture*, the *midtribulation rapture*, the *prewrath rapture*, and the *post-tribulation rapture*.

THE TRIBULATION

All but one of the names we have given the various theories include the word "tribulation," and understanding this time period is essential before we examine the main rapture-timing theories. Like the term "the rapture," the term "the tribulation" does *not* appear in the Bible. It is the expression our culture frequently utilizes to specify the seven-year period of time that precedes the *physical* second coming of Jesus when he, once again, stands upon the earth.

Personally, I don't like the term "the tribulation." I prefer the biblical term, the Seventieth Week of Daniel. The seven-year time period immediately before the physical return of Jesus is derived from a passage in Daniel 9 where it is defined as a seven-year period set aside by God. It is called a week because the Bible on occasion measures time in seven-year increments called shabua that mimic the six days of work, and a Sabbath, comprising a week. In ancient Hebrew culture, God commanded Israel to cultivate the land for six years and then allow the land to remain fallow in the seventh year (Lev. 25:3–4, 8), just as work was not permitted on the Sabbath. This seventh year of the seven-year cycle is thus called the sabbatical year, or shmitah year. In Daniel 9, the angel Gabriel told Daniel:

> Seventy weeks [shabuim] have been decreed for your people and your holy city, to finish the transgression, to make an end of sin, to make atonement for iniquity, to bring in everlasting righteousness, to seal up vision and prophecy and to anoint the most holy place. (Dan. 9:24 NASB, clarification mine)

We see that at the completion of Daniel's Seventieth Week almost all prophecy will be fulfilled, all sin will be atoned for, and an everlasting righteousness will be obtained for those who are in Jesus. This will be fulfilled upon the physical second coming of the Lord. During his earthly ministry, Jesus indicated to us that this period of seventy shabua (seventy weeks, which is seventy times seven years = 490 years) is a time period during which forgiveness will be granted:

> Then Peter came and said to Him, "Lord, how often shall my brother sin against me and I forgive him? Up to seven times?" Jesus said to him, "I do not say to you, up to seven times, but up to *seventy times seven*." (Matt. 18:21–22 NASB, emphasis mine.)

Toward the end of this period of *seventy times seven* years, the judgment of God will come upon the unrepentant, but those declared righteous in Jesus will be saved by the rapture.

The evaluation of the passage in Daniel 9 in light of history indicates that sixty-nine of these shabua have already occurred. This period began with the decree to rebuild Jerusalem following the Babylonian destruction. There is some controversy among Bible commentators about the exact events that frame the *beginning* and *end* of this time period. Regardless of which understanding proves correct, one week still remains. That final shabua, the Seventieth Week of Daniel, is pictured in these verses:

> And he will make a firm covenant with the many for *one week*, but *in the middle of the week* he will put a stop to sacrifice and grain offering; and on the wing of abominations will come one who makes desolate, even until a complete destruction, one that is decreed, is poured out on the one who makes desolate. (Dan. 9:27 NASB, emphasis mine)

Most Bible commentators believe this seven-year period is marked by two halves separated by a midpoint. Each half of the period will be three and a half years long. The first half may include what Jesus termed "the beginning of the birth pangs" (Matt. 24:8). Many commentators call the second half of the period the "great tribulation." However, Jesus never called the second half of the seven-year period the "great tribulation;" he only stated that after the midpoint there would *be* "great tribulation" (Matt. 24:21).

At the midpoint that separates the two halves, several important events occur. The man who is known as the Antichrist is revealed by him sitting in the newly constructed temple of God in Jerusalem (2 Thess. 2:3–4). He will also set up an idol or an abomination of some kind known as the abomination of desolation within the temple (Matt. 24:15). Immediately after these midpoint events, the Antichrist begins the greatest period of persecution the world has ever known—the great tribulation. At the end of the Seventieth Week of Daniel, Jesus will redeem and save the Jews who repent and judge the Antichrist and the False Prophet at an event known as the physical second coming.

Based on this framework of understanding, we will examine the rapture-timing theories which depict how Jesus will save the church.

1) THE *PRETRIBULATION RAPTURE*

Once we understand the concept of the Seventieth Week of Daniel (so-called by some the "tribulation"), the meaning of the *pretribulation rapture* theory becomes apparent—believers are assumed to be raptured *prior* to the Seventieth Week beginning. This theory can be envisioned in the following graphic on the next page. At some point prior to the beginning of Seventieth Week, this theory proposes that Christians will be quietly caught up into the clouds with Jesus. From that point, they will return with Jesus to heaven

246

where they will spend the entire Seventieth Week (seven years) safe from the events taking place on the earth. At the conclusion of the Seventieth Week, most believers in this theory suggest that the Christians will return to the earth with Jesus at the physical second coming.

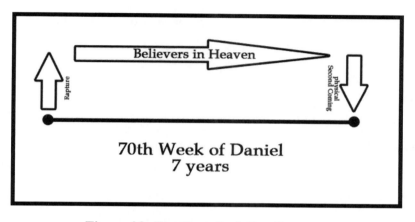

Figure 23: The Pretribulation Rapture

This theory is founded on the principal that God will not permit his followers to endure his wrath (which this theory defines as the *entire* Seventieth Week). This belief is based on the following verses:

> Wait for His Son from heaven, whom He raised from the dead, that is *Jesus, who rescues us from the wrath to come.* (1 Thess. 1:10 NASB, emphasis mine)

> For *God has not destined us for wrath*, but for obtaining salvation through our Lord Jesus Christ. (1 Thess. 5:9 NASB, emphasis mine)

The *pretribulation rapture* theory also supports the doctrine of imminence, which is defined as the rapture being able to occur at any time. This theory holds that no prophecies have to be fulfilled before the rapture, and that it may be (but doesn't have to be) the next event to occur on God's prophetic calendar.

In a 2016 Lifeway Research Survey, 36% of Protestant pastors (43% of Evangelical pastors) believe in a *pretribulation rapture*.

2) THE *POST-TRIBULATION RAPTURE*

The second most popular rapture-timing theory is the *post-tribulation rapture*, which is accepted by 18% of Protestant pastors.[117] As its name implies, this theory proposes that Christians will be caught up into the air at the conclusion of the Seventieth Week of Daniel. Most of the proponents of this theory believe this catching up is primarily a relocation of believers from all over the world so that they all can return with Jesus at the physical second coming. This theory is depicted in the following graphic:

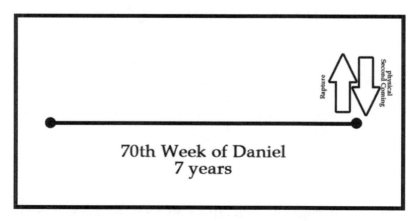

Figure 24: The Post-Tribulation Rapture

This theory suggests that Christians will be caught up into the clouds with Jesus only at the very end of the Seventieth Week of Daniel. Rather than being safe in heaven during the events taking place on the earth, advocates of this theory suppose Christians will endure those events. This theory assumes Christians will be subjected to the wrath of Satan and men, but will be protected from the wrath of God. Many different ideas exist among those who hold this rapture theory on how Christians are protected from God's wrath. Some believe God pours out his wrath after the completion of the Seventieth Week. Others believe that Christians are insulated from the wrath of God while it is poured out on unbelievers much as the ancient Israelites were protected in Goshen from the plagues that befell other parts of Egypt.

This theory also presupposes that the rapture is *not* imminent, but rather that many prophecies are yet to be fulfilled prior to the rapture.

3) THE *PREWRATH RAPTURE*

The *prewrath rapture* theory has, admittedly, by far the fewest proponents (4%),[118] but is rapidly growing in acceptance. Like the *pretribulation rapture* theory, this theory presupposes that God will rapture his church from the earth prior to pouring out his wrath (thus the name *prewrath rapture*). But unlike the *pretribulation rapture* theory, this theory defines the wrath of God as including only the trumpet and bowl judgments described in Revelation, not as being the entire Seventieth Week. In this way, this theory presupposes that Christians will be subjected to the wrath of men (tribulation), including the Antichrist during the Seventieth Week before the rapture occurs, just as the *post-tribulation rapture* theory holds. This rapture theory is depicted in a graphic on the following page:

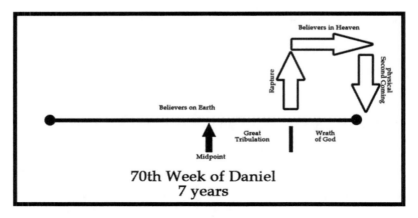

Figure 25: The Prewrath Rapture

The *prewrath rapture* pictures Christians as enduring great tribulation, and then as Jesus said, "Unless those days had been cut short, no life would have been saved; but for the sake of the elect *those days will be cut short*" (Matt. 24:22 NASB, emphasis mine). According to this theory, after the shortening of the great tribulation (so it does not last the entire final three and a half years for Christians), Jesus raptures his church.

Just as the *post-tribulation rapture* theory proposes, this theory presupposes many prophecies will be fulfilled before the return of Jesus. The *prewrath rapture* theory also does not assume the return of Jesus is imminent.

The *prewrath rapture* position has mistakenly been referred to as a *midtribulation rapture* by some. By definition, a *midtribulation rapture* occurs at the midpoint of the Seventieth Week of Daniel. To my understanding, although the *midtribulation rapture* used to be considered a viable theory, there are no longer any major proponents of it. Thus from five theories, we will only seriously examine three of them: The *pretribulation rapture*, *post-tribulation rapture*, and *prewrath rapture*.

WHAT DIFFERENCE DOES IT MAKE?

Two differences between these three theories in particular will impact the church. Those differences can be stated as answers to the following questions: 1) Will the church endure the great tribulation? and 2) Will the return of Jesus be imminent (could it occur at any time)? The church will wittingly or unwittingly develop a strategy to approach the return of our Lord based on what it believes about the answers to these two questions. Let's examine the two most popular church strategies in light of these two important questions.

1) THE *PRETRIBULATION RAPTURE* CHURCH STRATEGY

The *pretribulation rapture* theory presupposes that the church will not endure the great tribulation and that the return of Jesus is imminent. Based on these two assumptions, the strategy of the church in regard to end times should be both simple and clear: evangelize the lost and encourage the saved. In contrast to the other theories, if the *pretribulation rapture* theory is correct, needless worry will be spent on issues like preparing to face the Antichrist and concerning oneself about what signs precede the return of Jesus. Rather, all effort can be applied to getting as many lost souls in the lifeboat as possible (evangelism)—which is, of course, all important no matter what rapture position is taken.

Frankly, if this theory (the *pretribulation rapture*) is true, only a minimal amount of teaching needs to be spent on end-time prophecy (which comprises 25% of the Bible!) because it will be unnecessary for those who will be raptured in advance of those prophecies being fulfilled. Pastor Rick Warren, author of *The Purpose Driven Life*, encapsulates this teaching perfectly in his book that has sold over thirty million copies and spent years on the *New York Times* best-seller list. Many refer to him as America's foremost spiritual advisor.[119] On page 285 of this million-selling book he makes this bold statement:

> When the disciples wanted to talk about prophecy, Jesus quickly switched the conversation to evangelism. He wanted them to concentrate on their mission in the world. He said in essence, "The details of my return are none of your business. What is your business is the mission I have given you." —Pastor Rick Warren

Pastor Warren was obviously referring to Acts 1:6–8 where Jesus instructs his disciples that they cannot know the *timing* of his return with absolute precision. Whether Jesus actually said to not prepare for or think about his return is highly debatable.

The other advantage of a *pretribulation rapture* is the belief by its adherents that it won't "rob the joy" from believers as they pointlessly worry about facing tribulation and martyrdom. Pastor Brian Dellinger has preached a sermon, "Post-Trib. Rapture Thieves,"[120] in which he states that anything but belief in a *pretribulation rapture* steals the joy from a believer. David Stewart considers that the following verse refers to the joy that won't be taken away by the tribulation.[121]

> Therefore you too have grief now; but I will see you again and your heart will rejoice, and *no one will take your joy away*. (John 16:22 NASB, emphasis mine)

Most believers in this theory also consider the *pretribulation rapture* to be the blessed hope expressed in this verse:

Looking for the *blessed hope* and the appearing of the glory of our great God and Savior, Christ Jesus. (Titus 2:13 NASB, emphasis mine)

This final point is so important to many who hold this position that some individual churches and even some denominations (Calvary Chapel)[122] make belief in a *pretribulation rapture* an essential doctrine.[123]

2) POST-TRIBULATION AND PREWRATH RAPTURE CHURCH STRATEGIES

Both the *post-tribulation rapture* and *prewrath rapture* theories hold that the church will endure the entire great tribulation and that the return of Jesus is *not* imminent (it is preceded by events foretold by prophecy). Because of these similarities, we can consider their church strategies to prepare for the return of Jesus as one and the same.

The most significant aspect of preparation for proponents of these theories is to be ready to face the Antichrist and his great tribulation. Preparing to face imprisonment, persecution, and martyrdom requires emotional and spiritual readiness. Believers in these theories are of the opinion that proponents of the *pretribulation rapture* may "fall away" (commit apostasy) when faced with intense tribulation that they were not prepared to encounter. Others state that Christians may become disenchanted with their leaders and churches asking, "If you were wrong about something as important as the rapture, can I trust you about Jesus and other Bible teachings?" Some even call the *pretribulation rapture* theory the greatest threat to Christians today.[124]

Additionally, advocates of these theories do not believe in the imminent return of Jesus. If Jesus's return is not imminent, there will be *specific signs* to watch for prior to that event. Supporters of these theories believe that Jesus was speaking of these signs when he commanded Christians to watch.

> *Therefore keep watch* because you do not know when the owner of the house will come back—whether in the evening, or at midnight, or when the rooster crows, or at dawn. If he comes suddenly, do not let him find you sleeping. What I say to you, I say to everyone: *"Watch!"* (Mark 13:35–37 NIV, emphasis mine)

In the next sections, we will discuss how I approached this Bible study.

THE ROSETTA STONE

> They received the word with great eagerness, examining the Scriptures daily to see whether these things were so. (Acts 17:11 NASB)

Pierre-François rubbed his bad eye. He could barely focus. He thought back to the experiment gone wrong. He could almost feel the hot hydrogen gas exploding across his face. He could almost hear his buddy Nicolas-Jacques screaming. Earlier that morning they had been so excited. They were the ones who would present General Bonaparte with a new military advantage: an observation balloon inflated with hydrogen gas. Their promotions and careers were assured. What could go wrong? Then he thought back to the hospital and the day the doctors took off the bandages; the horror of realizing his right eye would never be "right" again.

Oh, but he needed that eye now. Hot July sweat mixed with the dust clouds of Rosetta, Egypt; the mixture burned like sulfuric acid as he rubbed both his good and his bad eye. He squinted at the stone lying in the garbage dump.

He needed that stone. The Ottomans were closing in. He was in charge of rebuilding and fortifying Fort Julien. His men needed every stone they could lay their hands on. Using old building stones for a new building was a time-honored Middle Eastern tradition, but maybe not this stone. Pierre-François poured the precious, life-giving water from his canteen onto the stone. Pulling out his dagger, he dug at the softened muddy surface.

"Bring me more water. Louis, I need water," the lieutenant barked. "Don't look at me like I'm crazy, soldier; just get me some water!"

With his one good eye, Pierre-François Bouchard stared at the stone in front of him. Yes, those were hieroglyphics. But more than just hieroglyphics were on that stone. The message was written in Greek as well. The last Egyptian who could read hieroglyphics had died more than 1,400 years earlier. The ancients called those symbols "gods' words" (Gk: *heiro*: meaning "sacred"; *glypho*: meaning "engraving"), but the meanings of the words were now hidden. Could the Greek found on the stone be a translation of the hieroglyphics? Pierre-François knew the value of this stone. "I need to take this to the general," he whispered. "I must take this to Bonaparte."

The discovery of the Rosetta Stone unlocked the ancient written language of the Egyptians found on pyramids and stele throughout the nation. It was one of the most significant archaeologic discoveries of all time. Although the Bible is written in known languages—Hebrew, Aramaic, and Koine Greek—at times when I read it I wish I had a Rosetta Stone to interpret its strange-sounding phrases.

RUMORS OF WAR

The desire to completely understand the Bible and its prophecies has never been stronger for me than right now. The world is on fire. Rumors of war and terrorism swirl around us like flickering tongues of flames. Economies teeter on the brink of collapse. According to a recent Barna survey,[125] 77% of Evangelical Christians believe we are already living in the end times. In fact, 41% of *all* Americans agree.

Even the staunchest atheist sees the growing chaos. Famed physicist Stephen Hawking has repeatedly warned us that we are in danger of destroying life as we know it and that an escape to another planet is the only hope to eventually save humanity.[126] Obviously Christians know that it is only Jesus who will save humanity, but nearly the entire civilized population of the planet is aware that times have become critical. If there was ever a need for a Rosetta Stone for Bible prophecy, especially rapture prophecy, now is the time.

Unfortunately, there is no foolproof magic interpretative system of Bible study to employ. That is because the Bible is not just a collection of man's words, like hieroglyphics are. The Bible truly is *God's* Word: "All Scripture is inspired by God" (2 Tim. 3:16 NASB). Not only were the words of the Bible breathed out by God himself, but the words are alive: "For the word of God is living and active" (Heb. 4:12 NASB). The *living* Word of God can't be broken down like some code. Only the Holy Spirit residing within a Christian can help us understand what living words truly mean.

This book is the recorded journey of one such Christian, no better and probably no worse than any other, just an average believer in Jesus the Messiah. I have shared with you what I've been taught by the Holy Spirit in regard to the event we call the rapture. I've shared the Scriptures, the actual living words of God, that led me to these conclusions. Then it is up to you to inquire of the Holy Spirit living within *you* if these conclusions are correct. This book and I are far from inerrant, but the Scriptures within the book are. Trust them as if your eternal life depends upon them, because it does.

SCRIPTURE INTERPRETING SCRIPTURE

So if we don't possess a Rosetta Stone for the Bible, what are we to do? I am sure that somewhere in your spiritual journey you have heard that we should allow Scripture to interpret Scripture. But what does this cryptic phrase truly mean? It sounds good. If Scripture is God's living words, then allowing some of his living words to interpret other living words is the way to go. Obviously, God knows more about what Scripture means than you or I do. Although there isn't a Rosetta Stone for the Bible, this is as close as we will get. But how do we accomplish it? Unfortunately, letting Scripture interpret Scripture is a lost art, and only a few commentators or pastors practice it, but the technique dates back to well before the days of Jesus.

The Jewish rabbi Hillel the Elder (110–10 BC) was the first to suggest the idea that the Holy Spirit has spread "bread crumbs" (quoted words and phrases) throughout Scripture to help us find our way (discover the meaning of passages). He called this methodology of letting one Scripture interpret another *gezerah shavah*,[127] or literally "equal testimonies/equal judgments." This methodology teaches that *a symbol or quoted passage in Scripture means the same thing everywhere it is found.*

As an example, a common symbol is "the rock." Jesus *is* the rock. Most Christians know that, but not all Christians know to apply this meaning of the symbol when we see the word rock in Scripture. For example, in the account of Moses striking the rock at Horeb to obtain water (Exod. 17:4–6), God allowed Moses to perform this miracle of supplying water for his people and employed strong *symbolism*. God provided them

257

physical water and at the same time *symbolically* showed that one day Jesus (the rock) would be struck (crucified) and would provide people with "living water."

Understanding this symbol is important. Later, Moses struck a rock again to provide water, but that time he did so contrary to the Lord's instruction to *speak* to the rock (Num. 20:8). God was angry with Moses for disobeying, and it was this very act of striking the rock twice which led God to forbidding Moses to enter the Promised Land, his lifelong dream. Why was God so angry with Moses? Symbolically, striking the rock *twice* was like crucifying Jesus twice. Jesus was crucified *once for all* (Rom. 6:10). Moses's disobedience destroyed the teachable moment that God was trying to use to instruct Israel about the coming Messiah.

Gezerah shavah is an ancient Bible interpretation technique. A more modern version taught in most seminaries is sense and reference. This discipline teaches that every Bible passage has a sense, which is its obvious meaning upon reading, what the text actually says. The passage may also have a reference, however, which is another Bible passage(s) that it quotes or refers to that helps expand the meaning.[128] This is a useful technique in gaining proper interpretation of Scripture.

APPLYING WHAT WE'VE LEARNED

Let's do an exercise and apply these new techniques to interpreting a word that is relevant to this book. It is a word that we looked at previously in this appendix A: "Summary of Rapture Timing Theories."

The Lord Himself will descend from heaven with a shout, with the voice of the archangel and with the trumpet of God, and the dead in Christ will rise first. Then we who are alive and remain

will be *caught up* [Gk: harpazo] together with them in the clouds
to meet the Lord in the air, and so we shall always be with the
Lord. (1 Thess. 4:16–17 NASB, emphasis mine)

Any study on the "catching up" or rapture must include an
examination of this Greek word harpazo. We have already seen that it means
a forcible, visible, and sudden snatching up, as in a hostage rescue. That is
the *sense* of the word. Let us now examine the *references* to this word found
throughout Scripture. The New Testament writers based their use of words
on *references* found in the Old Testament, so Old Testament uses are
extremely important in any word study. Most English Bible translations
utilize Hebrew words and cannot be compared with the Greek words found
in the New Testament. However, if we use the Greek Old Testament (the
Septuagint) as a reference, we can compare word-for-word between the
testaments. Readers might not be aware of this, but the Septuagint was the
primary Old Testament of the first-century church, and most or all of the
Old Testament quotes found in the New Testament are from the
Septuagint.[129]

The rapture was a mystery until after the resurrection of Jesus. So it
is not surprising that the vast majority of the thirty-seven uses of harpazo in
the Old Testament refer to theft or to a lion seizing its prey. There are two
references, however, that may prefigure the rapture. In the Book of Judges
(Jud. 21:21), we see this word used in connection with taking a wife. Jesus
will be returning for the bride of Christ, so this is a relevant reference. Of
greatest interest, however, is this prophecy from Hosea:

A lion to the house of Judah: and I will tear (Gk: harpazo), and
go away; and I will take, and there shall be none to deliver. I will

go and return to my place [heaven], until they [the Jews] are brought to naught, and then shall they seek my face. In their affliction [during the Seventieth Week] they will seek me early, saying, Let us go, and return to the Lord our God; for he has torn [Gk. harpazo, meaning "snatched us away"], and will heal us; he will smite, and bind us up. After two days [two thousand years] he will heal us: in the third day we shall arise and live before him, and shall know him. Let us follow on to know the Lord: we shall find him ready as the morning, *and he will come to us as the early and latter rain to the earth.* (Hos. 5:14–6:3 LXX, clarification and emphasis mine)

This is truly one of the most amazing and neglected prophecies in the Old Testament. In these five verses, the prophet tells us that Jesus will come to the earth as the early and latter rain (his first coming and his second coming). The prophet also foretells that Jesus, the Lion of the Tribe of Judah (Rev. 5:5), will return to heaven ("return to my place") after his first coming. It tells us he will leave in a hazpazo (the Ascension) until the Jews seek his face. Then he will harpazo them (the righteous Jews and Gentiles who will be resurrected and raptured) so they can "live before him." Did Paul have this use of harpazo in mind when he wrote 1 Thessalonians 4:16–17? Led by the Holy Spirit, he probably did.

In the New Testament Jesus used this word, harpazo, in the following famous example:

Can anyone enter the strong man's house and carry off [harpazo] his property, unless he first binds the strong man? And then he will plunder his house. (Matt. 12:29 NASB)

In this passage, Jesus shows that he will rescue and free Satan's property (the saints) by first binding the "strong man" (Satan).

There are also three individual examples in the New Testament of a harpazo. The first involved our Lord, the second involved Phillip, and the third involved the apostle Paul:

> She gave birth to a son, a male child, who is to rule all the nations with a rod of iron; and her child was caught up [Gk: harpazo] to God and to His throne. (Rev. 12:5 NASB)

> They both went down into the water, Philip as well as the eunuch, and he baptized him. When they came up out of the water, the Spirit of the Lord snatched [Gk: harpazo] Philip away; and the eunuch no longer saw him, but went on his way rejoicing. (Acts 8:38–39 NASB)

> I know a man in Christ who fourteen years ago—whether in the body I do not know, or out of the body I do not know, God knows—such a man was caught up [Gk: harpazo] to the third heaven. (2 Cor. 12:2 NASB)

What can we learn from all this? In all of these Scripture passages, we see the power of sense and reference to derive the proper interpretation. If we simply study 1 Thessalonians 4:16–17 in its context, we become aware of some of the nuances of what harpazo was meant to mean. But, it is only when we look at this word in the *broader* context of all of Scripture that we see the full meaning and use of the word. From the Old Testament we saw that the majority of the uses of the word were in regard to theft or seizing prey. Then in the New Testament we saw how Jesus used this same concept to teach about how he would seize Satan's property (the saints). We also learned that the ultimate example of a harpazo was the ascension of Jesus. Two other individuals experienced a harpazo as well (Philip and the apostle Paul). Finally, of course, we also saw that amazing prophecy from Hosea that encompassed both the first and second comings of Jesus, and how harpazo will be used as part of Jesus's method of healing. From this study, then, we are able to deduce far more than we would have without the references.

We have learned that harpazo was not just a concept that appeared upon the scene in a letter of Paul's, but was woven into the tapestry of both testaments. This understanding is significant for proper interpretation of Paul's well-known rapture passage of 1 Thessalonians 4:16–17.

The important lesson to be grasped here is that we learn more about the passage from *other Scriptures* than we would learn by just looking at the one individual passage, and that studying individual Scriptures cut off from the broader testimony of all of the Bible is *one of the greatest mistakes of Bible interpretation*. It is a primary reason we are trapped in the rapture-timing debate we now find ourselves engaged in.

SUMMARY

There isn't a biblical Rosetta Stone to help us interpret prophecy. Proper interpretation requires diligent Bible study and inspiration from the Holy Spirit. We have learned that one of the most reliable methods of interpretation is to use sense and reference. We first examine the *sense* of the passage in its context, what the passage literally says and what the words mean. Next, we let other Scripture interpret Scripture by examining *references* to common words, phrases, and symbols found elsewhere in the

Bible. The *gezerah shavah* methodology assures us that symbols and phrases carry the same meaning wherever they are found.

Appendix B

SUMMARY OF RAPTURE PROOFS

RAPTURE: CASE CLOSED!

> *"Because of the proof given by this ministry, they will glorify*
> *God for your obedience to your confession of the gospel of*
> *Christ"* (2 Cor. 9:13 NASB)

This book has presented many proofs that the Bible clearly testifies to a *prewrath rapture*, dispelling arguments for either a *pretribulation* or *post-tribulation* event. It is my hope that every person who desires to know the truth about the Seventieth Week of Daniel will prayerfully consider the evidence that has been presented in this book. If you do so, then I trust that you, too, will conclude that the rapture case is truly closed.

Although I have made every effort to be concise in the presentation of the proofs, arguments, and other discussions in this book, I realize that there is much to digest. It is therefore essential that I leave no doubt about what I have found the truth to be and make it as easy as possible to embrace that truth. It is just too important to get wrong. For this reason, I have selected and summarized essential biblical proofs and arguments presented in this book in the following graphics. The following header background and font key will help further clarify the grouping of the three proofs:

Proofs for prewrath	Proofs against pretrib.	Proofs against post-trib.

Proof	Summary	Scripture	Chapter	Section
The return of Jesus must precede the trumpet and bowl judgments	Because Jesus does not mention the extreme details of the trumpet and bowl judgments in the Olivet Discourse, they occur **after** Jesus has returned for the rapture.	Matt. 24:4–7; Rev. 8–11, 16	Two	Signs of His Return
The Olivet Discourse is an exact depiction of the *prewrath rapture*	The event depicted in Matt. 24:30–31 is the rapture of the faithful, which occurs after the sixth seal and prior to the trumpet and bowl judgments.	Matt. 24:4–7	Two	The Olivet Discourse = the *Prewrath Rapture*
Jesus manifestly appears to every inhabitant of	After the sixth seal, the exact same six events are depicted in Matt. 24:29–30	Rev. 6:12–17; Matt. 24:30	Three	Every Eye Shall See Him

Proof	Summary	Scripture	Chapter	Section
the earth after the sixth seal	and Rev. 6:12–17. The final of these events is the appearance of Jesus coming on the clouds			
The *prewrath rapture* is explicitly depicted in Revelation 5–7	Two nearly identical scenes are found in Rev. 5 and Rev. 7. The only difference is the addition of a great multitude (the raptured saints) to the second scene	Rev. 5:9–12; Rev. 7:9–17	Three	"Moving Picture" of the Rapture
Fire falls at the first trumpet judgment, and this marks the day of the Lord	There is one time where fire falls from heaven in judgment that could be on the day of the Lord, and that is at the	Luke 8:7	Four	Fiery Judgment

Proof	Summary	Scripture	Chapter	Section
	first trumpet judgment			
Multiple assorted proofs that Matt. 24:30–31 is the rapture	Multiple proofs based on the teaching of Alan Kurschner	Matt. 24:30–31	Five	Other Reasons Matthew 24:30–31 Is the Rapture
Rapture passages in 1 and 2 Thessalonians are parallel to rapture passages in Matt. 24	Fifteen parallel passages are presented based on a table by Alan Kurschner		Five	Paul's Thessalonian Letters — Further Proof of the *Prewrath Rapture*
The word episunago (gather together upwards) indicates the rapture	The "gathering together upwards" is of resurrected and living saints not the Jewish remnant	Matt. 24:31 2 Thess. 2:1, Mark 13:27, Isa. 66:18-20	Five	The Gathering Together
Jesus's teaching on	Based on the teaching of		Five	The "End"

Proof	Summary	Scripture	Chapter	Section
the "end of the age" precludes a pretribulation rapture and supports a prewrath rapture	Marvin Rosenthal			

Figure 26: Proofs for a *Prewrath Rapture*

Proof	Summary	Scripture	Chapter	Section
Rev. 7:14 does not indicate the great multitude come out of the great tribulation continually	The Greek word "come" is a participle, not a verb, and doesn't show continual action	Rev. 7:14	Three	*Pretribulation Rapture* Arguments
The great multitude in Revelation 7 are not souls but are in resurrected bodies	The great multitude exhibit what bodies do: they stand, wave palm branches, and wear their white robes. They are no longer beneath the altar but before the throne	Rev. 6:9–11; Rev. 20:4–5; Rev. 7:9–17	Three	*Pretribulation Rapture* Arguments
The 24 elders are not the newly raptured church or	The elders are only 24 in number; all saints must always be with	Rev. 5:9–12	Three	The Elders

Proof	Summary	Scripture	Chapter	Section
representatives of the church	the Lord after the rapture			
Rev. 3:10 terminology proves the occurrence of the rapture; however; it does not point to a *pretribulation rapture*	The Greek word for perseverance is used in association with the great tribulation, and the Greek word *ek* is used, which indicates coming out from the middle of something	Rev. 3:10; Rev. 14:9–10, 12; Rev. 13:10; Rev. 7:14	Six	The Backfire Effect
The day of the Lord is not the entire *Seventieth Week of Daniel*	The celestial earthly disturbance and silence in heaven precede the day of the Lord. Since these occur upon the opening of the sixth and	Joel 2:30–31; Zeph. 1:7; Matt. 24:29 Rev. 6:12–17; Rev. 8:1	Seven	The *Wrath of God* Considerations

Proof	Summary	Scripture	Chapter	Section
	seventh seal, the day of the Lord cannot be the entire Seventieth Week			
The day of the Lord is the day of salvation, however.	Several Scriptures indicate that salvation occurs on the day of the Lord.	1 Cor. 1:8; 1 Cor. 5:5; 2 Tim. 4:8	Six	The *Wrath of God* Considerations
All seven seals cannot be the wrath of God	At the opening of the fifth seal, it is explicitly stated that God had not yet begun to judge or to seek vengeance (wrath).	Rev. 6:9–11	Six	Are the Seals God's Wrath?
1 Thess. 5:2–4 demonstrates that the day of the Lord occurs after	Three separate proofs show that the death of the two witnesses are	1 Thess. 5:2–4; Rev. 11:9–12;	Six	1 Thessalonians 5

Proof	Summary	Scripture	Chapter	Section
the celestial earthly disturbance	the "peace and safety" the world claims, the day of the Lord comes like a thief via the celestial earthly disturbance, and that the labor pains listed come after the celestial earthly disturbance	Matt. 24:8; Isa. 13:6–10		
The apostasy and the appearance of the Antichrist must both precede the rapture and the day of the Lord	The rapture cannot occur until after the midpoint of the Seventieth Week of Daniel, because the abomination of the Antichrist and the great apostasy must both occur first; apostasia means	2 Thess. 2:1–4	Six	Will the Church Face the Antichrist?

Proof	Summary	Scripture	Chapter	Section
	revolt, not departure.			
The Olivet Discourse is not just for the Jews, but for Christians as well	Matt. 24:36 is understood by most to refer to a rapture that unbelieving Jews will not participate in. This is circular reasoning. The *Didache* also clearly indicated that the early church believed the Olivet Discourse was for Christians	Matt. 24:9; Matt. 24:36	Six	Is the Olivet Discourse (Matthew 24) for the Jews or Christians?
The church is not absent from Revelation after chapter 3	The term *ekklesia* (church) only appears in Revelation 1–3 in association with the seven	Rev. 1–19	Six	Is the Church Present in Revelation after Chapter 3?

Proof	Summary	Scripture	Chapter	Section
	churches. Elsewhere in Revelation, the church is referred to as saints, bond servants, and bride; but there is no mention of them during the trumpet and bowl judgments, since at this point the church has been raptured, consistent with *prewrath rapture* theory.			
Imminence ignores the evidence in which Jesus commands the church to	The three versions of the Olivet Discourse in Matt., Mark, and Luke	Matt 24–25; Mark 13; Luke 21; Rev. 3:3;	Six	Imminence

Proof	Summary	Scripture	Chapter	Section
watch for signs of his return.	contain over 30 references to watch, see, and be observant. In Jesus's letter to the church of Sardis, he states that *if* believers are watchful he won't come as a thief to them; consistent with 1 Thess. 5:4	1 Thess. 5:4		
Ancient Jewish wedding customs do not support a seven-year period of the saints in heaven	The marriage of the Lamb is "time-stamped" by the bride of Christ wearing of white garments, which takes place after the sixth seal.	Rev. 19:7–8; Rev. 7:9–17	Six	Ten Virgins and a Jewish Wedding
The Jewish idiom "a thief in the night" is	A "thief in the night" refers to the temple guards catching	Rev. 3:3; 1 Thess. 5:1–6;	Six	Imminence

Proof	Summary	Scripture	Chapter	Section
not proof of imminence	priests asleep during their duties of maintaining the temple fire. It is a reference to watchfulness, not imminence.	Rev. 16:15		
Matt. 24:36 *cannot* refer to a *pretribulation rapture*	Jesus's use of the phrase "that day" can only be in reference to a day that was previously stated (Matt. 24:29–31) not to an unstated *pretribulation rapture*. The reference to Noah that follows shows God provided Noah with a specific timing of the flood	Matt. 24:36	Six	That Day

Proof	Summary	Scripture	Chapter	Section
	seven days prior to it.			
There is only one first resurrection which includes those martyred during the Seventieth Week	According to 1 Cor. 15, "we will *all* be changed, in a moment, in the twinkling of an eye, at the last trumpet." We are told that this resurrection happens at Jesus's return, not at multiple times.	Rev. 20:4–5; 1 Cor 15: 51–52; 1 Cor 15: 22–26	Six	The First Resurrection

Figure 27: Proofs Against a *Pretribulation Rapture*

Proof	Summary	Scripture	Chapter	Section
The order of the seals, trumpets, and bowls is consecutive	If the Olivet Discourse includes only the seals before the return of Jesus, the seals must precede the trumpet and bowl judgments; also see table in chapter seven.	Matt. 24:4–30	Two	Seals, Trumpets, and Bowls
The seventh trumpet cannot be the last trumpet	The trumpet judgments precede the bowl judgments; therefore it is impossible for the seventh trumpet to be the last trumpet. Additionally, the last trumpet is referred to as the "trumpet of God" in Thessalonians, to be blown by	1 Cor. 15:52; 1 Thess. 4:16; Rev. 11:15–19; Zech. 9:14	Seven	Last Trumpet = the Seventh Trumpet?

Proof	Summary	Scripture	Chapter	Section
	God (Zech. 9:14); the seventh trumpet is blown by an *angel*.			
The days of the great tribulation (1,260) are shortened	The Antichrist is ordained a set number of days (1,260), and Jesus references this by saying "those days" will be shortened.	Rev. 13:5–7; Dan. 7:25; Matt. 24:21–22, 29	Seven	The Days Shall Be Shortened
The harvests in Rev 14 are not chronologically listed and do not take place after the seventh trumpet	Rev 14 is a parenthetical chapter in Revelation that contains three visions that occur in reverse chronological order	Rev 14	Seven	The Harvests in Revelation 14
Jesus has only one parousia that occurs at the rapture	The arrival or parousia of Jesus is the rapture when he is revealed; it lasts	Matt. 24:27–31;	Seven	Does Jesus Have a Third Coming?

Proof	Summary	Scripture	Chapter	Section
	one year, ten days.	1 Cor. 15:22–23; 1 Cor. 4:15–17; 2 Thess. 2:1		
The resurrection does not occur on the last day of the Seventieth Week	Jesus may have referred to the last day as meaning the day of the Lord (1 year, 10 days long) or the final 1000-year "day."	John 6:39–54; 2 Pet. 3:3–10; Heb. 1:2; Isa. 34:8; Isa. 61:2; Isa. 63:4	Seven	A Fourfold "Last-Day" Resurrection
Christians are not sealed in Rev 7	God selectively keeps his wrath from Christians by rapturing them (as in Rev. 7:7–19); sealing is reserved for the twelve tribes of	Rev. 7, Ezek. 9:1–11; Rev. 9:3–4	Seven	Sealing of the Saints

Proof	Summary	Scripture	Chapter	Section
	Israel who endure God's wrath			
The righteous are "taken" and the unrighteous are "left"	In the cases of Noah, Lot, the parable of the ten virgins, and at the parousia, it is clear that the righteous will be the ones to be removed from judgment. *Paralambano* and *aphiemi* also indicate the righteous are "taken."	Luke 17:26–30; Matt. 25:1–13; Matt. 24:30–31	Seven	Left Behind or Taken
The illustration of the vultures and the body is about the rapture, not about Armageddon	The two occurrences of this illustration point to *angels* (referred to as eagles) who "gather together" the living and dead body (the	Matt. 24:27–31; Luke 17:36–37; Rev. 19:17–18; Rev. 4:7; Rev. 8:13;	Seven	Vultures and a Body

Proof	Summary	Scripture	Chapter	Section
	resurrection and rapture)	Rev. 12:14; 2 Thess. 2:1		
Apantesis does not mean to "meet and then return home"	The Greek word *apantesis* is not a technical term and is not used in the context (1 Thess. 4:16–17) of a hellenistic reception	1 Thess. 4:16–17; Matt. 25:1; John 14:2–3; 2 Cor. 4:14; Isa. 26: 19–21	Eight	Do the Saints Rise and Then Immediately Descend during the Rapture?

Figure 28: Proofs against a Post-tribulation Rapture

Appendix C: SCRIPTURE INDEX

287

289

END NOTES

END NOTES

Chapter One

[1] "Pastors: The End of the World is Complicated," Lifeway Research, last modified April 26, 2016, accessed January 22, 2017, http://lifewayresearch.com/2016/04/26/pastors-the-end-of-the-world-is-complicated/

[2] "What We Believe," Calvary Chapel, last modified unknown, accessed April 2, 2016, https://calvarychapel.com/about/doctrine/view/doctrine/

[3] Marvin Rosenthal, *The Pre-Wrath Rapture of the Church*, (Thomas Nelson, Nashville, 1990), pp. 24-32.

[4] Robert Van Kampen, *The Rapture Question Answered,* (Revell, Grand Rapids, MI, 1997), p. 199.

[5] Joseph Lenard, personal email to Nelson Walters, May 8, 2016

Chapter Two

[6] "Missing Masterpiece Lost for Ninety Years . . . " *Dailymail.com*, last modified November 28, 2014, accessed January 26, 2016, http://www.dailymail.co.uk/news/article-2852842/Missing-masterpiece-lost-90-years-discovered-background-Stuart-Little-Art-historian-finds-painting-watching-children-s-film-daughter.html

[7] Nelson Walters, *Revelation Deciphered*, (Ready for Jesus Publications, Wilmington, 2016), Chapter 3

[8] John Walvoord, Mark Hitchcock, and Phillip Rawley, *Revelation*, (Moody Publishers, Chicago, 2011), Chapter 6

[9] Andreas J. Köstenberger, L. Scott Kellum, and Charles L Quarles, *The Cradle, the Cross, and the Crown* (B&H Academic, Nashville, 2009), p. 834.

[10] "A Comparison of the Olivet Discourse and Revelation," Pre-Trib. Research Center, last modified: unknown, accessed April 7, 2016, http://www.pre-trib.org/articles/view/comparison-of-olivet-discourse-and-book-revelation

[11] "Rapture Debate between Alan Kurschner (Pre-Wrath) and Thomas Ice (Pre-Trib.)," Eschatos Ministries, last modified September 27, 2015, accessed April 6, 2016, http://www.alankurschner.com/2015/09/27/rapture-debate-between-alan-kurschner-prewrath-and-thomas-ice-pretrib/ TIME: 1:17:15.

[12] William Daniel Kelly, *Shadow of Things to Come*, (Westbow Press, Bloomington, 2013), p.42.

[13] "Seals, Trumpets, Bowls in the Book of Revelation: Concurrent-Recapitulation or Consecutive-Progressive? (Part 1 of 2) – Ep. 36," Eschatos Ministries, last modified

May 28, 2015, accessed October 11, 2015,
http://www.alankurschner.com/2015/05/28/seals-trumpets-bowls-in-the-book-of-revelation-concurrent-recapitulation-or-consecutive-progressive-part-1-of-2-ep-36/

[14] Nelson Walters, Chapter 14

[15] Charles Cooper, *God's Elect and the Great Tribulation* (Strong Tower Publishing, Belfonte, PA, 2008), p. 158.

Chapter Three

[16] "World's Most Expensive Animation Cels," *Your3dSource*, last modified 2008, accessed April 3, 2016, http://www.your3dsource.com/most-expensive-animation-cels.html

[17] "Rapture Debate between Alan Kurschner (Pre-Wrath) and Thomas Ice (Pre-Trib.)," Eschatos Ministries, last modified September 27, 2015, accessed April 6, 2016, http://www.alankurschner.com/2015/09/27/rapture-debate-between-alan-kurschner-prewrath-and-thomas-ice-pretrib/ TIME: 1:08:55 – 1:09:20

[18] Marvin Rosenthal, *The Pre-Wrath Rapture of the Church*, (Thomas Nelson, Nashville, 1990), pp. 184-185

[19] Renald E. Showers, *The Pre-Wrath Rapture View*, (Kregel Publications, Grand Rapids, 2001), p. 139.

[20] Showers, pp. 147-151.

[21] Alan Kurschner, personal email to Nelson Walters, June 23, 2017.

[22] "The Rapture in Revelation," *Pre-Trib* , last modified 2007, accessed April 3, 2016, http://www.pre-trib.org/data/pdf/Hocking-TheRaptureinRevelati.pdf

[23] Marvin Rosenthal, pp. 251-253

[24] Dr. Michael Heiser, *The Unseen Realm*, (Lexham Press, Bellingham WA, 2015), pp. 157-158.

[25] Michael Snyder, Rapture Verdict, (Michael Snyder, 2016), p.170

[26] Sheila Sternberg, personal email to Nelson Walters, July 24, 2017

Chapter Five

[27] "Marbury v. Madison," Wikipedia, last modified April 10, 2016, accessed April 23, 2016, https://en.wikipedia.org/wiki/Marbury_v._Madison

[28] Robert Van Kampen, *The Rapture Question Answered*, (Revell, Grand Rapids, MI, 1997), p. 47.

[29] Van Kampen, p. 56-57.

[30] "Rapture Debate between Alan Kurschner (Pre-Wrath) and Thomas Ice (Pre-Trib.)," Eschatos Ministries, last modified September 27, 2015, accessed April 6, 2016, http://www.alankurschner.com/2015/09/27/rapture-debate-between-alan-kurschner-prewrath-and-thomas-ice-pretrib/ TIME: 1:34:10 – 1:34:20.

[31] "A Reply to Jim McClarty's Selective Use of Passages to Fit His Unbiblical Construct of a Pretrib Rapture: Matthew 24, Israel, and the Church – Ep. 50'" Eschatos Ministries, last modified Dec. 7, 2015, accessed June 20, 2015,

http://www.alankurschner.com/2015/12/07/a-reply-to-jim-mcclartys-selective-use-of-passages-to-fit-his-unbiblical-construct-of-a-pretrib-rapture-matthew-24-israel-and-the-church-ep-50/

[32] Alan Kurschner, *Antichrist Before the Day of the Lord*, (Eschatos, Pompton Lakes, 2013), p.91-94.

[33] Ibid. p. 94-100.

[34] Van Kampen, p. 184-185,

[35] "Thomas Ice: Part 28 - Matthew 24:31 An Angelic Gathering," Blue Letter Bible, last modified: unknown, accessed March 31, 2017, https://www.blueletterbible.org/Comm/ice_thomas/Mat24-25/Mat24-25_Part28.cfm

[36] Van Kampen, pp. 79-80

[37] Van Kampen, pp 79-81.

[38] Van Kampen, pp. 80-81.

[39] William Varner, "Didache Apocalypse and Matthew 24," last modified: unknown, accessed October 29, 2016, http://www.academia.edu/4206817/Didache_Apocalypse_and_Matthew_24

[40] Ibid. p. 179.

[41] Marvin Rosenthal, pp.225-230.

[42] "John Walvoord, The Rapture Question, 1st Edition, (Findlay, Ohio: n.p. 1957) p. 148

[43] "Pastors: The End of the World is Complicated," *Lifeway Research*, last modified April 26, 2016, accessed June 4, 2016, http://lifewayresearch.com/2016/04/26/pastors-the-end-of-the-world-is-complicated/

Chapter Six

[44] "When Corrections Fail: The persistence of political misperceptions'" *Dartmouth.edu*, last modified unknown, April 5, 2016, http://www.dartmouth.edu/~nyhan/nyhan-reifler.pdf

[45] "The Backfire Effect: Why Facts Don't Win Arguments," *The Big Think*, last modified , accessed April 5, 2016, http://bigthink.com/think-tank/the-backfire-effect-why-facts-dont-win-arguments

[46] Richard Mayhue, *The Prophet's Watchword, The Day of the Lord*, (Ph.D. diss., Grace Theological Seminary, 1981), pp. 181-182.

[47] Robert Van Kampen, The Rapture Question Answered: Plain and Simple, (Revell, Grand Rapids, 1997), pp. 177

[48] David Mathewson, Revelation, A Handbook on the Greek Text (Baylor University Press, Waco, 2016), p. 49.

[49] "The Apostasy as it relates to the Lord's Return," *Pre-Trib. Research Center*, last modified unknown, accessed April 7, 2016, http://www.pre-trib.org/articles/view/apostasy-as-it-relates-to-lords-return

[50] David L. Mathewson and Elodie Ballantine Emig, *Intermediate Greek Grammar* (Baker Publishing Group, Grand Rapids, 2016), p. 92.

[51] Marvin Rosenthal, pp. 235-237.

[52] "Rapture Debate between Alan Kurschner (Pre-Wrath) and Thomas Ice (Pre-Trib.)," Eschatos Ministries, last modified September 27, 2015, accessed April 6, 2016, http://www.alankurschner.com/2015/09/27/rapture-debate-between-alan-kurschner-prewrath-and-thomas-ice-pretrib/ TIME: 1:08:30

[53] Marvin Rosenthal, pp. 1555-160.

[54] "The Pre-Wrath Rapture: is there any validity in it," *Lion and Lamb Ministries*, last modified: unknown, accessed April 6, 2016, http://www.lamblion.com/articles/articles_rapture10.php

[55] "The Prewrath Confusion," Middletown Bible Church, last modified: unknown, asscessed April 14, 2017, http://www.middletownbiblechurch.org/proph/prewrath.htm

[56] "Abortion Statistics," *Right to Life of Holland*, last modified: unknown, accessed April 7, 2016, http://rtlofholland.org/abortion-statistics/

[57] "Tears of Jihad," *Political Islam* , last modified May 3, 2008 , accessed April 7, 2016, https://www.politicalislam.com/tears-of-jihad/

[58] "Rapture Debate between Alan Kurschner (Pre-Wrath) and Thomas Ice (Pre-Trib.)," Eschatos Ministries, last modified September 27, 2015, accessed April 6, 2016, http://www.alankurschner.com/2015/09/27/rapture-debate-between-alan-kurschner-prewrath-and-thomas-ice-pretrib/ TIME: 1:09:30-1:14:30

[59] "An Overview of Pre-Tribulational Arguments," Pre-Trib. Research Center, last modified unknown, accessed May 4, 2016, http://www.pre-trib.org/articles/view/an-overview-of-pretribulatonal-arguments

[60] "Rapture Debate between Alan Kurschner (Pre-Wrath) and Thomas Ice (Pre-Trib.)," Eschatos Ministries, last modified September 27, 2015, accessed April 6, 2016, http://www.alankurschner.com/2015/09/27/rapture-debate-between-alaecn-kurschner-prewrath-and-thomas-ice-pretrib/ TIME: 1:09:30-1:14:30

[61] Dr. Renald Showers as quoted by John Ankerberg in "The Pre-Wrath Rapture View," *The John Ankerberg Show*, last modified unknown, accessed January 17, 2017

[62] "When Will the Believing be Leaving?" *Understanding the Times with Jan Markel*, last modified Jan. 14, 2017, accessed June 7, 2017, http://www.oneplace.com/ministries/understanding-the-times/custom-player

[63] "The Apostasy as it relates to the Lord's Return," *Pre-Trib. Research Center*, last modified unknown, accessed April 7, 2016, http://www.pre-trib.org/articles/view/apostasy-as-it-relates-to-lords-return

[64] "646. Apostasia," *Bible Hub*, last modified unknown, accessed April 17, 2016, http://biblehub.com/greek/646.htm

[65] Duncan W. McKenzie, *The Antichrist and the Second Coming*, (Xulon, 2009), p. 349.

[66] "Rapture Debate between Alan Kurschner (Pre-Wrath) and Thomas Ice (Pre-Trib.)," *Eschatos Ministries*, last modified September 27, 2015, accessed April 6, 2016, http://www.alankurschner.com/2015/09/27/rapture-debate-between-alan-kurschner-prewrath-and-thomas-ice-pretrib/

[67] "A Defense of the Rapture in 2 Thessalonians 2:3," *Pre-Trib. Research Center*, last modified: unknown, accessed May 8, 2016, http://www.pre-trib.org/articles/view/a-defense-of-the-rapture-in-2-thessalonians-23

[68] "2nd Thessalonians 2 and the Rapture," *Pre-Trib. Research Center*, last modified unknown, accessed July 17, 2016, http://www.pre-trib.org/data/pdf/Feinberg-TheRaptureand2Thessa.pdf

[69] "Matthew 24 is for the Jews," *Yeshua.org*, last modified: unknown, accessed April 7, 2016, http://yeshua.org/who/matthew-24-is-for-the-jews-2/

[70] "The Didache," Early Christian Writings, last modified: unknown, accessed April 7, 2016, http://www.earlychristianwritings.com/didache.html

[71] Ibid. http://www.academia.edu/4206817/Didache_Apocalypse_and_Matthew_24

[72] "Where is the Church in Rev. 4-19," Pre-Trib. Research Center, last modified: unknown, accessed April 8, 2016, http://www.pre-trib.org/articles/view/where-is-church-in-revelation-4-19

[73] Marvin Rosenthal, p. 245.

[74] "The Apocalypse of John and the Rapture of the Church: a Re-evaluation," Bible.org, last modified May 25, 2004, accessed May 31, 2017, https://bible.org/article/apocalypse-john-and-rapture-church-reevaluation#P32_9486

[75] "Origen's System of Interpretation," *Elijahnet*, last modified: unknown, accessed May 7, 2016, http://www.elijahnet.net/Origen%20System%20of%20Interpret.html

[76] "The Apocalypse of John and the Rapture of the Church: a Re-evaluation," *Bible.org*, last modified May 25, 2004, accessed May 31, 2017, https://bible.org/article/apocalypse-john-and-rapture-church-reevaluation#P32_9486

[77] Ibid.

[78] "Perhaps Today: The Imminent Return of Christ," *Rapture Ready*, last modified , accessed April 7, 2016, https://www.raptureready.com/featured/ice/tt7.html

[79] John F. Walvoord, *The Rapture Question: Revised and Enlarged Edition* (Grand Rapids: Zondervan, 1979), p. 273.

[80] Nelson Walters, *Are We Ready For Jesus*, (Seraphina Press, Minneapolis, 2015), pp. 109-111.

[81] "Jesus's Warning to Watch: What Did He Mean?" *Beyond Today*, last modified January 26,2011, accessed April 7, 2016, http://www.ucg.org/the-good-news/jesus-warning-to-watch-just-what-did-he-mean

[82] "Bible Study: The Thief in the Night vs. the Thief," Calvary Bible Church, last modified January 8, 2011, accessed December 23, 2014, http://www.cbcmidway.org/2011/01/08/bible-study-the-thief-in-the-night-vs-the-thief/.

[83] "Defending the Pre-Trib. Rapture," Rapture Ready, last modified: unknown, accessed April 8, 2016, https://www.raptureready.com/rr-pre-trib-rapture.html

Chapter Seven

[84] Fraser, Craig G. *The Cosmos: A Historical Perspective*. (Greenwood, 2006). p. 14.

[85] "Great Astronomers," *Star Teach Astronomy*, last modified , accessed April 9, 2016, http://www.starteachastronomy.com/astronomers.html

[86] Bernard R. Goldstein, "Saving the Phenomena: The Background to Ptolemy's Planetary Theory", Journal for the History of Astronomy, 28 (1997):pp. 1–12

[87] Edward Chumney, *The Seven Festivals of the Messiah* (Shippensburg, PA: Treasure House, an Imprint of Destiny Image Publishers, Inc. 2001), pp. 92-93.

[88] "Yom Teruah," *Hoshana Rabbah*, last modified September 26, 2006 , accessed May 28, 2016, http://www.hoshanarabbah.org/pdfs/yom_teruah.pdf

[89] Snyder, p.70-71

[90] Ibid., p.71

[91] Ibid., p.75

[92] "If Those Days Were not Cut Short, No One Would Survive," *Last Days Mysteries*, last modified: unknown, accessed April 11, 2016, http://www.lastdaysmystery.info/if_those_days_where_not_cut_short.htm

[93] Showers, pp. 28-31.

[94] "The Prophetic Perfect," Truth or Tradition, last modified 2016, accessed March 17, 2017, http://www.truthortradition.com/articles/the-prophetic-perfect

[95] E. Kautzsch, editor, Gesenius' Hebrew Grammar (Clarendon Press, Oxford, 1910), pp. 312 - 313

[96] "Will There Be a Second and Third Coming of Christ?" *Sola Scriptura*, last modified: unknown, accessed April 11, 2016, http://www.solagroup.org/articles/faqs/faq_0011.html

[97] "3952-Parousia," Bible Hub, last modified: unknown, accessed April 11, 2016, http://biblehub.com/greek/3952.htm

[98] "The Post-Tribulation Resurrection-Rapture," *Endtime Pilgrim*, last modified: unknown, accessed April 11, 2016, http://endtimepilgrim.org/resrap.htm

[99] Snyder, p. 181

[100] "2 Peter 3:5," *Bible Hub*, last modified: unknown, accessed April 12, 2016, http://biblehub.com/commentaries/2_peter/3-5.htm

101 "Year 6000," *Wikipedia*, last modified: December 29, 2015, accessed April 12, 2016, https://en.wikipedia.org/wiki/Year_6000

[102] "Is the Creation Narrative a Prophecy?" *The Gospel in the End Times*, last modified January 10, 2015, accessed April 12, 2016, http://www.thegospelintheendtimes.com/pictures-of-end-times-in-the-bible/creation-narrative-prophecy/

[103] Snyder, pp.46-49

[104]" The Wrath of God and the Tribulation of the Church," last modified: unknown, accessed April 13, 2016, http://www.velocity.net/~edju70/wrathchu.htm

[105] "The 144,000 Jews Will not Evangelize," *The Ultimate Deception*, last modified: unknown, accessed April 12, 2016, http://www.frankcaw.com/144000-Jews.html

[106]"A Quick Reply to Postribulationists Michael Brown and Craig Keener and Their Misrepresentation
of Pre-Wrath," *Eschatos Ministries*, last modified October 17, 2014 , accessed April 13, 2016, http://www.alankurschner.com/2014/10/17/a-quick-reply-to-posttribulationists-michael-brown-and-craig-keener-and-their-misrepresentation-of-prewrath/

[107] "The Pre-Wrath Rapture of the Church," *Salvation by Grace* , last modified:unknown , accessed April 13, 2016, http://salvationbygrace.org/wp-content/uploads/2016/02/The-Pre-wrath-Rapture-of-the-Church-Jim-McClarty.pdf

[108] Dr. Craig Keener, *Matthew*, (Intervarsity Press, Downers Grove, 1997). p. 352.

[109]"Hellenistic Formal Receptions and Paul's Use of APANTESIS in 1 Thess. 4:17," *Bulletin for Biblical Research*, last modified: 1994 , accessed April 13, 2016, www.ibr-bbr.org/files/bbr/BBR_1994_02_Crosby-Apantesis1Thes.pdf

[110] "Where Do Believers Go after the Rapture," Eschatos Ministries, last modified February 15, 2014, accessed April 26, 2016, www.alankurschner.com/2014/02/15/where -do-believers-go-after-the-rapture/

Chapter Eight

[111] "Meet SARA, Our Emotional Response to Bad News," *Zenger-Folkman*, last modified: unknown, accessed April 21, 2016, http://zengerfolkman.com/meet-sara-our-emotional-response-to-bad-news/

[112] "Ex-Muslims Lighting the way for Islam's Collapse," *CBN News*, last modified: June 4, 2015 , accessed April 21, 2016, http://www1.cbn.com/cbnnews/world/2015/June/Ex-Muslims-Lighting-the-Way-for-Islams-Collapse

[113] "Corrie Ten Boom on Forgiveness," *Guideposts*, last modified: unknown, accessed April 21, 2016, https://www.guideposts.org/inspiration/stories-of-hope/guideposts-classics-corrie-ten-boom-on-forgiveness?nopaging=1

[114] Nelson Walters, *Are We Ready For Jesus*, (Seraphina Press, 2015, pp. 108-111)

[115] "Rapture Debate between Alan Kurschner (Pre-Wrath) and Thomas Ice (Pre-Trib.)," Eschatos Ministries, last modified September 27, 2015, accessed April 6,

2016, http://www.alankurschner.com/2015/09/27/rapture-debate-between-alan-kurschner-prewrath-and-thomas-ice-pretrib/ TIME: 1:19:10-1:19:30

[116] "726. Harpazo," Bible Hub, last modified: unknown, accessed April 10, 2016, http://biblehub.com/greek/726.htm

[117] "Pastors: The End of the World is Complicated," *Lifeway Research*, last modified April 26, 2016, accessed June 4, 2016, http://lifewayresearch.com/2016/04/26/pastors-the-end-of-the-world-is-complicated/

[118] Ibid.

[119] Rich Warren, *The Purpose Driven Life*, (Zondervan, 2002), p. 246

[120] "Post-Tribulation Thieves of Joy," *SermonAudio.com*, last modified May 9, 2014, accessed April 2, 2016, (38 second mark) http://www.sermonaudio.com/sermoninfo.asp?SID=59141434550

[121] "Is the Pre-Tribulation Rapture a New Teaching," *Jesus is Savior*, last modified unknown, accessed April 28, 2016, www.jesus-is-savior.com/end%20of%20the%20World/rapture_not_new.htm

[122] "What We Believe," Calvary Chapel, last modified unknown, accessed April 2, 2016, https://calvarychapel.com/about/doctrine/view/doctrine/

[123] "Can We Still Believe in the Rapture," *Southwest Baptist Theological Seminary*, last modified August 26, 2014, accessed April 2, 2016, http://media.swbts.edu/item/982/can-we-still-believe-in-the-rapture

[124] "The Greatest Threat to Christians Today is the Pre-Tribulation Rapture," *Judeo Christian Church*, last modified Feb. 1, 2014, accessed April 2, 2016, http://judeochristianchurch.com/biggest-threat-christians-teaching-pre-tribulation-rapture/

[125] "SHOCK POLL: Startling Numbers of Americans Believe World Now in the "End Times" Religion News Service, last modified September 11, 2013, accessed January 26, 2016, http://pressreleases.religionnews.com/2013/09/11/shock-poll-startling-numbers-of-americans-believe-world-now-in-the-end-times/#sthash.mbc7OZoq.dpuf

[126] "Stephen Hawking Warns Humanity Could Destroy Itself in the Next Hundred Years," *IFLScience*, last modified January 19, 2016, accessed January 26, 2016, http://www.iflscience.com/space/stephen-hawking-warns-humanity-could-destroy-itself-next-100-years

[127] "Talmudical Hermeneutics'" *Wikipedia*, last modified Dec. 25, 2014, accessed June 21, 2015, https://en.wikipedia.org/wiki/Talmudical_hermeneutics

[128] "Sense and Reference" *Wikipedia*, last modified January 29, 2015, accessed March 3, 2015, http://en.wikipedia.org/wiki/Sense_and_reference

[129] "Table of Old Testament Quotes in the New Testament, in English Translation," *Septuagint Online*, last modified 2013, accessed April 3, 2016, http://www.kalvesmaki.com/LXX/NTChart.htm

CONTINUE YOUR STUDY

An accompanying ten-week, small group Bible study is available
(Amazon.com) to complement this book. Assemble a group and expand
your study of this topic.